STREET FIGHTER® LEGENDS
IBUKI

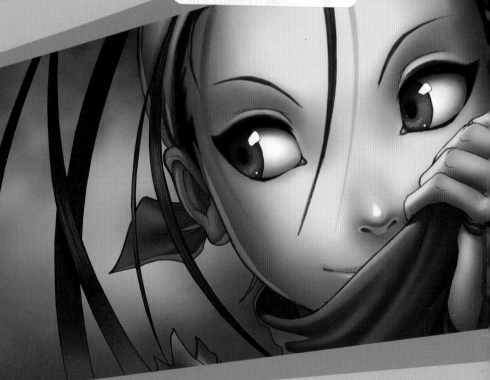

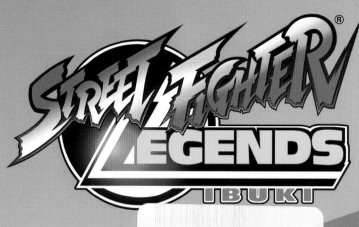

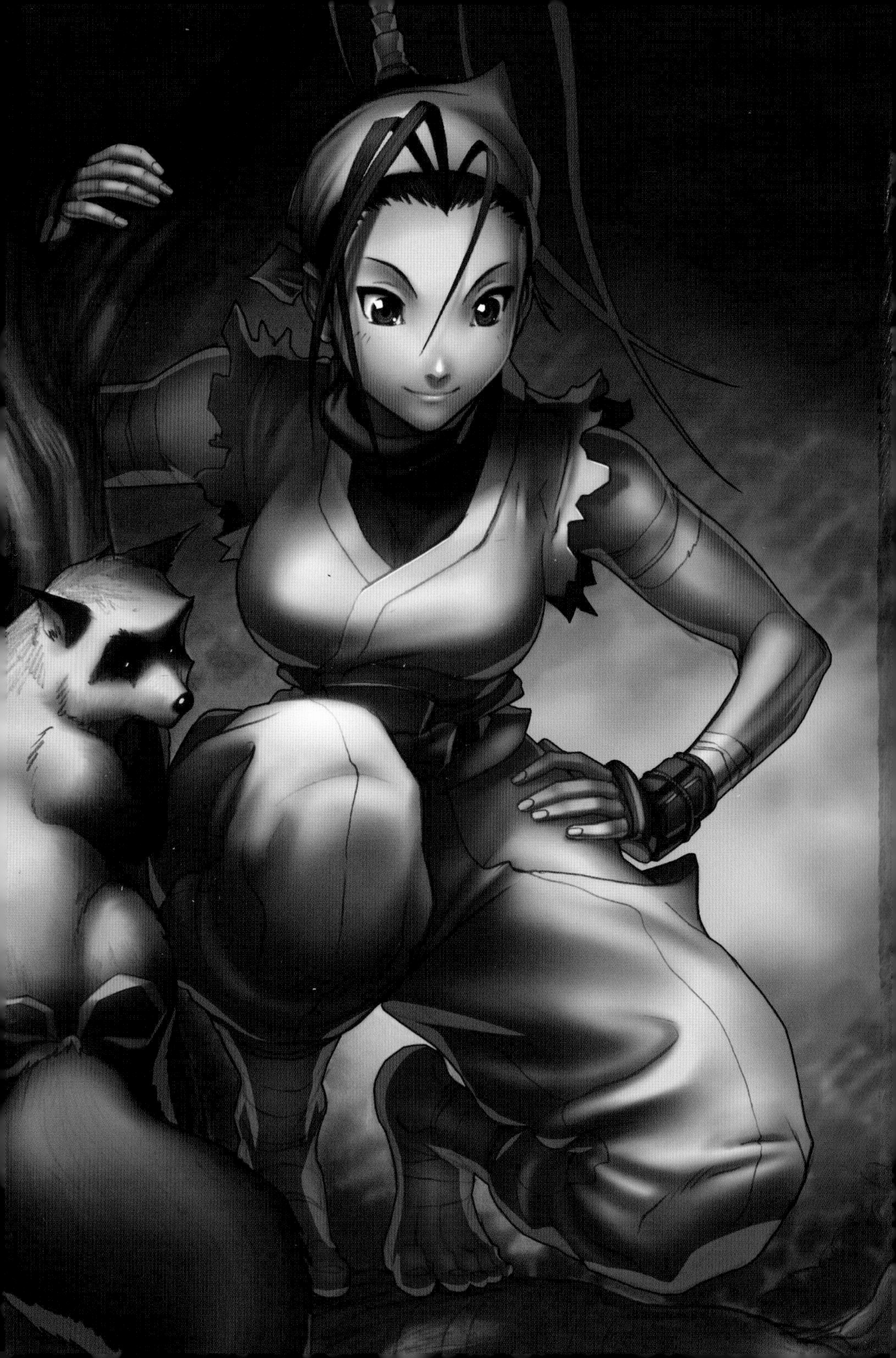

Prelude: AMBUSH!

Art by: Omar Dogan

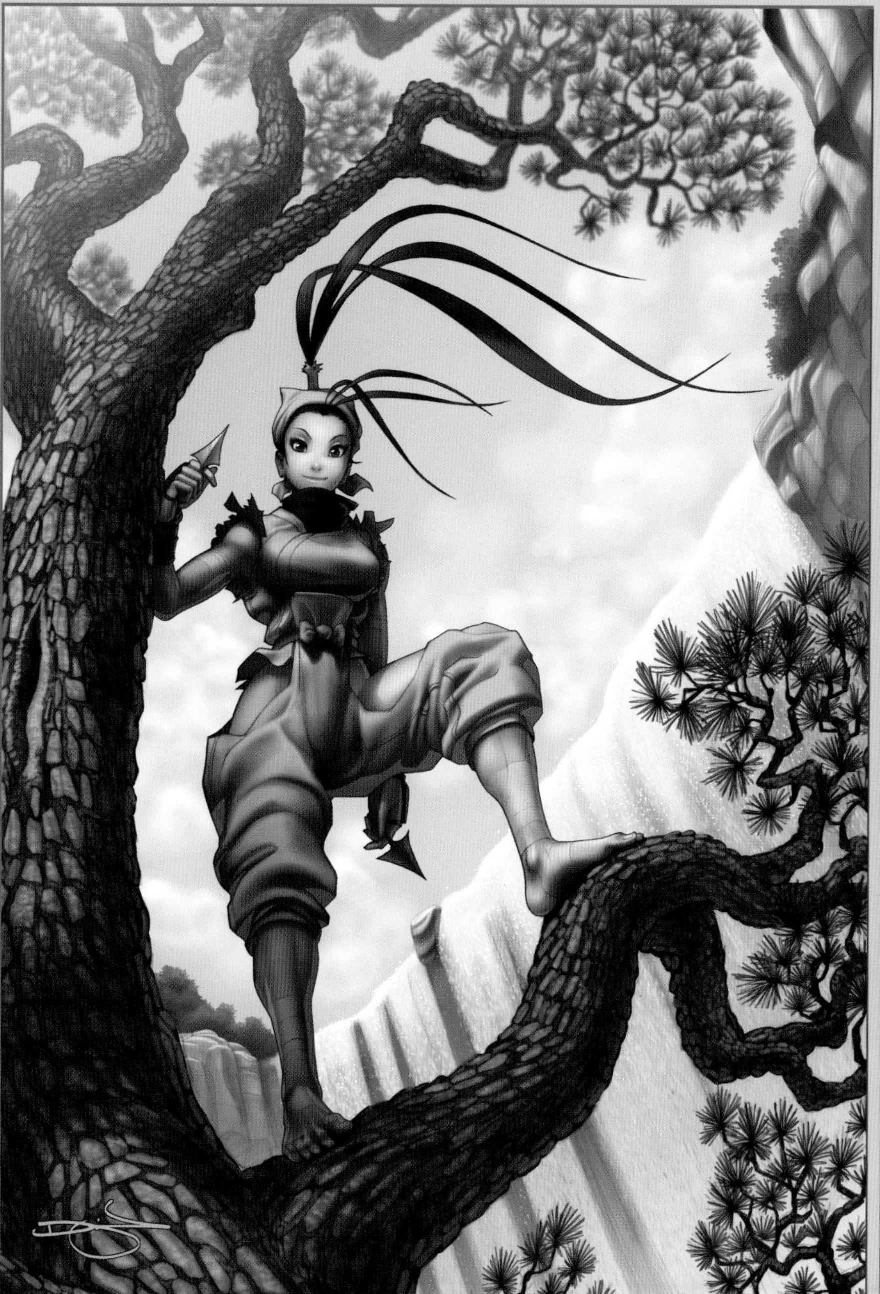

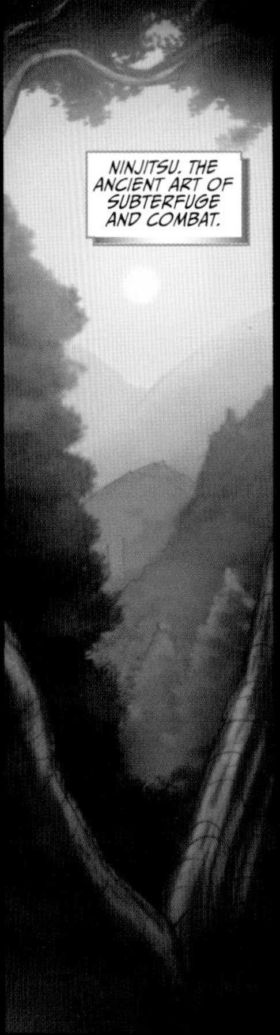
NINJITSU. THE ANCIENT ART OF SUBTERFUGE AND COMBAT.

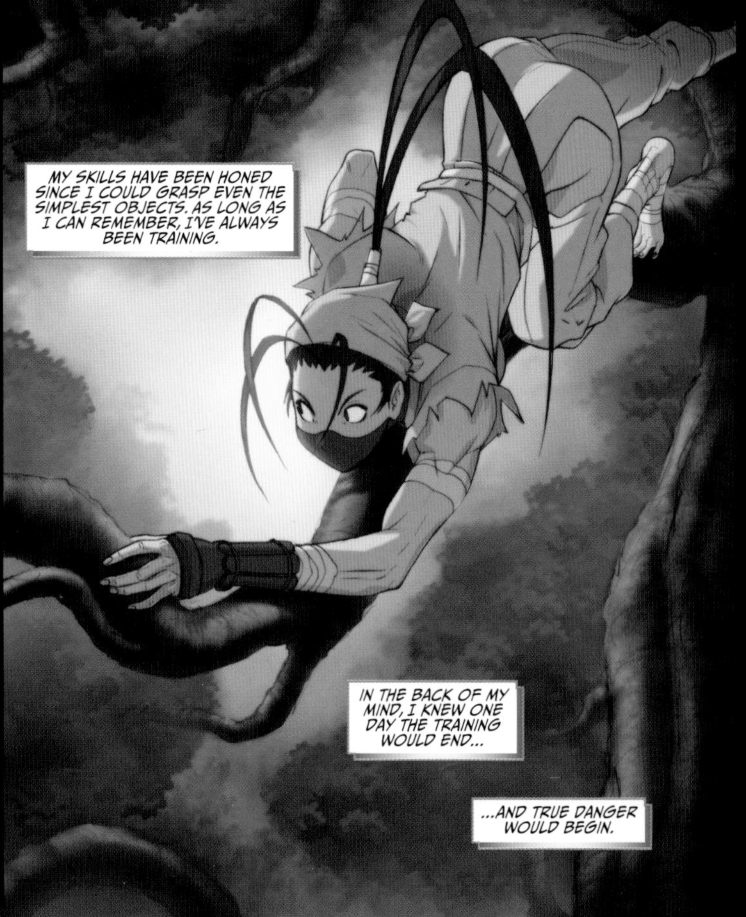
MY SKILLS HAVE BEEN HONED SINCE I COULD GRASP EVEN THE SIMPLEST OBJECTS. AS LONG AS I CAN REMEMBER, I'VE ALWAYS BEEN TRAINING.
IN THE BACK OF MY MIND, I KNEW ONE DAY THE TRAINING WOULD END...
...AND TRUE DANGER WOULD BEGIN.

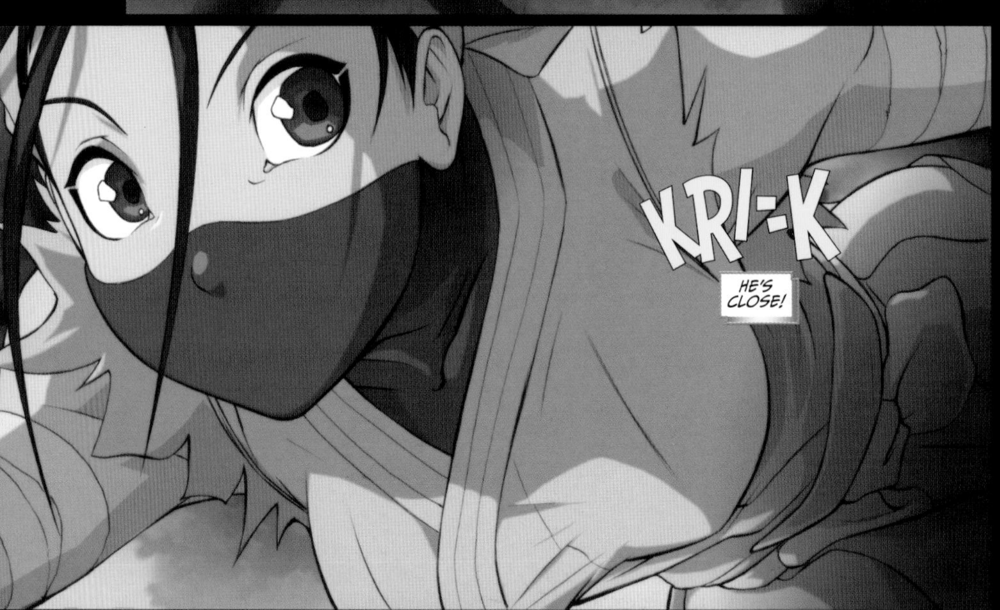
KRI-K
HE'S CLOSE!

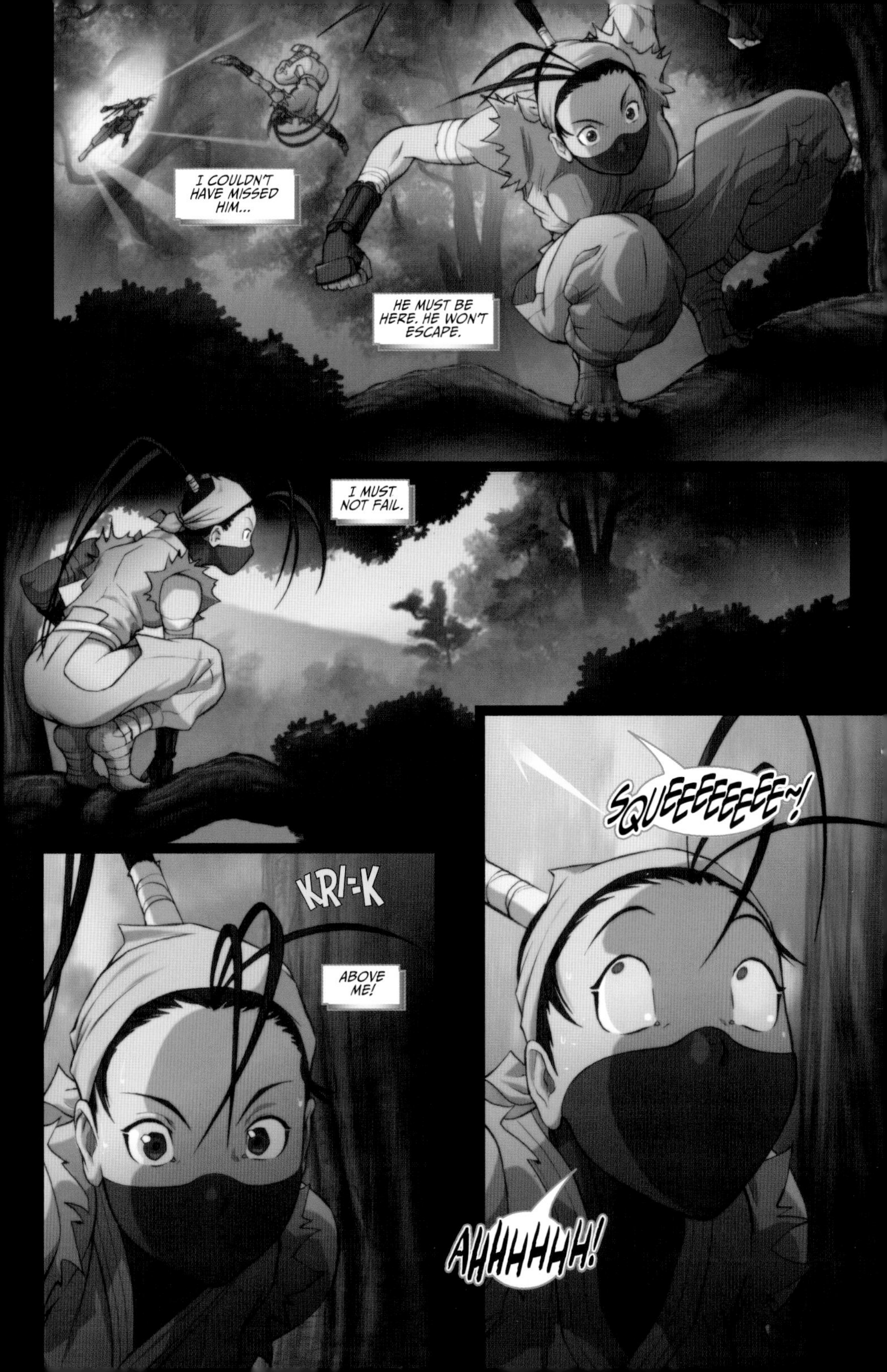
I COULDN'T HAVE MISSED HIM...
HE MUST BE HERE. HE WON'T ESCAPE.
I MUST NOT FAIL.
KRI-K
ABOVE ME!
SQUEEEEEEEEE~!
AHHHHHH!

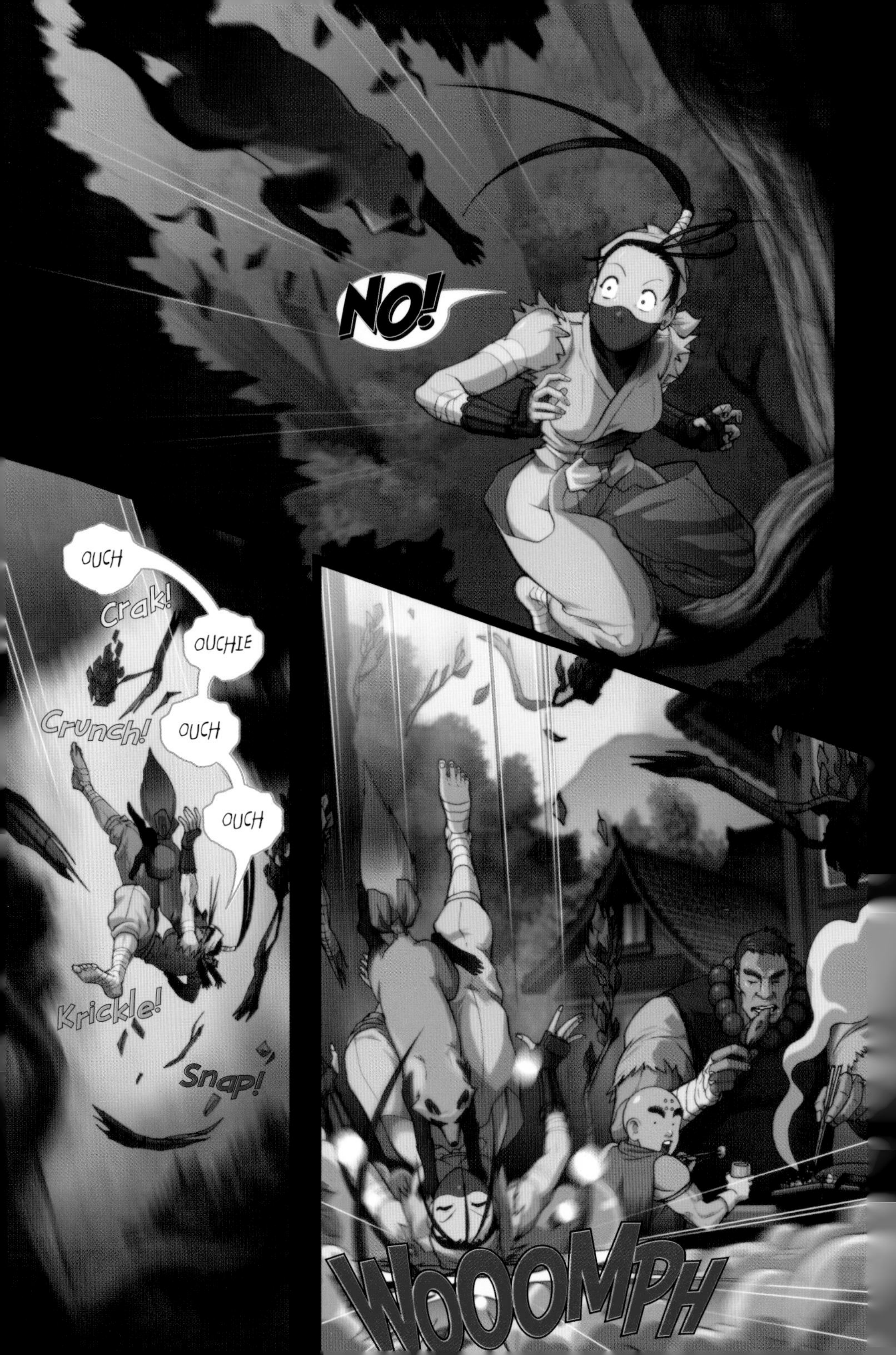
NO!
OUCH
Crak!
OUCHIE
Crunch!
OUCH
OUCH
Krickle!
Snap!
WOOOMPH

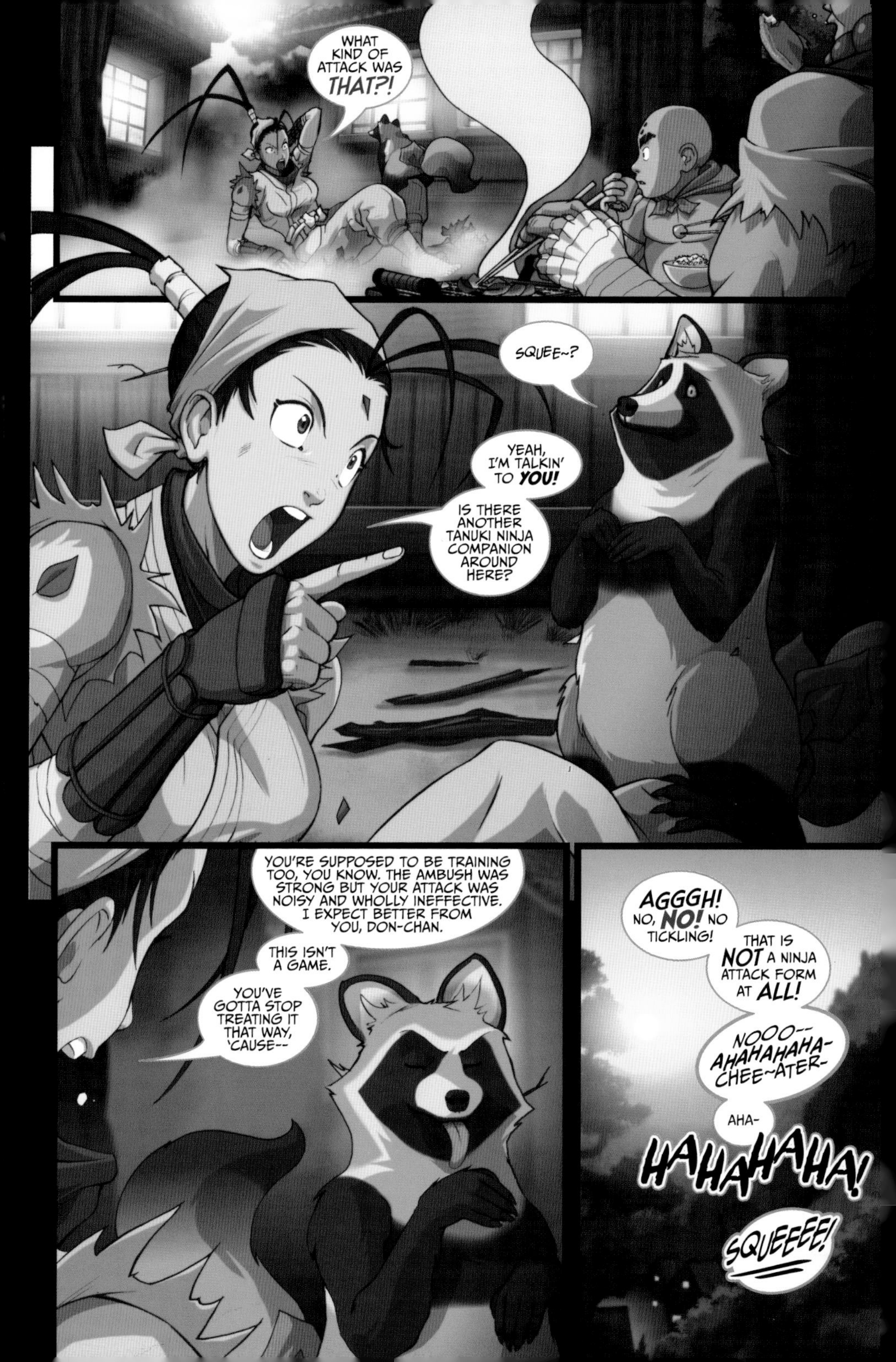
WHAT KIND OF ATTACK WAS THAT?!
SQUEE~?
YEAH, I'M TALKIN' TO YOU!
IS THERE ANOTHER TANUKI NINJA COMPANION AROUND HERE?
YOU'RE SUPPOSED TO BE TRAINING TOO, YOU KNOW. THE AMBUSH WAS STRONG BUT YOUR ATTACK WAS NOISY AND WHOLLY INEFFECTIVE. I EXPECT BETTER FROM YOU, DON-CHAN.
THIS ISN'T A GAME.
YOU'VE GOTTA STOP TREATING IT THAT WAY, 'CAUSE--
AGGGH! NO, NO! NO TICKLING!
THAT IS NOT A NINJA ATTACK FORM AT ALL!
NOOO--AHAHAHAHA-CHEE~ATER-
AHA-
HAHAHAHA!
SQUEEEE!

Art by: Omar Dogan

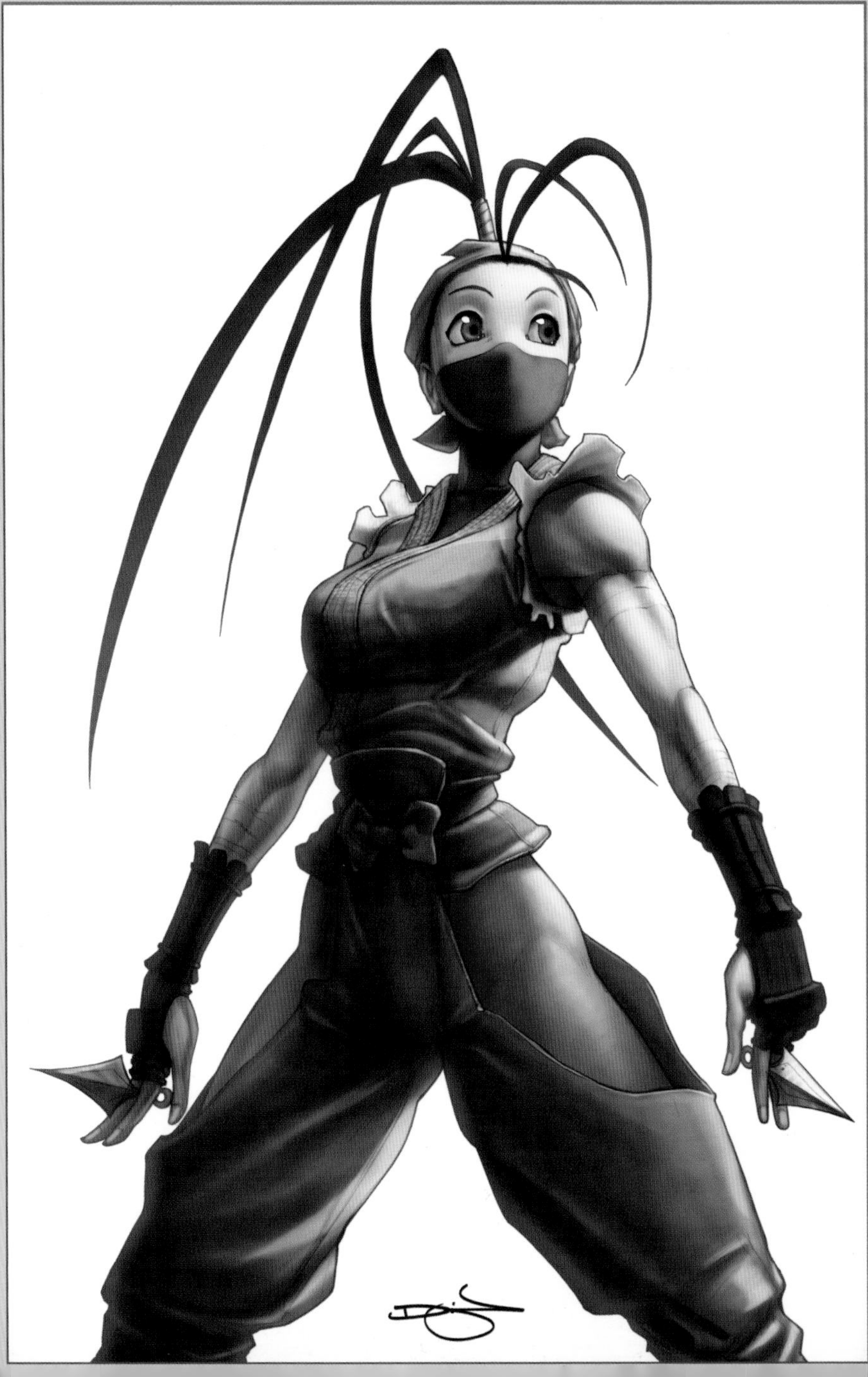

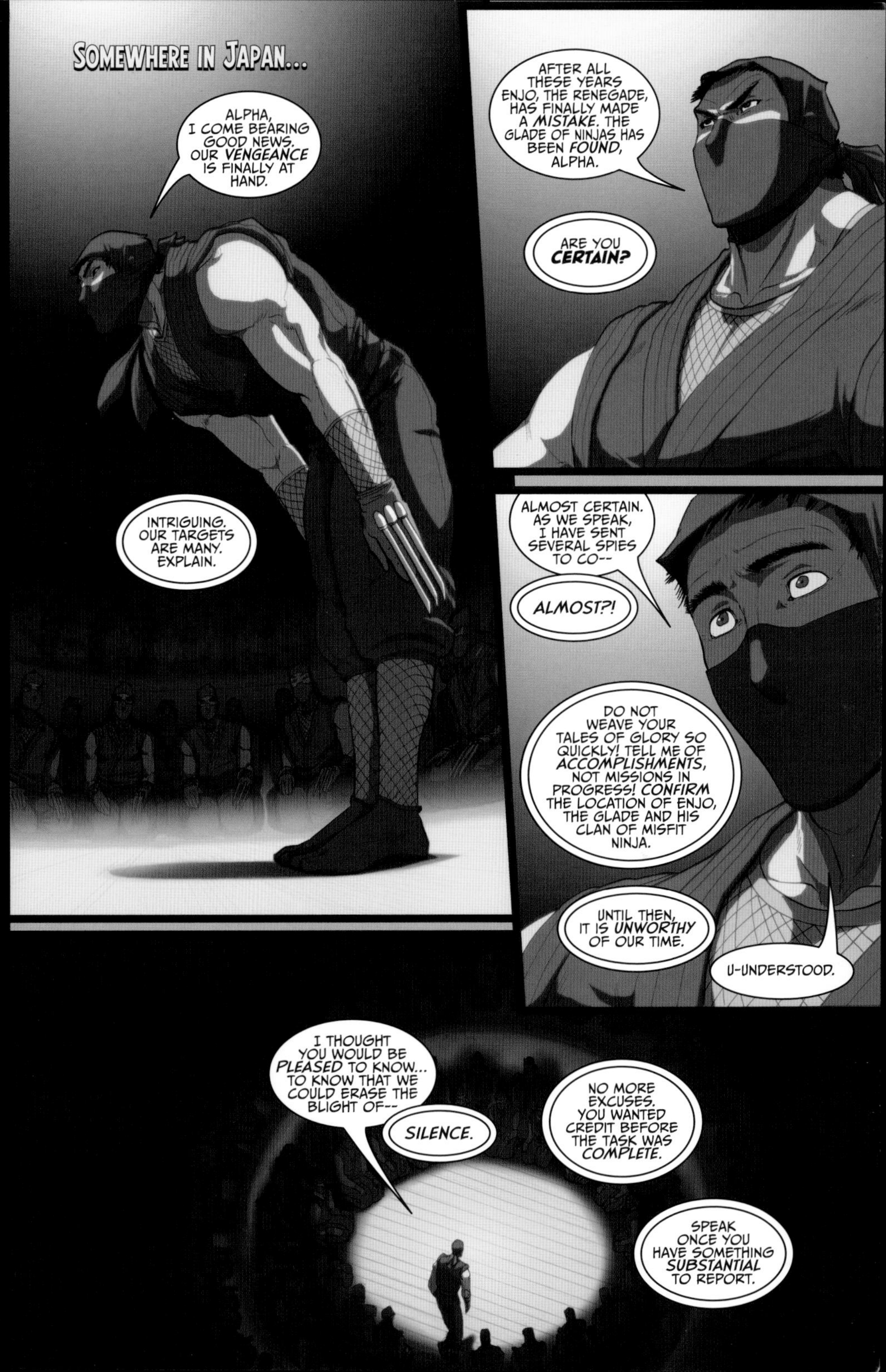
SOMEWHERE IN JAPAN...
ALPHA, I COME BEARING GOOD NEWS. OUR VENGEANCE IS FINALLY AT HAND.
INTRIGUING. OUR TARGETS ARE MANY. EXPLAIN.
AFTER ALL THESE YEARS ENJO, THE RENEGADE, HAS FINALLY MADE A MISTAKE. THE GLADE OF NINJAS HAS BEEN FOUND, ALPHA.
ARE YOU CERTAIN?
ALMOST CERTAIN. AS WE SPEAK, I HAVE SENT SEVERAL SPIES TO CO--
ALMOST?!
DO NOT WEAVE YOUR TALES OF GLORY SO QUICKLY! TELL ME OF ACCOMPLISHMENTS, NOT MISSIONS IN PROGRESS! CONFIRM THE LOCATION OF ENJO, THE GLADE AND HIS CLAN OF MISFIT NINJA.
UNTIL THEN, IT IS UNWORTHY OF OUR TIME.
U-UNDERSTOOD.
I THOUGHT YOU WOULD BE PLEASED TO KNOW... TO KNOW THAT WE COULD ERASE THE BLIGHT OF--
SILENCE.
NO MORE EXCUSES. YOU WANTED CREDIT BEFORE THE TASK WAS COMPLETE.
SPEAK ONCE YOU HAVE SOMETHING SUBSTANTIAL TO REPORT.

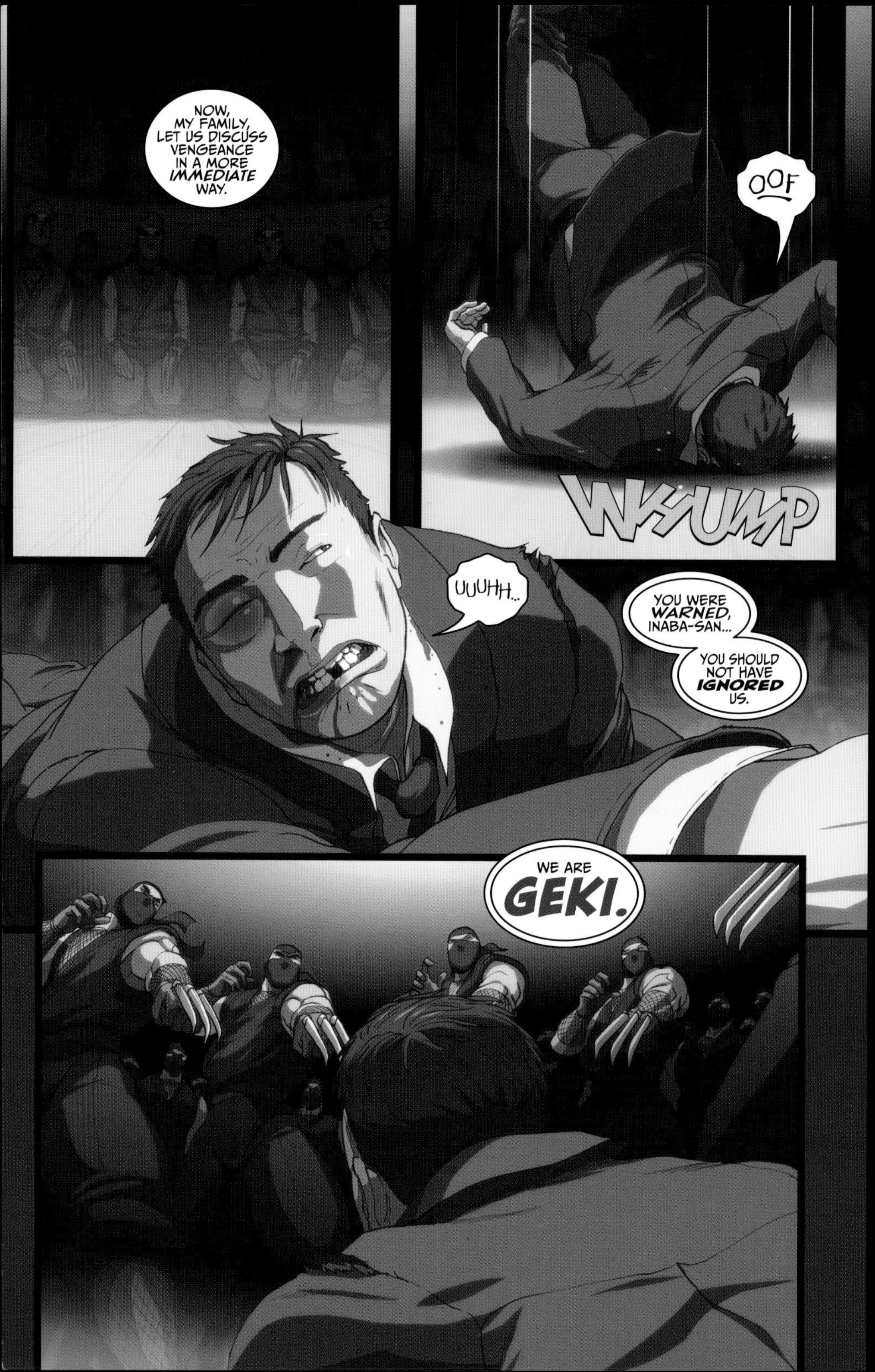
NOW, MY FAMILY, LET US DISCUSS VENGEANCE IN A MORE IMMEDIATE WAY.
OOF
WSUMP
UUUHH...
YOU WERE WARNED, INABA-SAN...
YOU SHOULD NOT HAVE IGNORED US.
WE ARE GEKI.

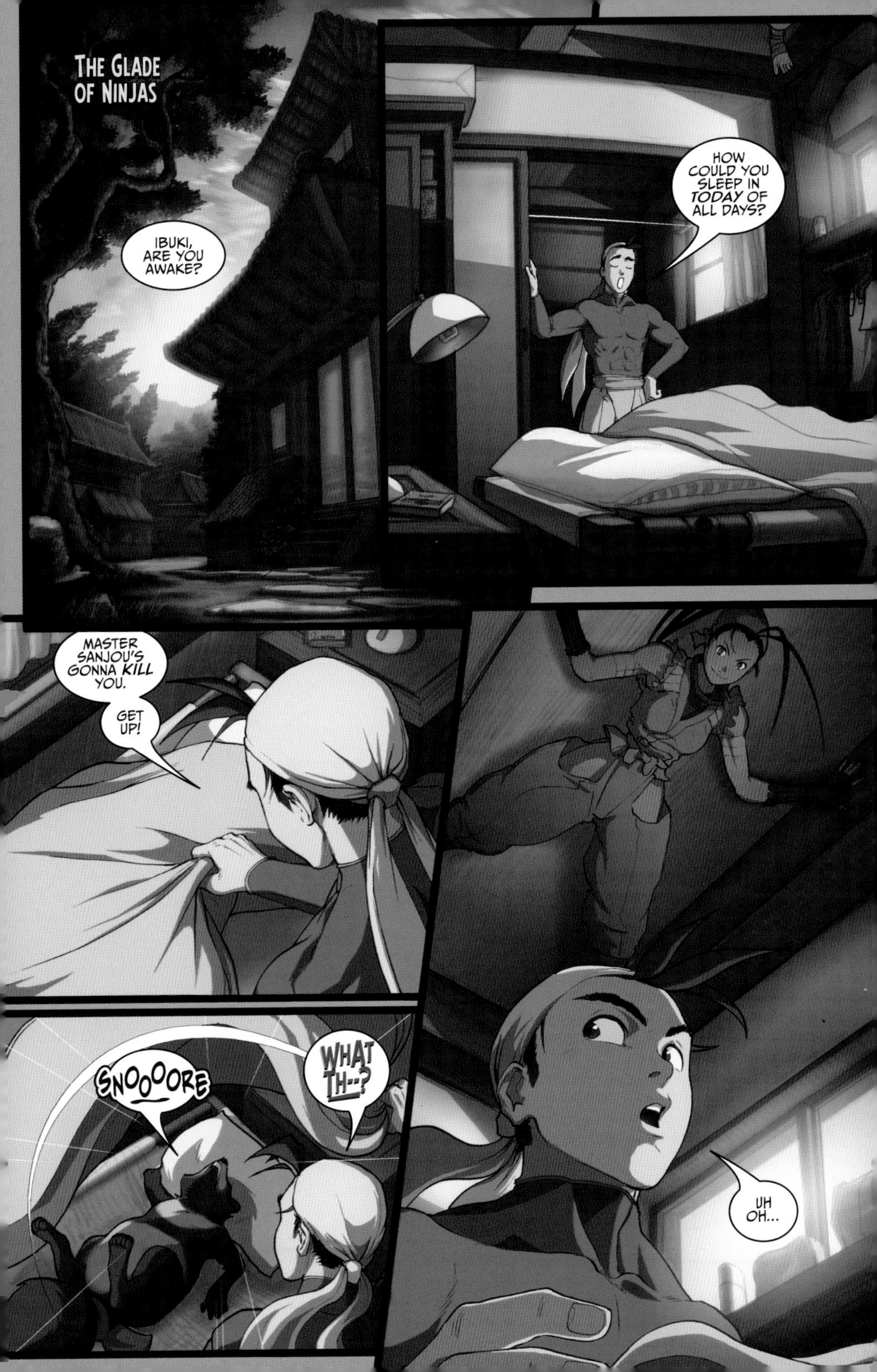

THE GLADE OF NINJAS
IBUKI, ARE YOU AWAKE?
HOW COULD YOU SLEEP IN *TODAY* OF ALL DAYS?
MASTER SANJOU'S GONNA **KILL** YOU.
GET UP!
SNOOOORE
WHAT TH--?
UH OH...

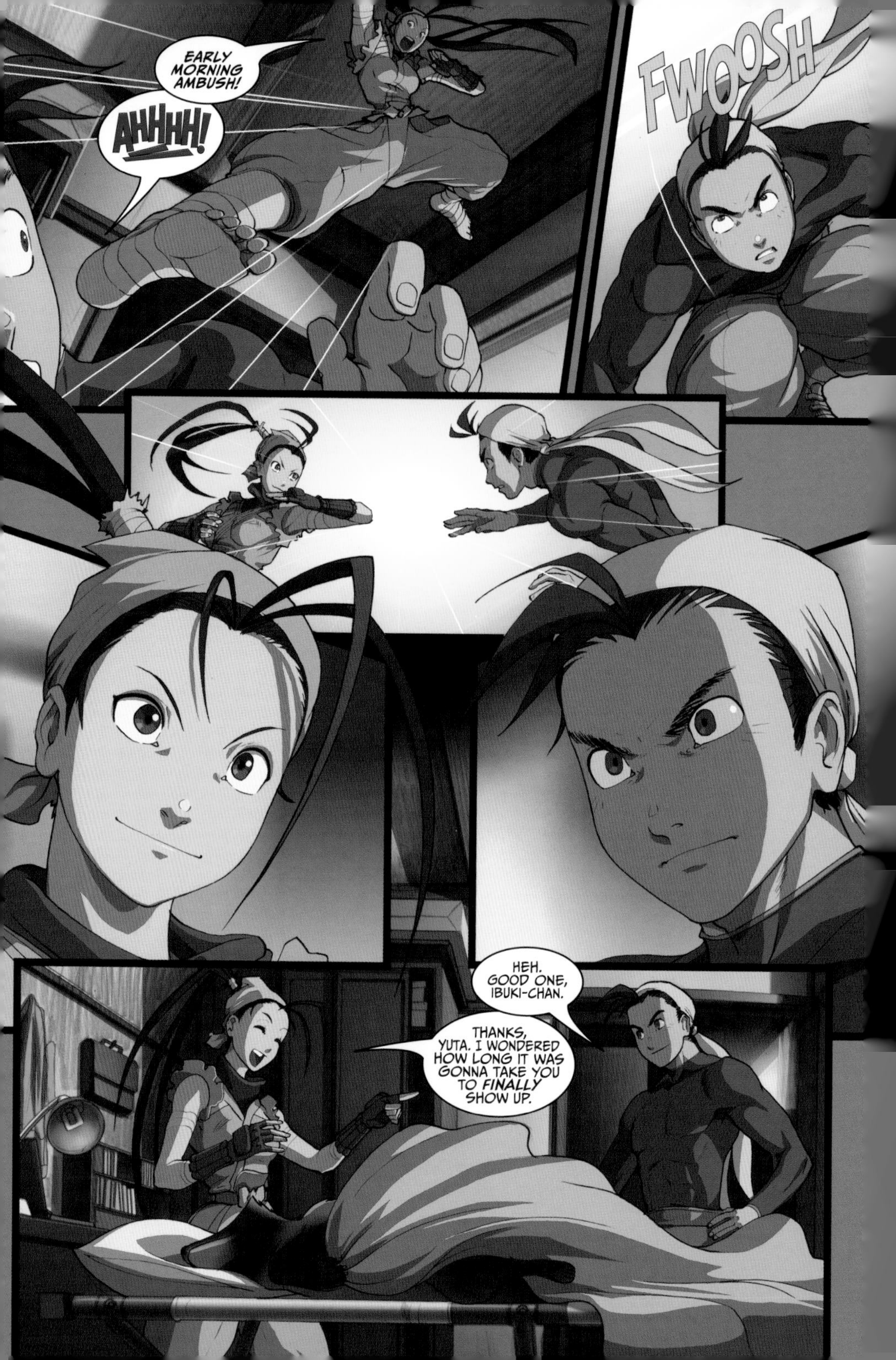
EARLY MORNING AMBUSH!
AHHHH!
FWOOSH
HEH. GOOD ONE, IBUKI-CHAN.
THANKS, YUTA. I WONDERED HOW LONG IT WAS GONNA TAKE YOU TO FINALLY SHOW UP.

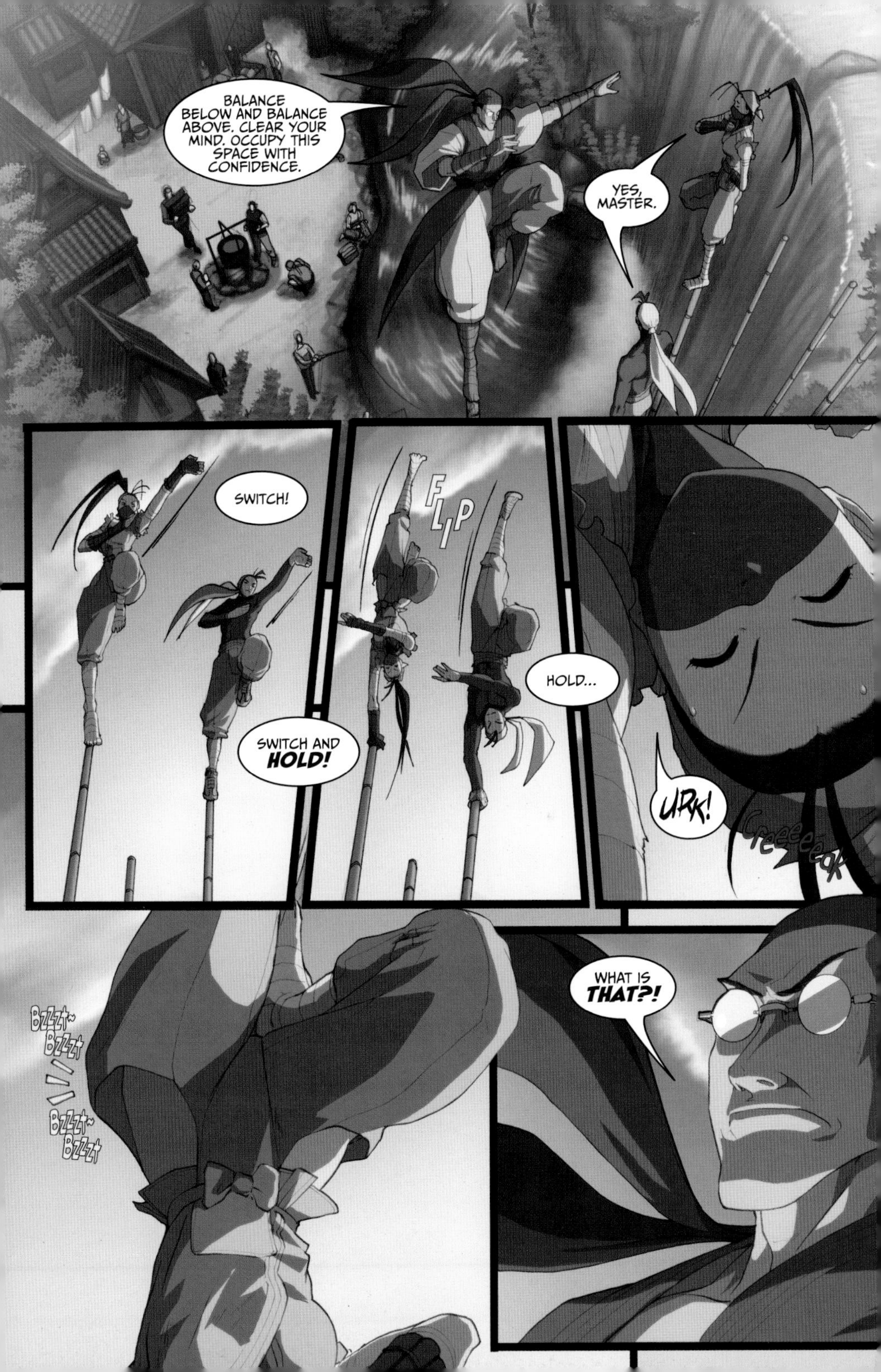
BALANCE BELOW AND BALANCE ABOVE. CLEAR YOUR MIND. OCCUPY THIS SPACE WITH CONFIDENCE.
YES, MASTER.
SWITCH!
SWITCH AND HOLD!
FLIP
HOLD...
URK!
Creeeeeak
Bzzzt~ Bzzzt
Bzzzt~ Bzzzt
WHAT IS THAT?!

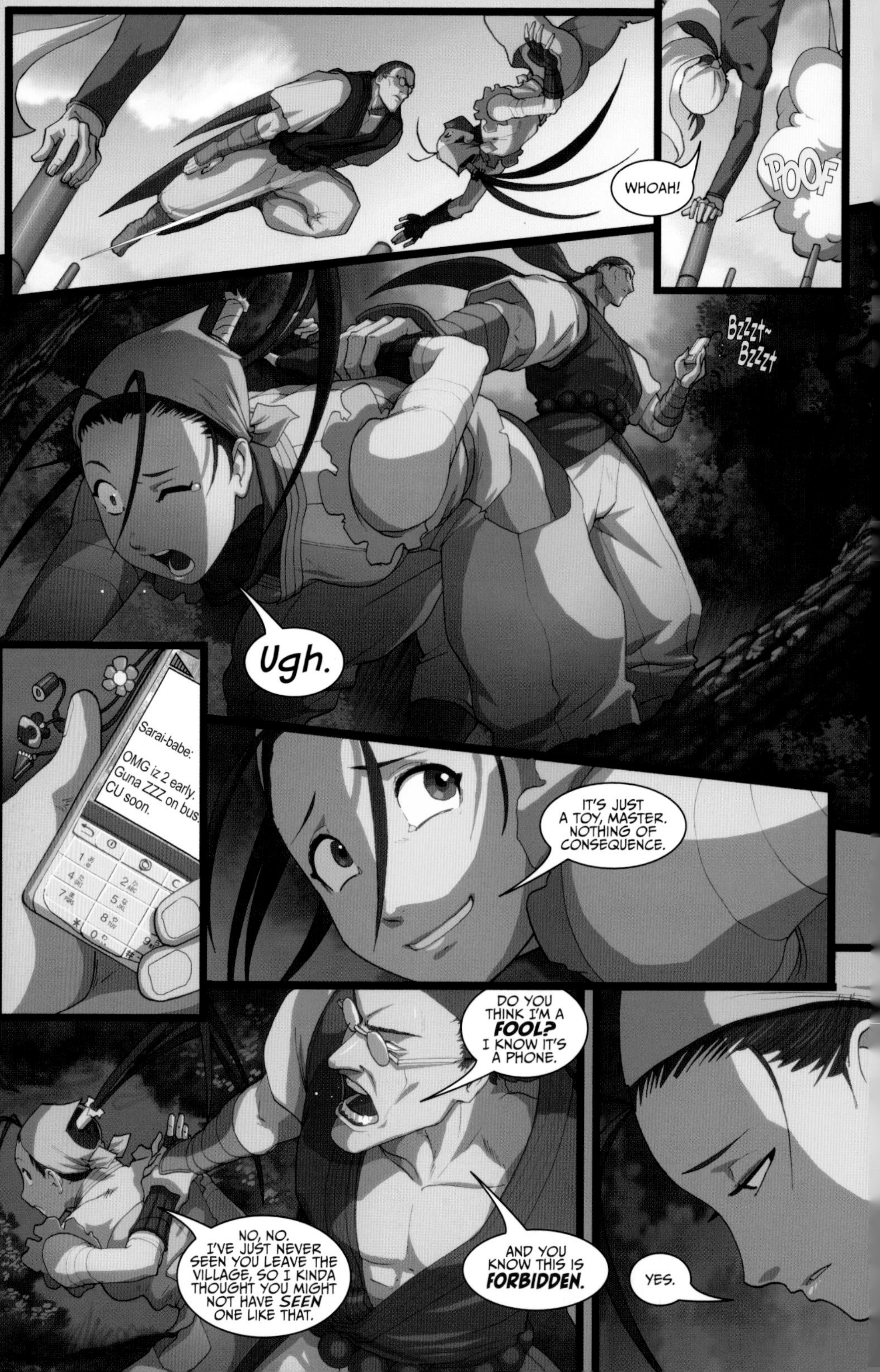
WHOAH!
POOF
Bzzzt~ Bzzzt
Ugh.
Sarai-babe:
OMG iz 2 early. Guna ZZZ on bus. CU soon.
IT'S JUST A TOY, MASTER. NOTHING OF CONSEQUENCE.
DO YOU THINK I'M A **FOOL?** I KNOW IT'S A PHONE.
NO, NO. I'VE JUST NEVER SEEN YOU LEAVE THE VILLAGE, SO I KINDA THOUGHT YOU MIGHT NOT HAVE *SEEN* ONE LIKE THAT.
AND YOU KNOW THIS IS **FORBIDDEN.**
YES.

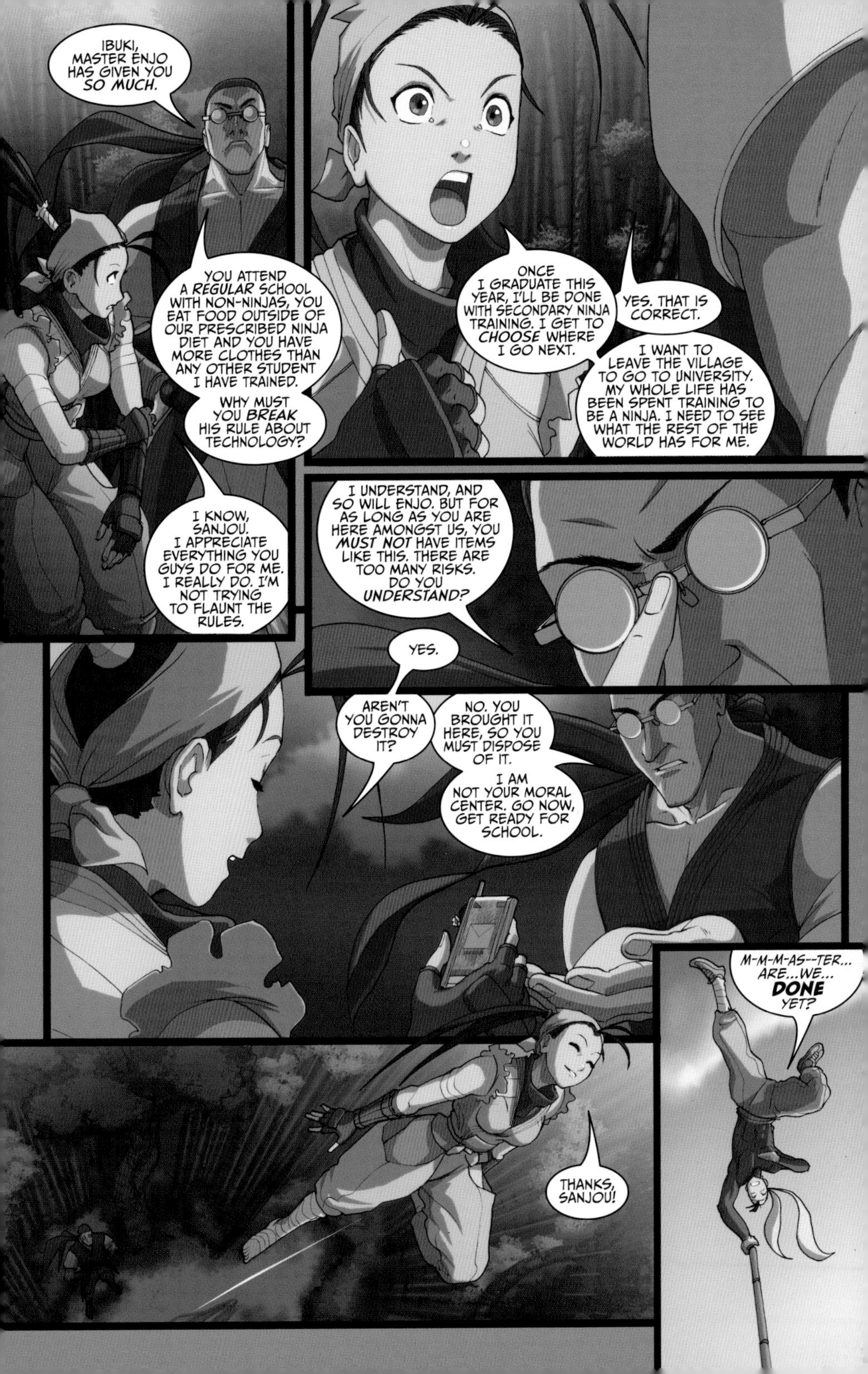
IBUKI, MASTER ENJO HAS GIVEN YOU SO MUCH.
YOU ATTEND A REGULAR SCHOOL WITH NON-NINJAS, YOU EAT FOOD OUTSIDE OF OUR PRESCRIBED NINJA DIET AND YOU HAVE MORE CLOTHES THAN ANY OTHER STUDENT I HAVE TRAINED.
WHY MUST YOU BREAK HIS RULE ABOUT TECHNOLOGY?
I KNOW, SANJOU. I APPRECIATE EVERYTHING YOU GUYS DO FOR ME. I REALLY DO. I'M NOT TRYING TO FLAUNT THE RULES.
ONCE I GRADUATE THIS YEAR, I'LL BE DONE WITH SECONDARY NINJA TRAINING. I GET TO CHOOSE WHERE I GO NEXT.
YES. THAT IS CORRECT.
I WANT TO LEAVE THE VILLAGE TO GO TO UNIVERSITY. MY WHOLE LIFE HAS BEEN SPENT TRAINING TO BE A NINJA. I NEED TO SEE WHAT THE REST OF THE WORLD HAS FOR ME.
I UNDERSTAND, AND SO WILL ENJO. BUT FOR AS LONG AS YOU ARE HERE AMONGST US, YOU MUST NOT HAVE ITEMS LIKE THIS. THERE ARE TOO MANY RISKS. DO YOU UNDERSTAND?
YES.
AREN'T YOU GONNA DESTROY IT?
NO. YOU BROUGHT IT HERE, SO YOU MUST DISPOSE OF IT.
I AM NOT YOUR MORAL CENTER. GO NOW, GET READY FOR SCHOOL.
THANKS, SANJOU!
M-M-M-AS--TER... ARE...WE... DONE YET?

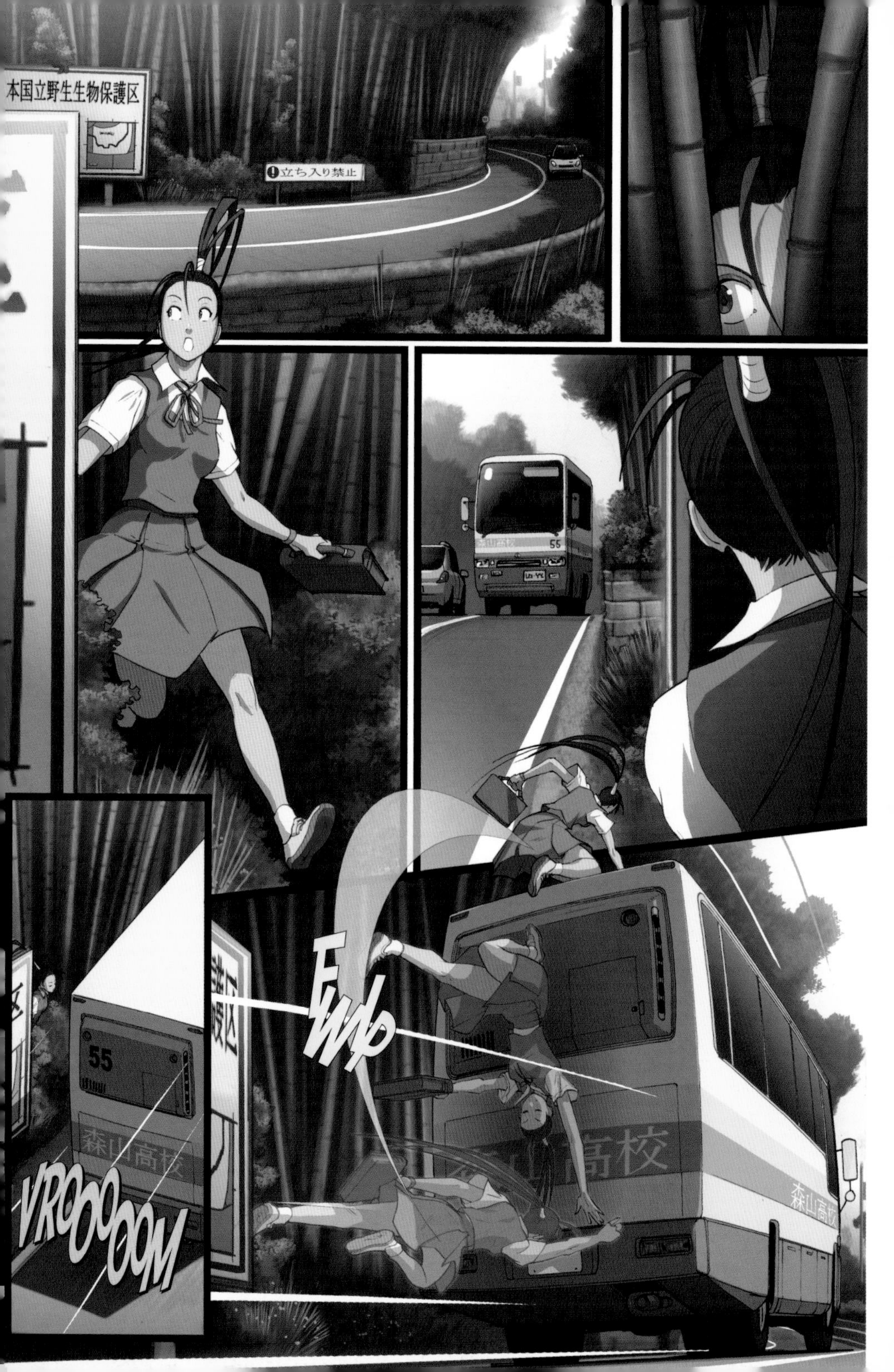
本国立野生生物保護区
立ち入り禁止
55
森山高校
FWIP
VROOOOOM
55
森山高校
森山高校

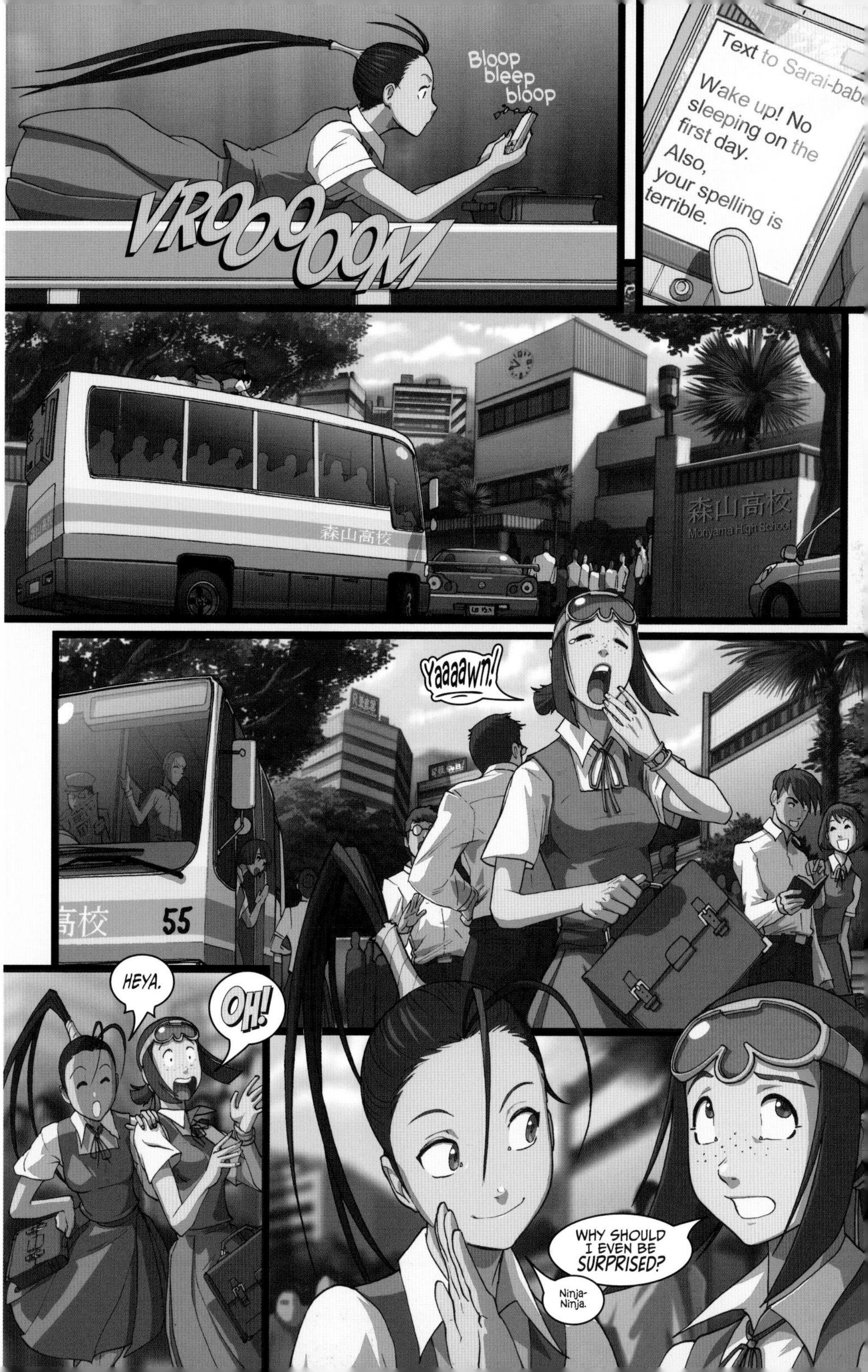
Bloop
bleep
bloop
VROOOOOM
Text to Sarai-babe
Wake up! No sleeping on the first day.
Also, your spelling is terrible.
森山高校
森山高校
Moriyama High School
Yaaaawn!
高校 55
HEYA.
OH!
WHY SHOULD I EVEN BE SURPRISED?
Ninja-Ninja.

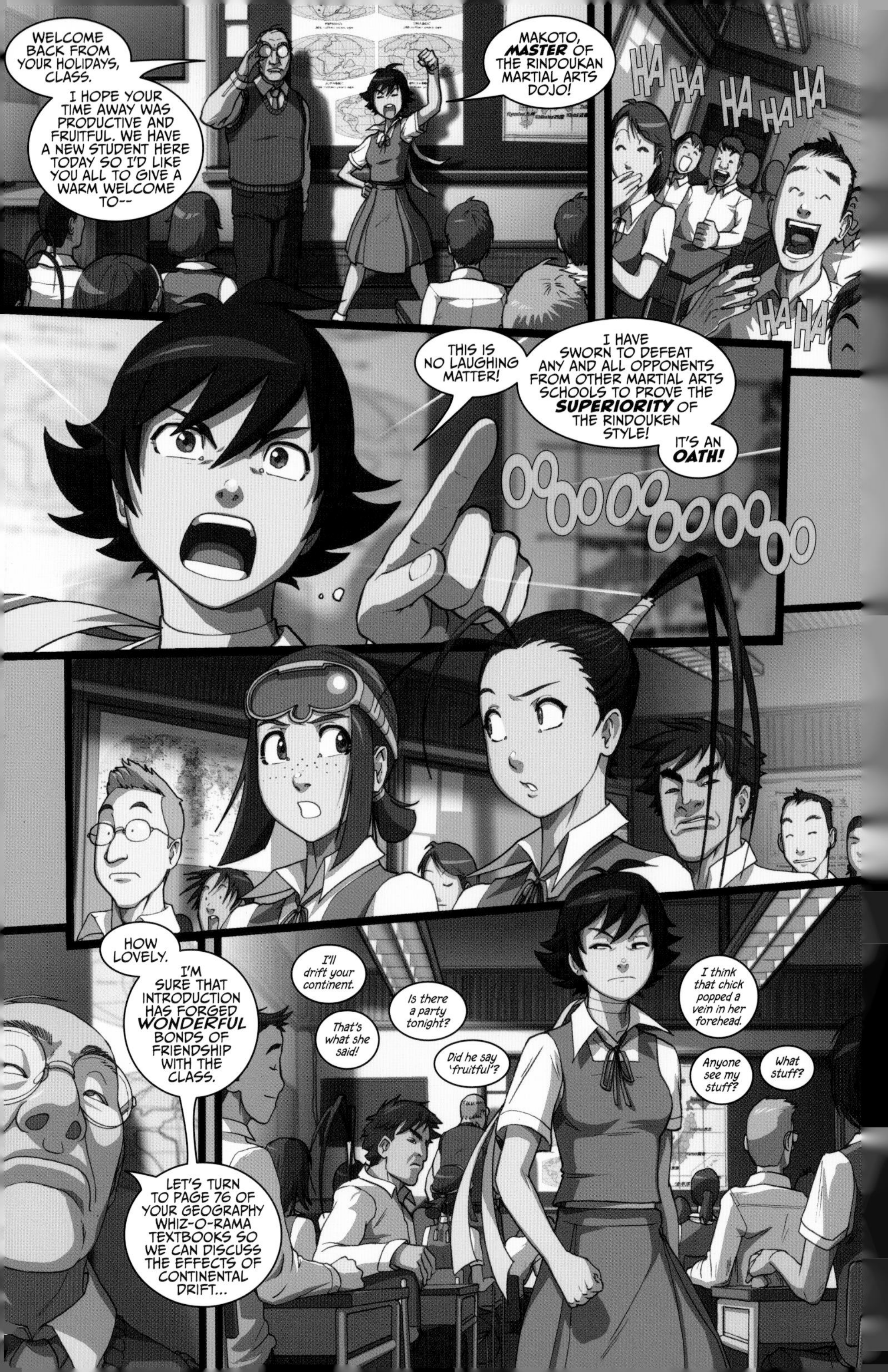
WELCOME BACK FROM YOUR HOLIDAYS, CLASS.
I HOPE YOUR TIME AWAY WAS PRODUCTIVE AND FRUITFUL. WE HAVE A NEW STUDENT HERE TODAY SO I'D LIKE YOU ALL TO GIVE A WARM WELCOME TO--
MAKOTO, **MASTER** OF THE RINDOUKAN MARTIAL ARTS DOJO!
HA HA HA HA HA
HA HA
THIS IS NO LAUGHING MATTER!
I HAVE SWORN TO DEFEAT ANY AND ALL OPPONENTS FROM OTHER MARTIAL ARTS SCHOOLS TO PROVE THE **SUPERIORITY** OF THE RINDOUKEN STYLE!
IT'S AN **OATH!**
OOOOOOOOOOOOOO
HOW LOVELY.
I'M SURE THAT INTRODUCTION HAS FORGED **WONDERFUL** BONDS OF FRIENDSHIP WITH THE CLASS.
I'll drift your continent.
That's what she said!
Is there a party tonight?
Did he say 'fruitful'?
I think that chick popped a vein in her forehead.
Anyone see my stuff?
What stuff?
LET'S TURN TO PAGE 76 OF YOUR GEOGRAPHY WHIZ-O-RAMA TEXTBOOKS SO WE CAN DISCUSS THE EFFECTS OF CONTINENTAL DRIFT...

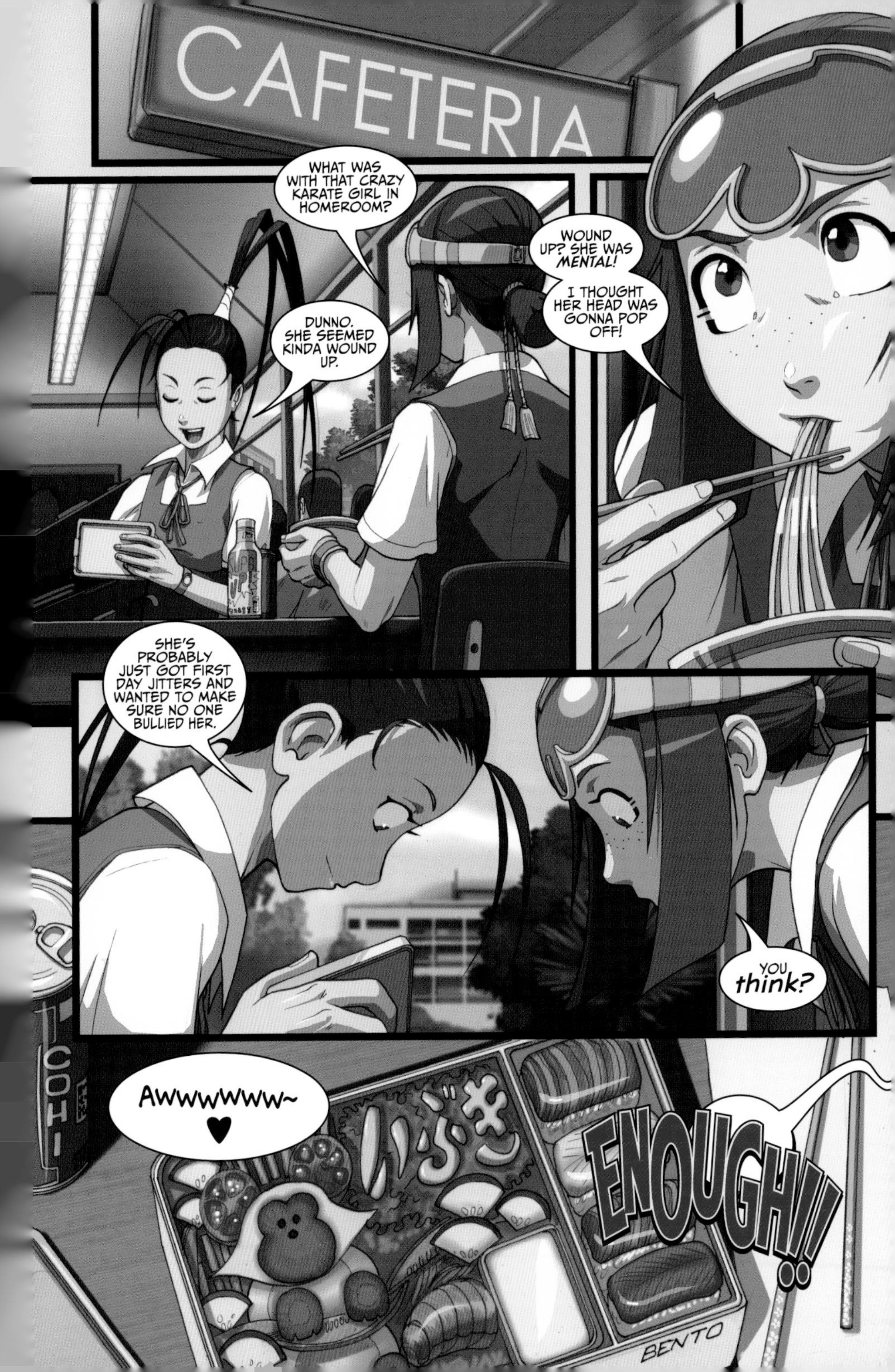
CAFETERIA
WHAT WAS WITH THAT CRAZY KARATE GIRL IN HOMEROOM?
DUNNO. SHE SEEMED KINDA WOUND UP.
WOUND UP? SHE WAS MENTAL!
I THOUGHT HER HEAD WAS GONNA POP OFF!
SHE'S PROBABLY JUST GOT FIRST DAY JITTERS AND WANTED TO MAKE SURE NO ONE BULLIED HER.
YOU think?
AWWWWWW~ ♥
ENOUGH!!
BENTO

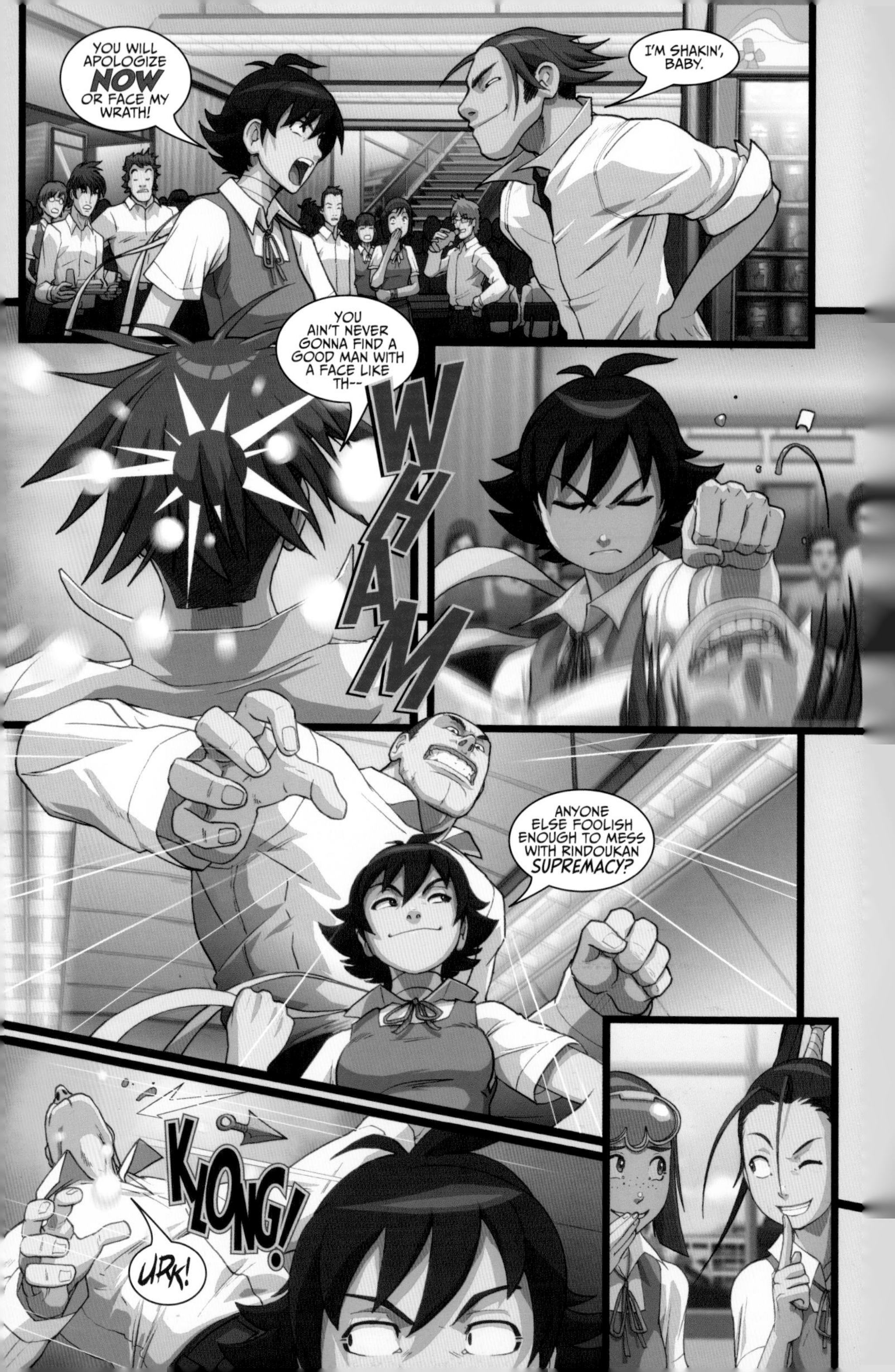
YOU WILL APOLOGIZE NOW OR FACE MY WRATH!
I'M SHAKIN', BABY.
YOU AIN'T NEVER GONNA FIND A GOOD MAN WITH A FACE LIKE TH--
WHAM
ANYONE ELSE FOOLISH ENOUGH TO MESS WITH RINDOUKAN SUPREMACY?
KLONG!
URK!

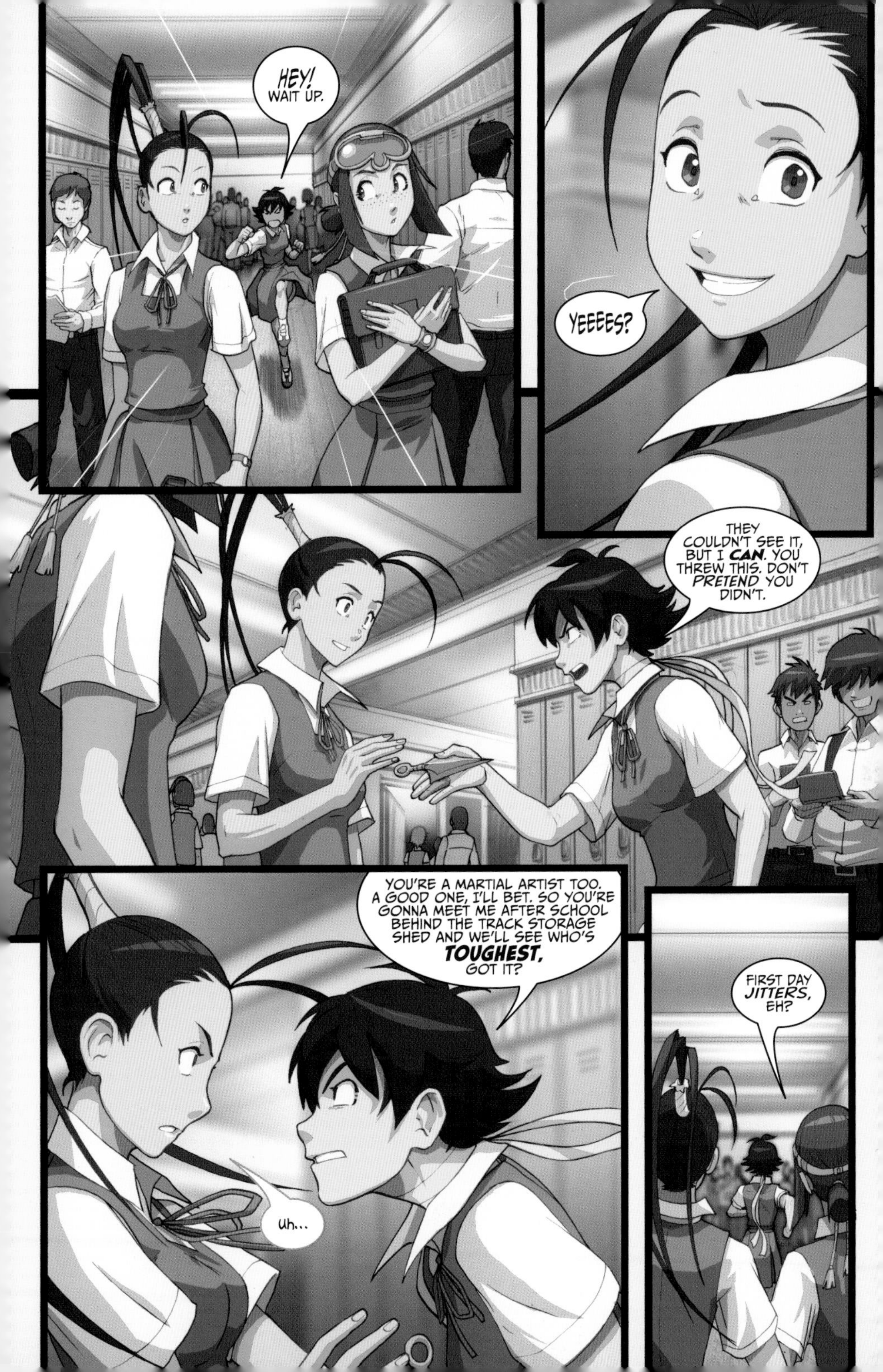

HEY! WAIT UP.
YEEEES?
THEY COULDN'T SEE IT, BUT I CAN. YOU THREW THIS. DON'T PRETEND YOU DIDN'T.
YOU'RE A MARTIAL ARTIST TOO. A GOOD ONE, I'LL BET. SO YOU'RE GONNA MEET ME AFTER SCHOOL BEHIND THE TRACK STORAGE SHED AND WE'LL SEE WHO'S TOUGHEST, GOT IT?
Uh...
FIRST DAY JITTERS, EH?

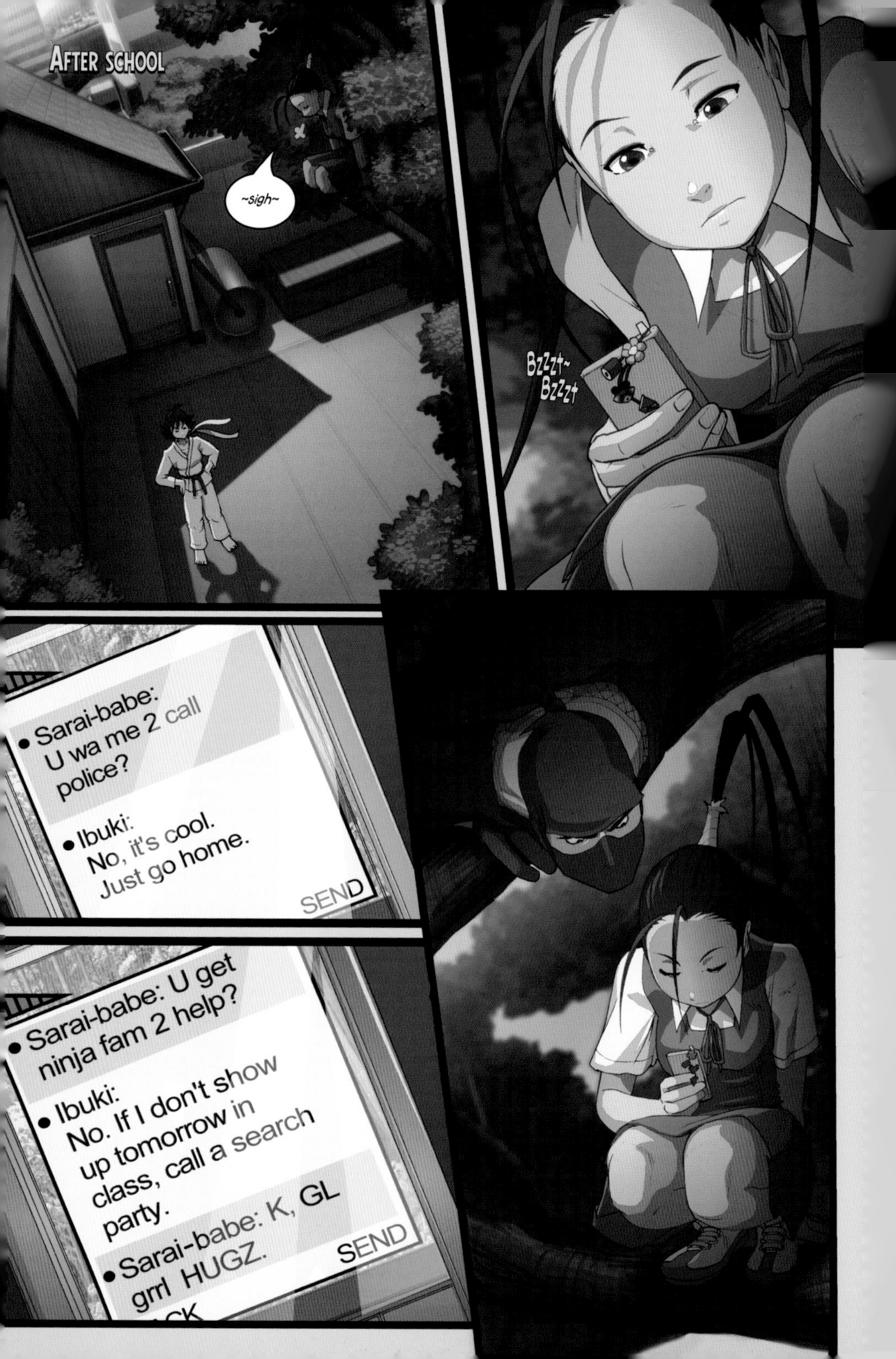

AFTER SCHOOL
~sigh~
Bzzzt~
Bzzzt
Sarai-babe: U wa me 2 call police?
Ibuki: No, it's cool. Just go home.
SEND
Sarai-babe: U get ninja fam 2 help?
Ibuki: No. If I don't show up tomorrow in class, call a search party.
Sarai-babe: K, GL grrl HUGZ.
SEND

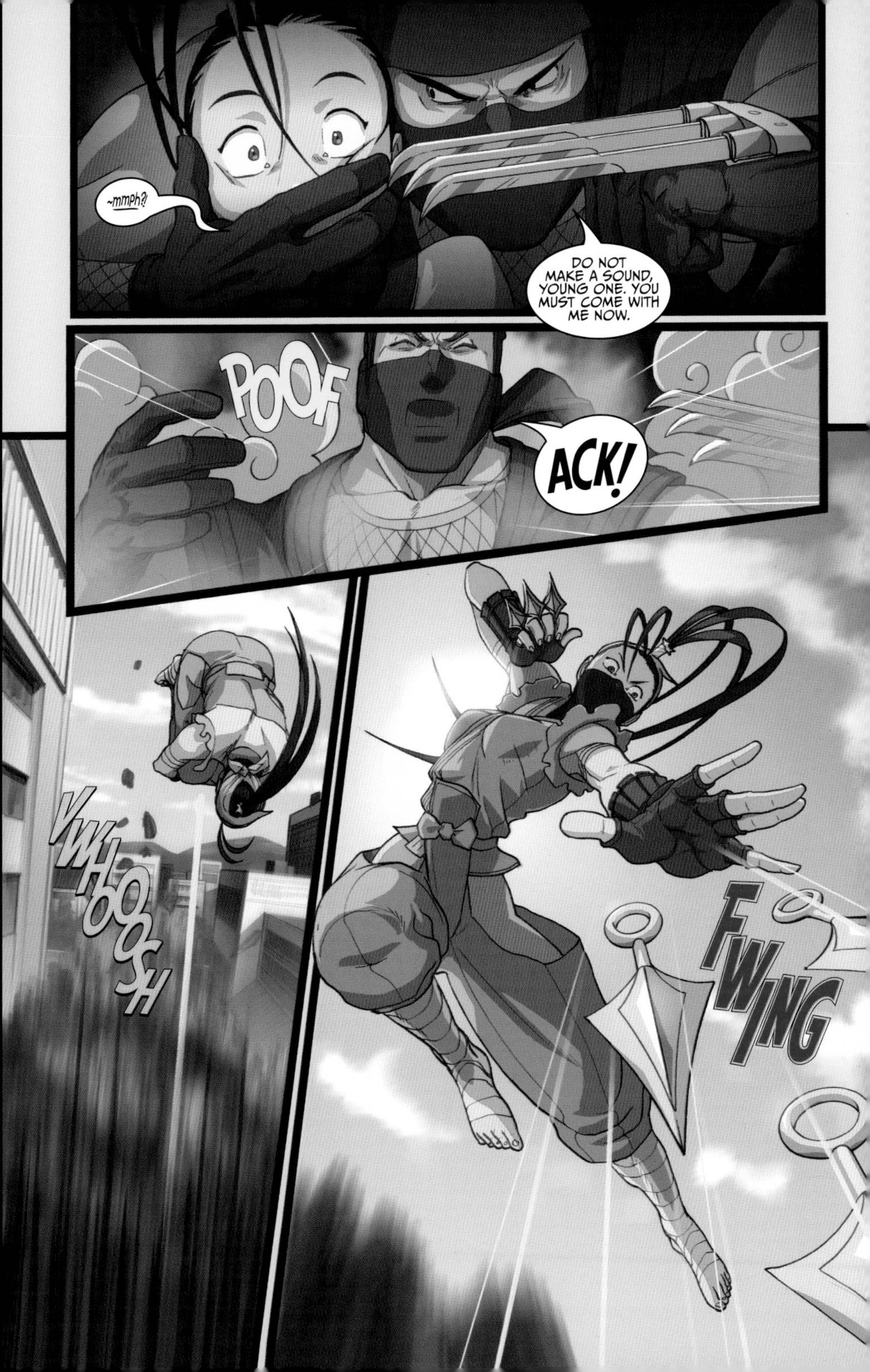
~mmph?!
DO NOT MAKE A SOUND, YOUNG ONE. YOU MUST COME WITH ME NOW.
POOF
ACK!
VWHOOSH
FWING

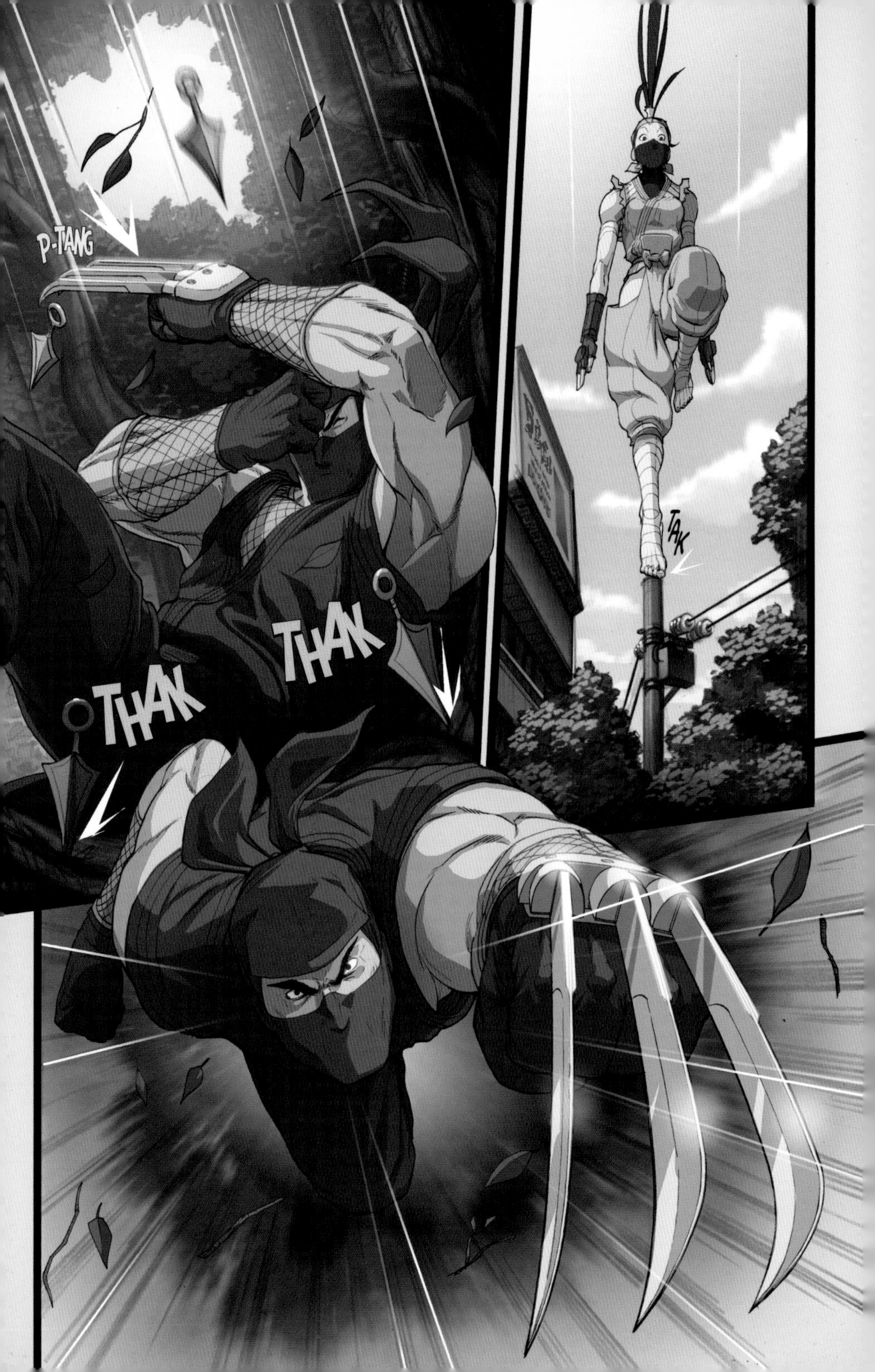
P-TANG
THAK
THAK
TAK

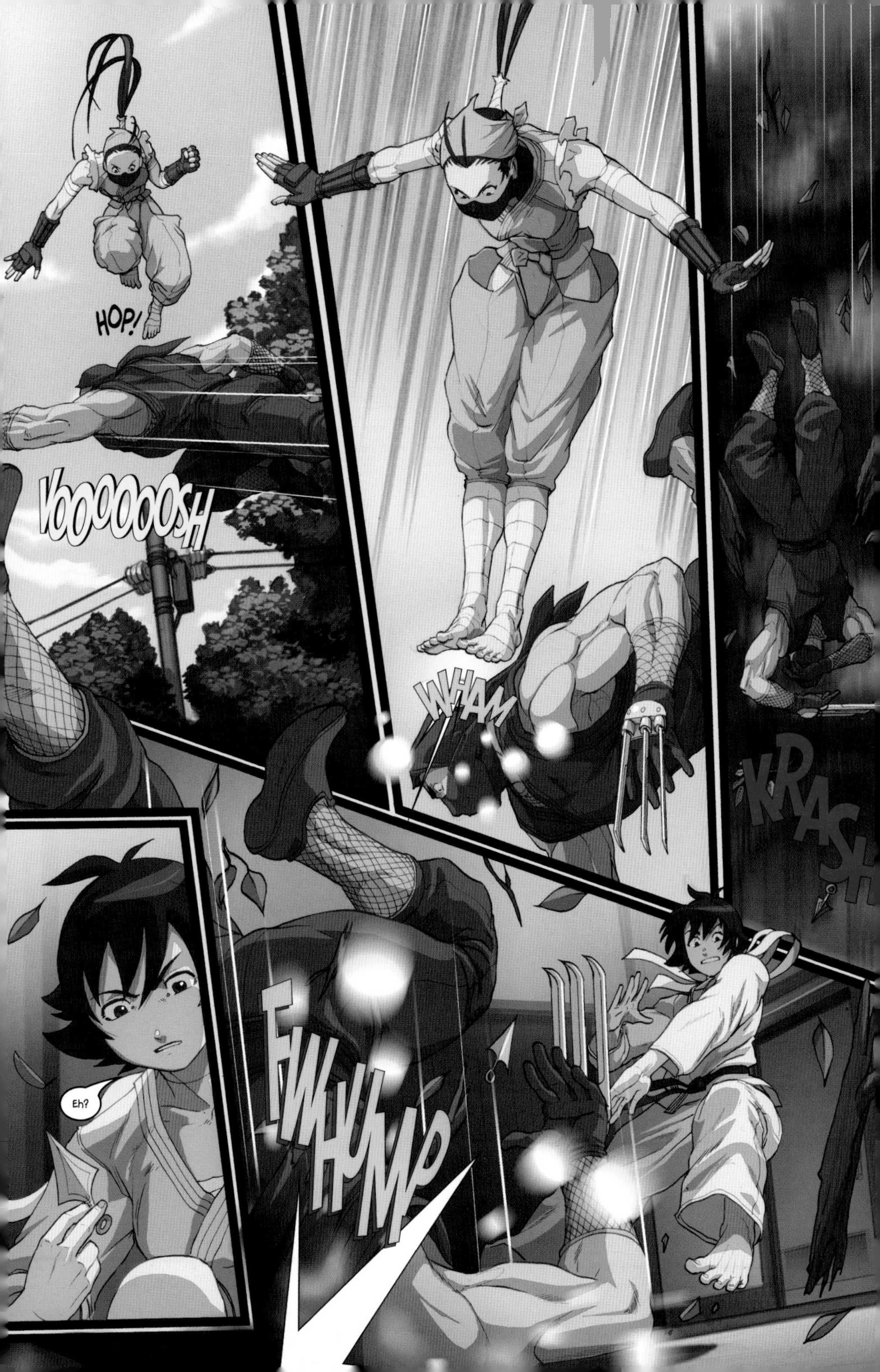
HOP!
VOOOOOOSH
WHAM
KRASH
Eh?
FWHUMP

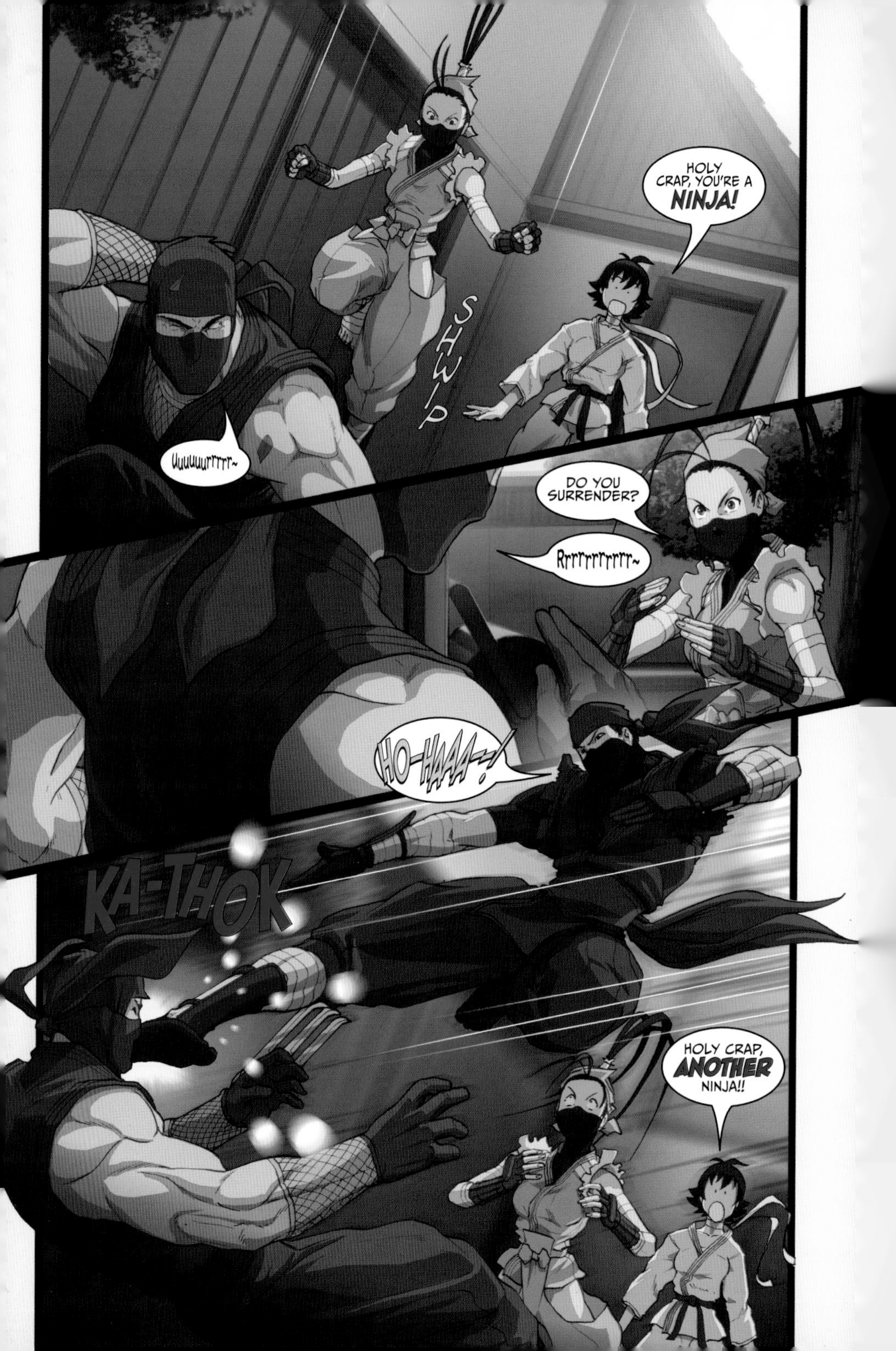
HOLY CRAP, YOU'RE A **NINJA!**
SHWIP
Uuuuuurrrr~
DO YOU SURRENDER?
Rrrrrrrrrrr~
HO-HAAA~!
KA-THOK
HOLY CRAP, **ANOTHER** NINJA!!

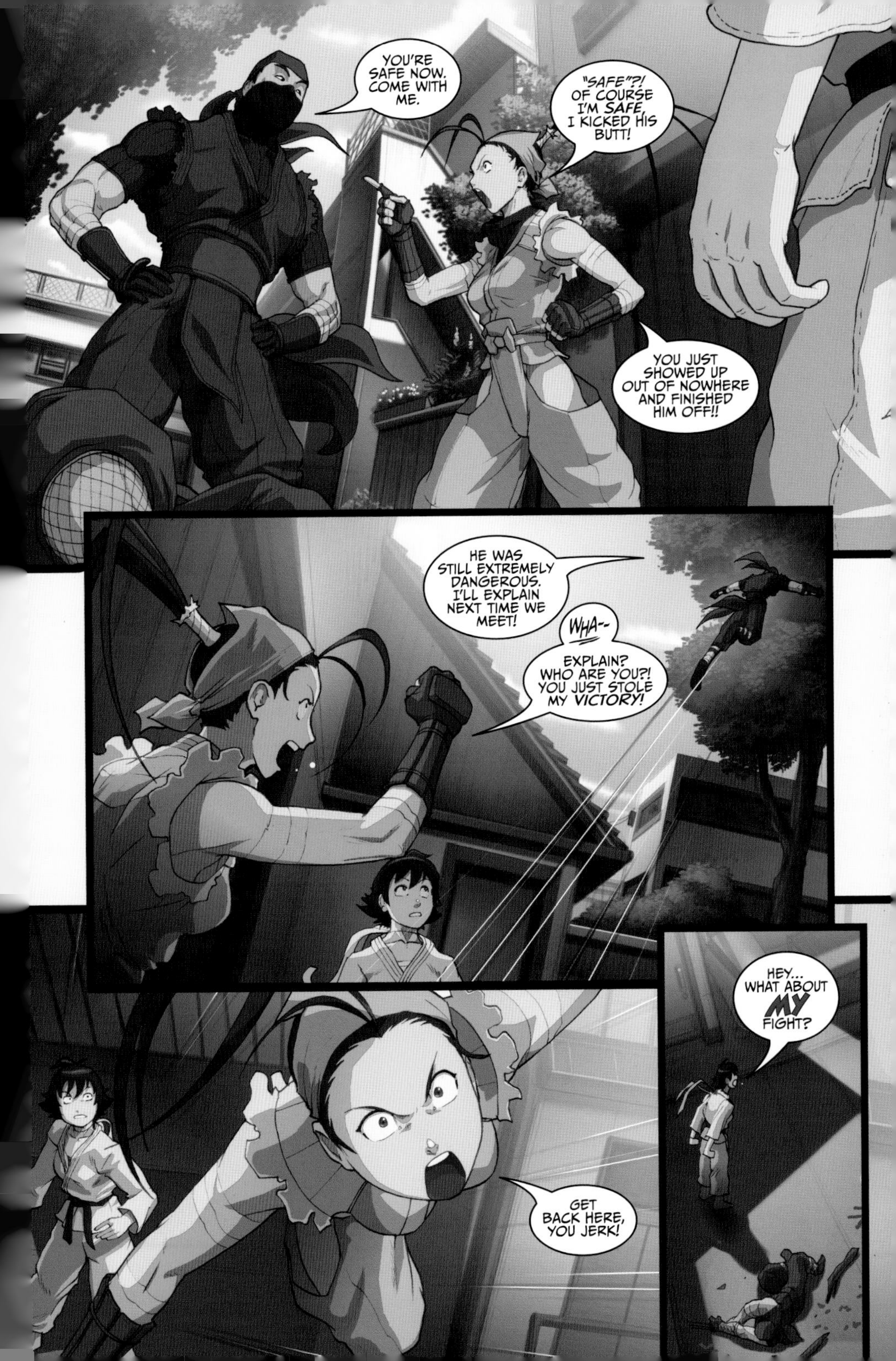
YOU'RE SAFE NOW. COME WITH ME.
"SAFE"?! OF COURSE I'M SAFE, I KICKED HIS BUTT!
YOU JUST SHOWED UP OUT OF NOWHERE AND FINISHED HIM OFF!!
HE WAS STILL EXTREMELY DANGEROUS. I'LL EXPLAIN NEXT TIME WE MEET!
WHA--
EXPLAIN? WHO ARE YOU?! YOU JUST STOLE MY VICTORY!
GET BACK HERE, YOU JERK!
HEY... WHAT ABOUT MY FIGHT?

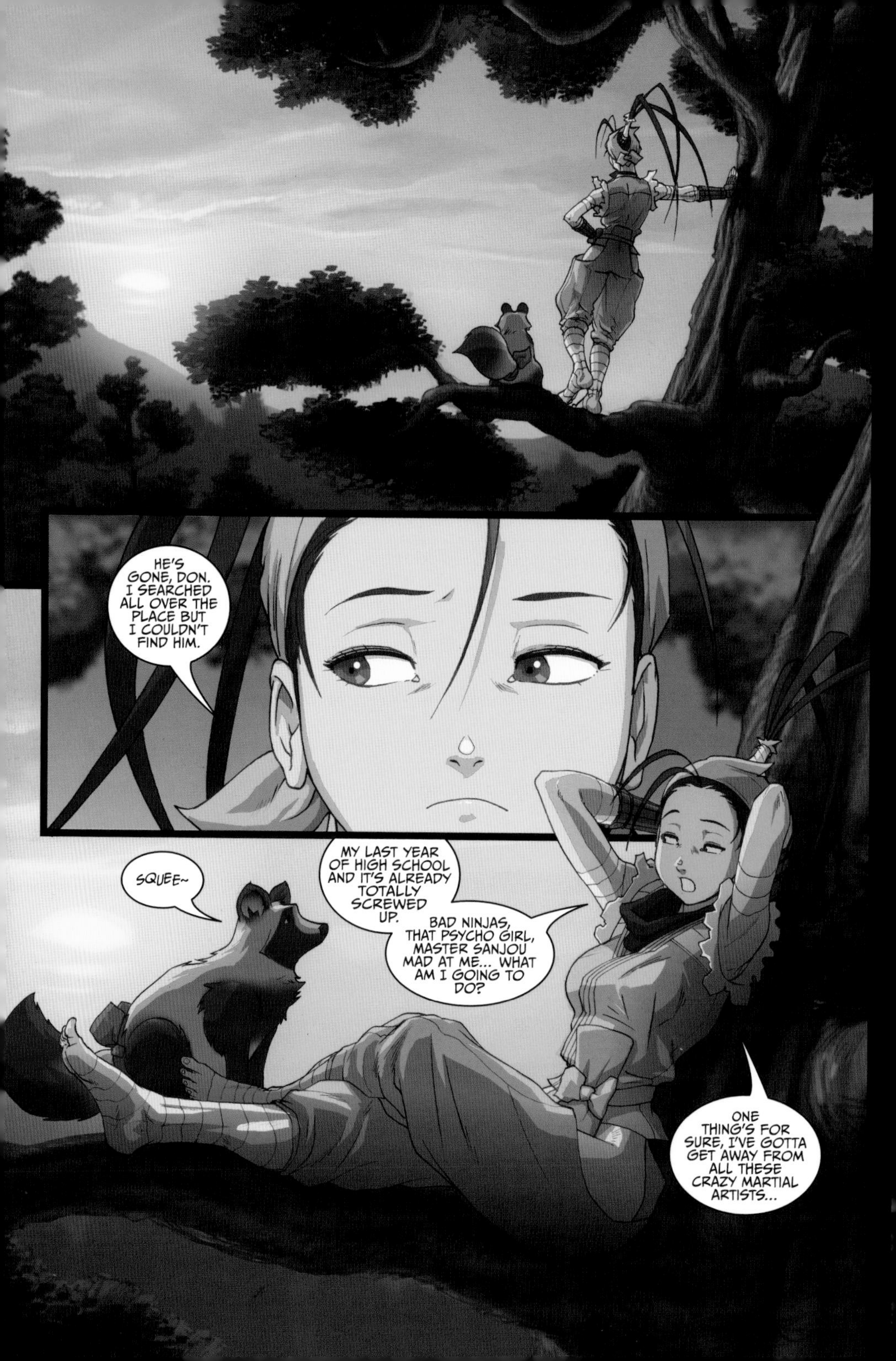
HE'S GONE, DON. I SEARCHED ALL OVER THE PLACE BUT I COULDN'T FIND HIM.
SQUEE~
MY LAST YEAR OF HIGH SCHOOL AND IT'S ALREADY TOTALLY SCREWED UP.
BAD NINJAS, THAT PSYCHO GIRL, MASTER SANJOU MAD AT ME... WHAT AM I GOING TO DO?
ONE THING'S FOR SURE, I'VE GOTTA GET AWAY FROM ALL THESE CRAZY MARTIAL ARTISTS...

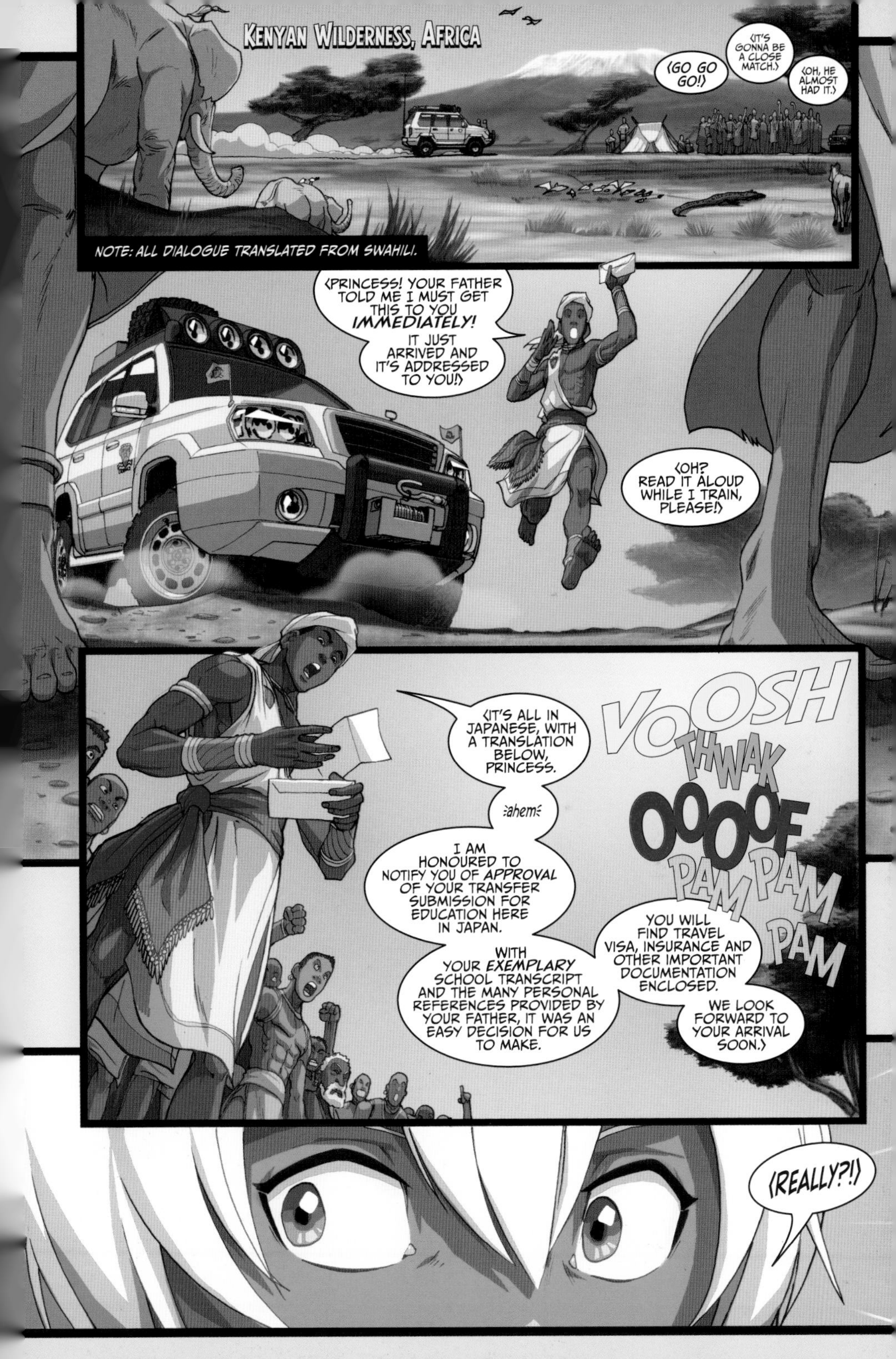
KENYAN WILDERNESS, AFRICA
⟨GO GO GO!⟩
⟨IT'S GONNA BE A CLOSE MATCH.⟩
⟨OH, HE ALMOST HAD IT.⟩
NOTE: ALL DIALOGUE TRANSLATED FROM SWAHILI.
⟨PRINCESS! YOUR FATHER TOLD ME I MUST GET THIS TO YOU IMMEDIATELY!
IT JUST ARRIVED AND IT'S ADDRESSED TO YOU!⟩
⟨OH? READ IT ALOUD WHILE I TRAIN, PLEASE!⟩
⟨IT'S ALL IN JAPANESE, WITH A TRANSLATION BELOW, PRINCESS.
ahem
I AM HONOURED TO NOTIFY YOU OF APPROVAL OF YOUR TRANSFER SUBMISSION FOR EDUCATION HERE IN JAPAN.
WITH YOUR EXEMPLARY SCHOOL TRANSCRIPT AND THE MANY PERSONAL REFERENCES PROVIDED BY YOUR FATHER, IT WAS AN EASY DECISION FOR US TO MAKE.
YOU WILL FIND TRAVEL VISA, INSURANCE AND OTHER IMPORTANT DOCUMENTATION ENCLOSED.
WE LOOK FORWARD TO YOUR ARRIVAL SOON.⟩
VOOSH
THWAK
OOOOF
PAM PAM PAM PAM
⟨REALLY?!⟩

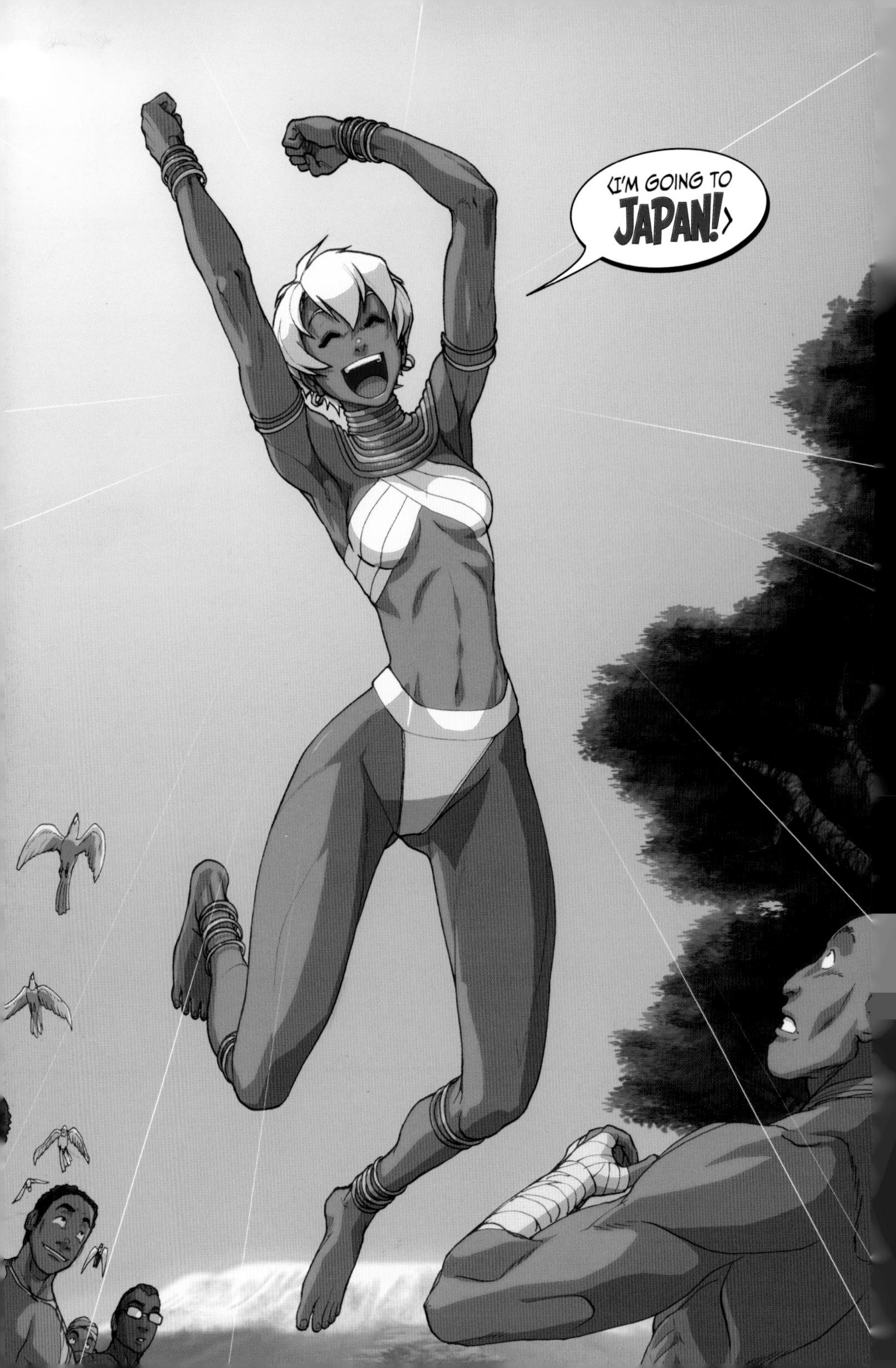
‹I'M GOING TO JAPAN!›

Bonus Story: MAKOTO

Art by: Gonzalo Ordóñez Arias

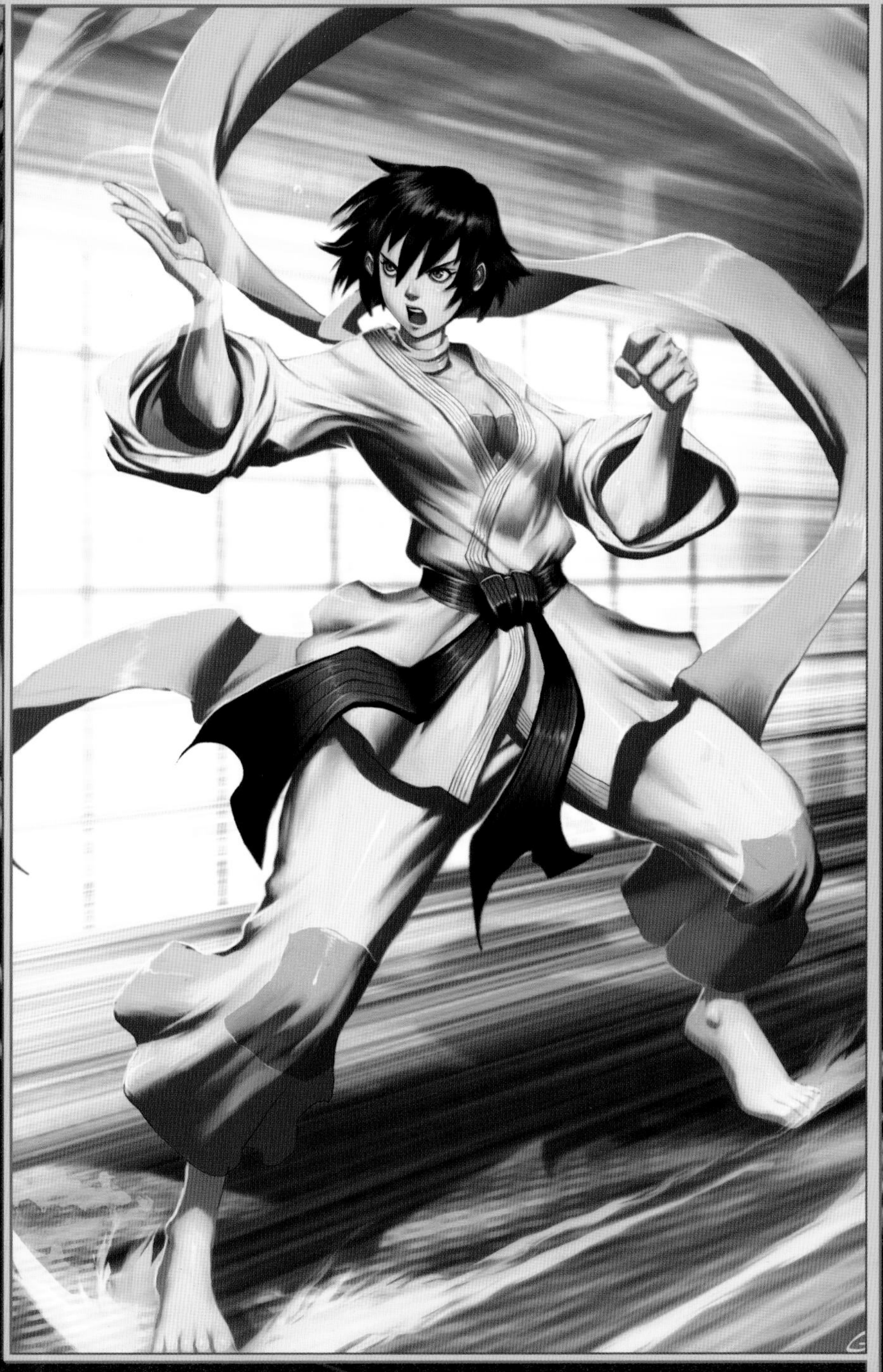

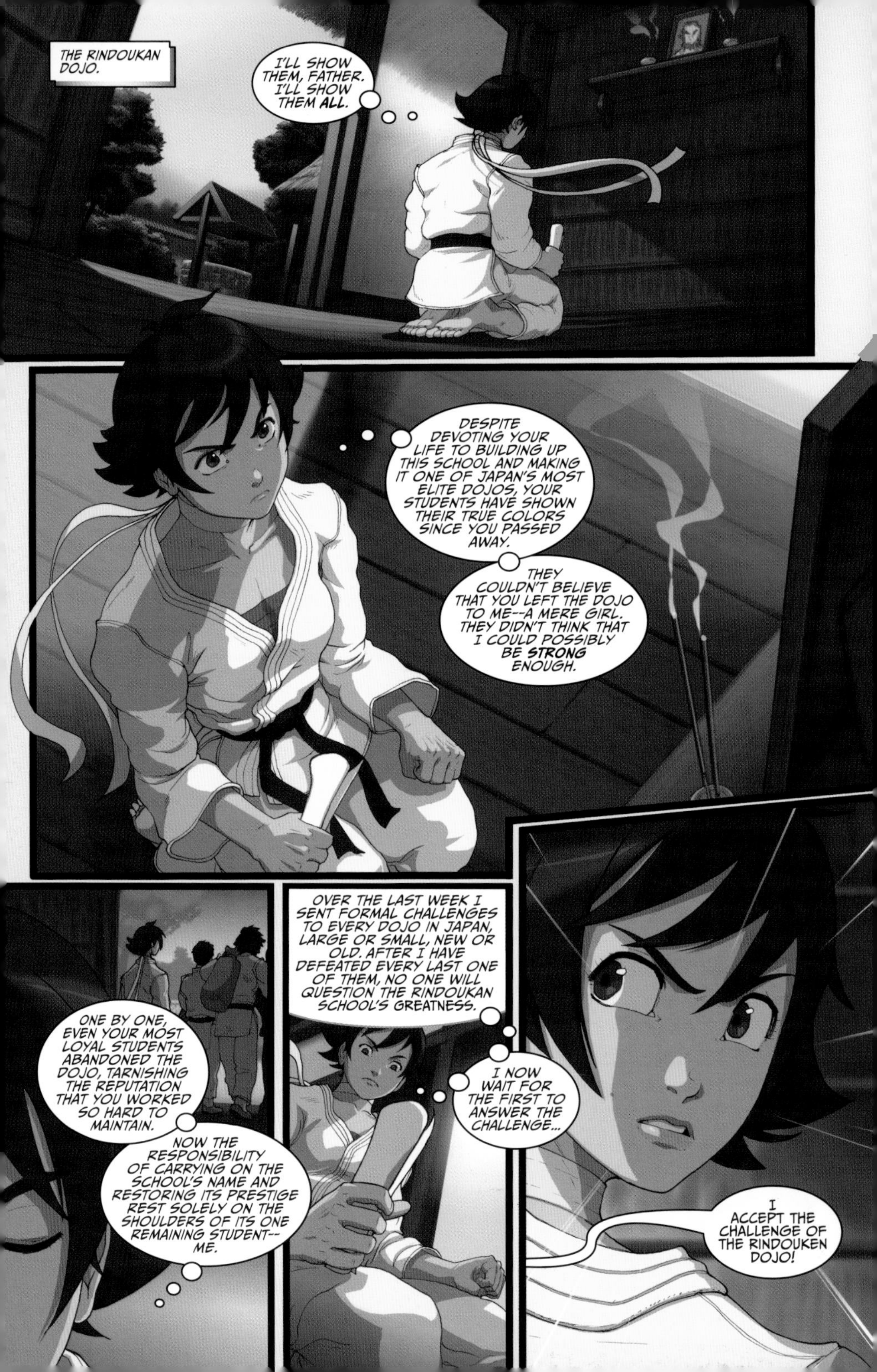
THE RINDOUKAN DOJO.
I'LL SHOW THEM, FATHER. I'LL SHOW THEM **ALL**.
DESPITE DEVOTING YOUR LIFE TO BUILDING UP THIS SCHOOL AND MAKING IT ONE OF JAPAN'S MOST ELITE DOJOS, YOUR STUDENTS HAVE SHOWN THEIR TRUE COLORS SINCE YOU PASSED AWAY.
THEY COULDN'T BELIEVE THAT YOU LEFT THE DOJO TO ME--A MERE GIRL. THEY DIDN'T THINK THAT I COULD POSSIBLY BE **STRONG** ENOUGH.
ONE BY ONE, EVEN YOUR MOST LOYAL STUDENTS ABANDONED THE DOJO, TARNISHING THE REPUTATION THAT YOU WORKED SO HARD TO MAINTAIN.
NOW THE RESPONSIBILITY OF CARRYING ON THE SCHOOL'S NAME AND RESTORING ITS PRESTIGE REST SOLELY ON THE SHOULDERS OF ITS ONE REMAINING STUDENT-- ME.
OVER THE LAST WEEK I SENT FORMAL CHALLENGES TO EVERY DOJO IN JAPAN, LARGE OR SMALL, NEW OR OLD. AFTER I HAVE DEFEATED EVERY LAST ONE OF THEM, NO ONE WILL QUESTION THE RINDOUKAN SCHOOL'S GREATNESS.
I NOW WAIT FOR THE FIRST TO ANSWER THE CHALLENGE...
I ACCEPT THE CHALLENGE OF THE RINDOUKEN DOJO!

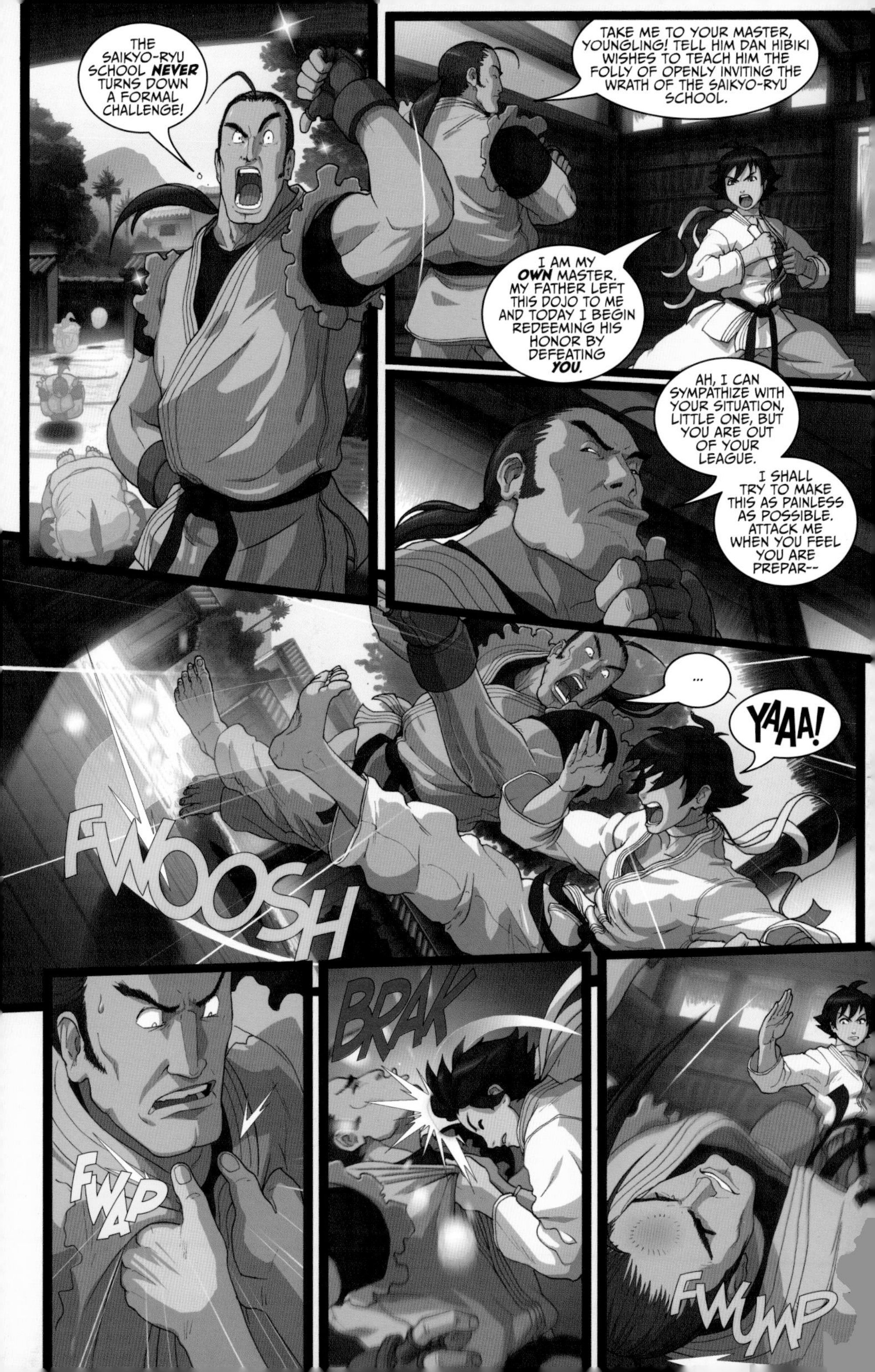
THE SAIKYO-RYU SCHOOL NEVER TURNS DOWN A FORMAL CHALLENGE!
TAKE ME TO YOUR MASTER, YOUNGLING! TELL HIM DAN HIBIKI WISHES TO TEACH HIM THE FOLLY OF OPENLY INVITING THE WRATH OF THE SAIKYO-RYU SCHOOL.
I AM MY OWN MASTER. MY FATHER LEFT THIS DOJO TO ME AND TODAY I BEGIN REDEEMING HIS HONOR BY DEFEATING YOU.
AH, I CAN SYMPATHIZE WITH YOUR SITUATION, LITTLE ONE, BUT YOU ARE OUT OF YOUR LEAGUE.
I SHALL TRY TO MAKE THIS AS PAINLESS AS POSSIBLE. ATTACK ME WHEN YOU FEEL YOU ARE PREPAR--
...
YAAA!
FWOOSH
FWAP
BRAK
FWUMP

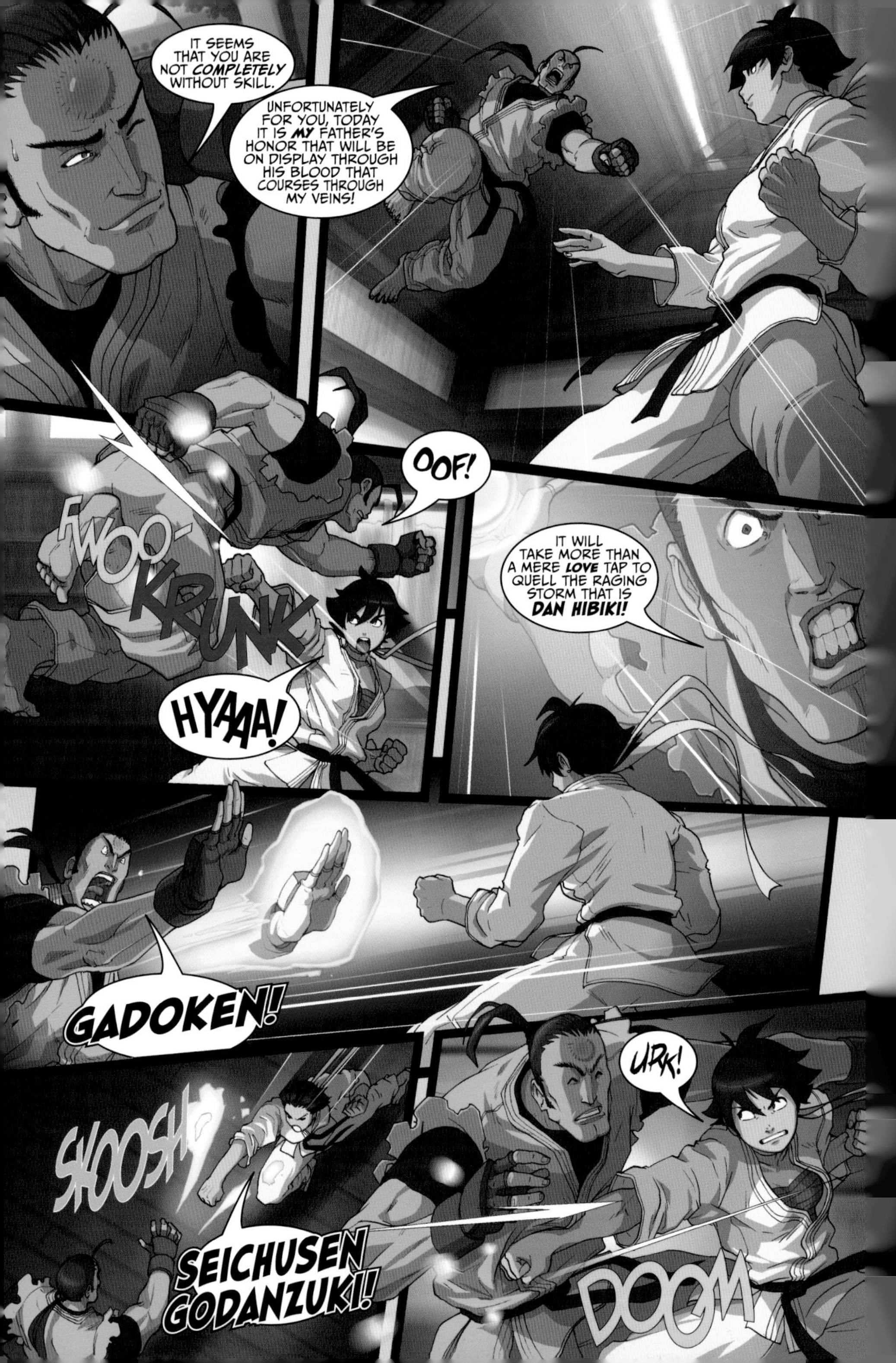

IT SEEMS THAT YOU ARE NOT COMPLETELY WITHOUT SKILL.
UNFORTUNATELY FOR YOU, TODAY IT IS MY FATHER'S HONOR THAT WILL BE ON DISPLAY THROUGH HIS BLOOD THAT COURSES THROUGH MY VEINS!
FWOO-KRUNK
OOF!
HYAAA!
IT WILL TAKE MORE THAN A MERE LOVE TAP TO QUELL THE RAGING STORM THAT IS DAN HIBIKI!
GADOKEN!
SHOOSH
SEICHUSEN GODANZUKI!
URK!
DOOM

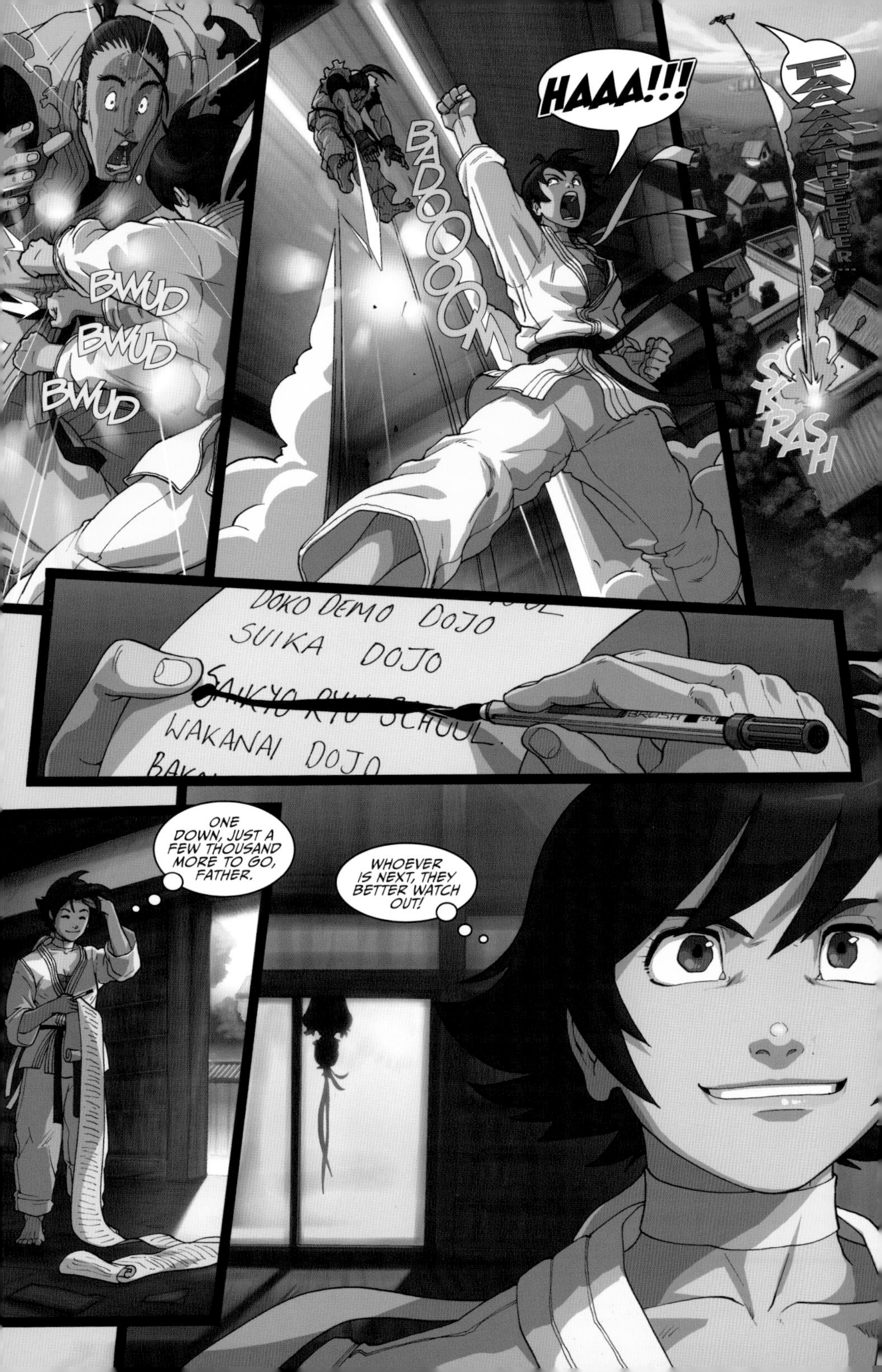
BWUD
BWUD
BWUD
BADOOOOM
HAAA!!!
FAAAAATHEEEEER...
SKRASH
DOKO DEMO DOJO
SUIKA DOJO
SAIKYO RYU SCHOOL
WAKANAI DOJO
ONE DOWN, JUST A FEW THOUSAND MORE TO GO, FATHER.
WHOEVER IS NEXT, THEY BETTER WATCH OUT!

Art by: Omar Dogan

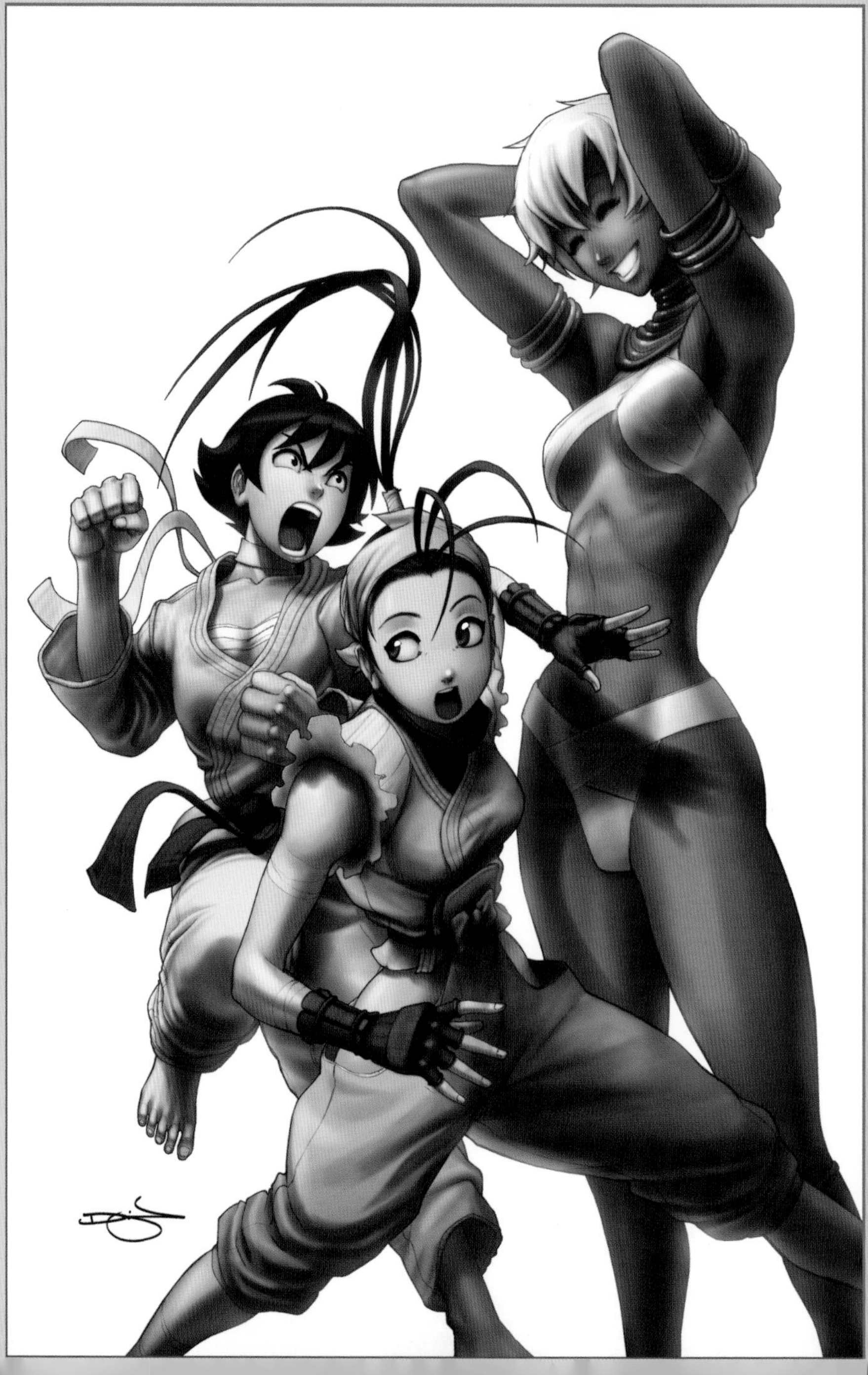

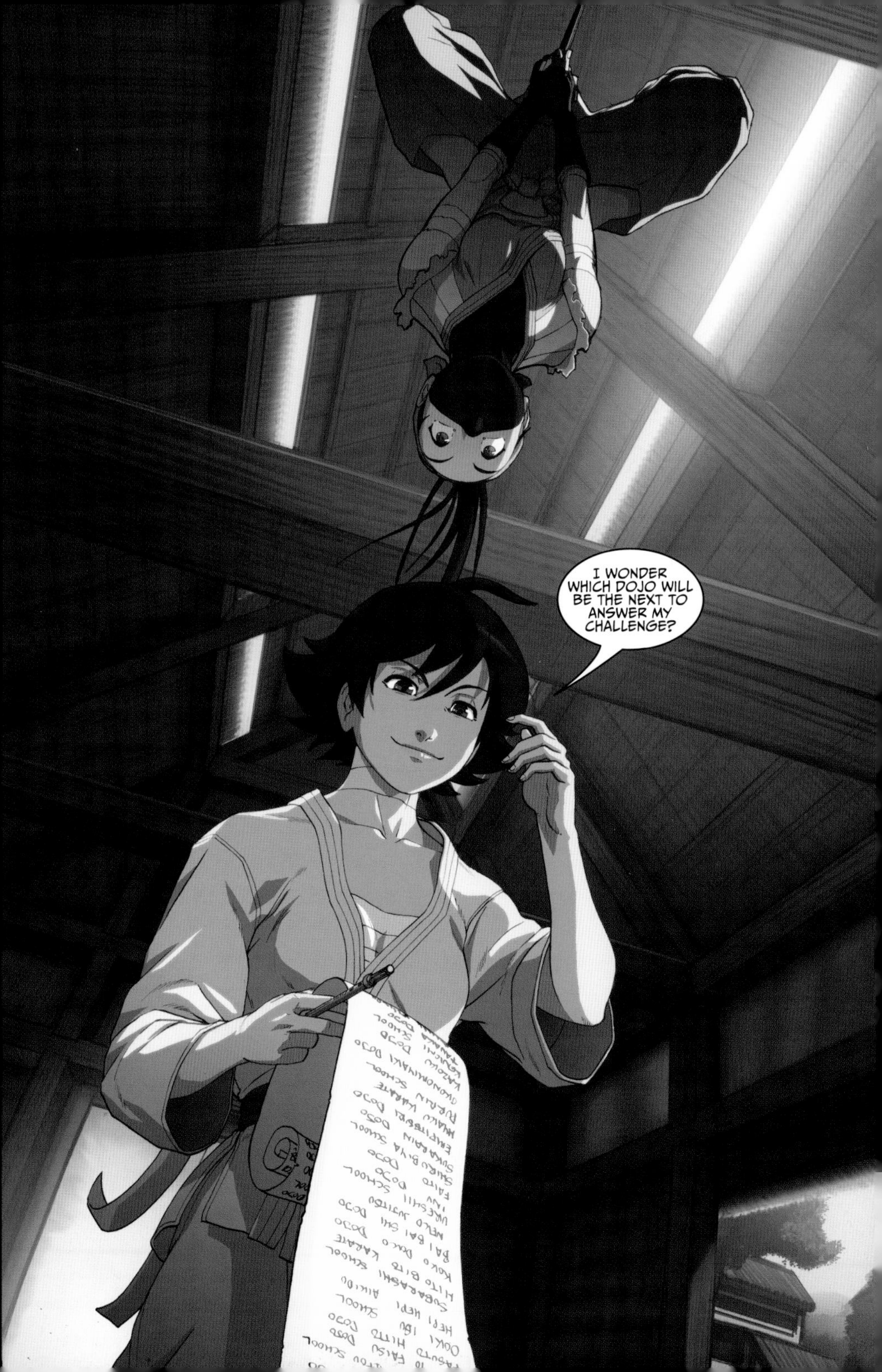
I WONDER WHICH DOJO WILL BE THE NEXT TO ANSWER MY CHALLENGE?

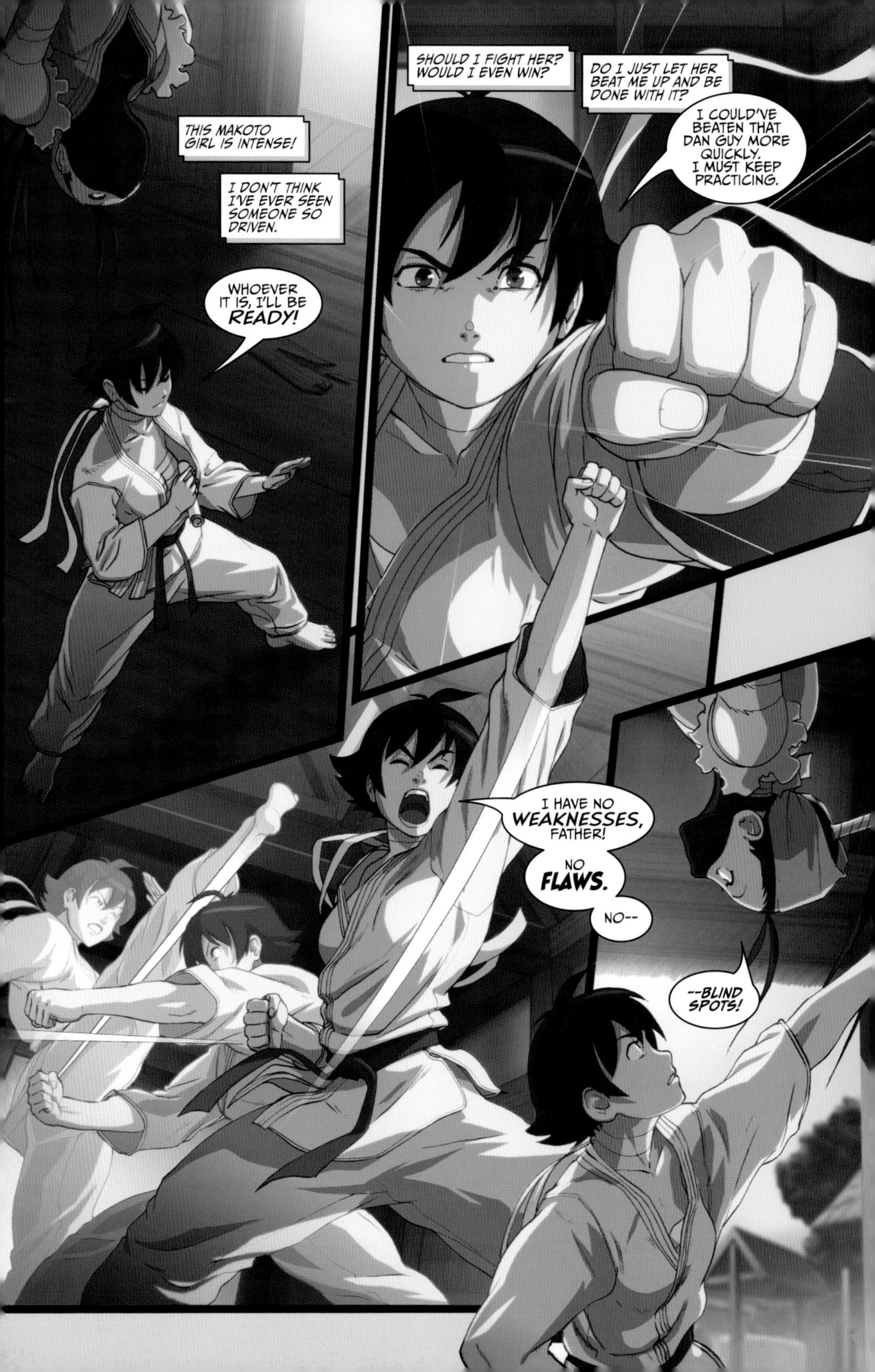

THIS MAKOTO GIRL IS INTENSE!
I DON'T THINK I'VE EVER SEEN SOMEONE SO DRIVEN.
WHOEVER IT IS, I'LL BE READY!
SHOULD I FIGHT HER? WOULD I EVEN WIN?
DO I JUST LET HER BEAT ME UP AND BE DONE WITH IT?
I COULD'VE BEATEN THAT DAN GUY MORE QUICKLY. I MUST KEEP PRACTICING.
I HAVE NO WEAKNESSES, FATHER!
NO FLAWS.
NO--
--BLIND SPOTS!

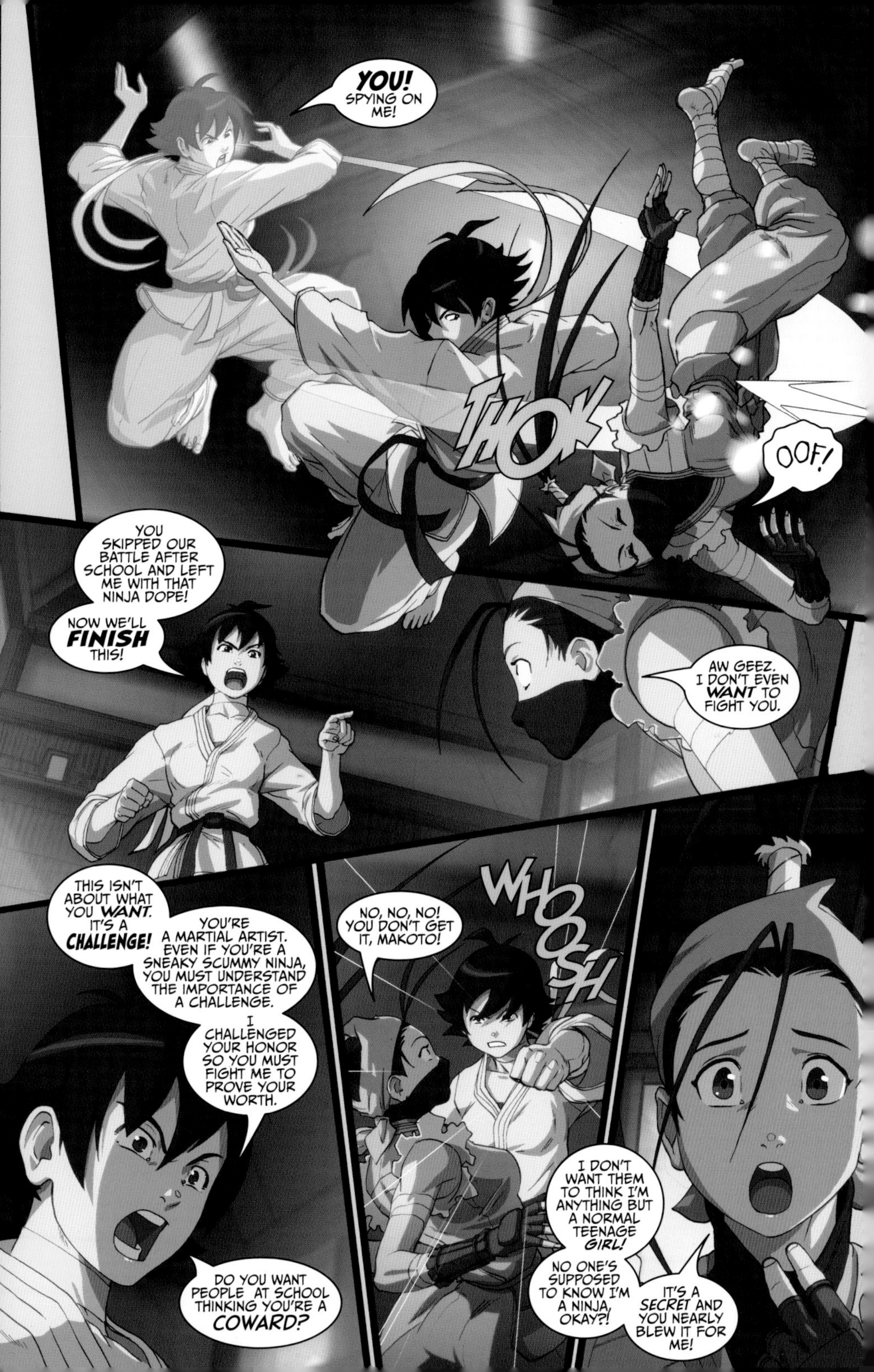
YOU! SPYING ON ME!
THOK
OOF!
YOU SKIPPED OUR BATTLE AFTER SCHOOL AND LEFT ME WITH THAT NINJA DOPE!
NOW WE'LL FINISH THIS!
AW GEEZ. I DON'T EVEN WANT TO FIGHT YOU.
THIS ISN'T ABOUT WHAT YOU WANT. IT'S A CHALLENGE!
YOU'RE A MARTIAL ARTIST. EVEN IF YOU'RE A SNEAKY SCUMMY NINJA, YOU MUST UNDERSTAND THE IMPORTANCE OF A CHALLENGE.
I CHALLENGED YOUR HONOR SO YOU MUST FIGHT ME TO PROVE YOUR WORTH.
DO YOU WANT PEOPLE AT SCHOOL THINKING YOU'RE A COWARD?
WHOOSH
NO, NO, NO! YOU DON'T GET IT, MAKOTO!
I DON'T WANT THEM TO THINK I'M ANYTHING BUT A NORMAL TEENAGE GIRL!
NO ONE'S SUPPOSED TO KNOW I'M A NINJA, OKAY?!
IT'S A SECRET AND YOU NEARLY BLEW IT FOR ME!

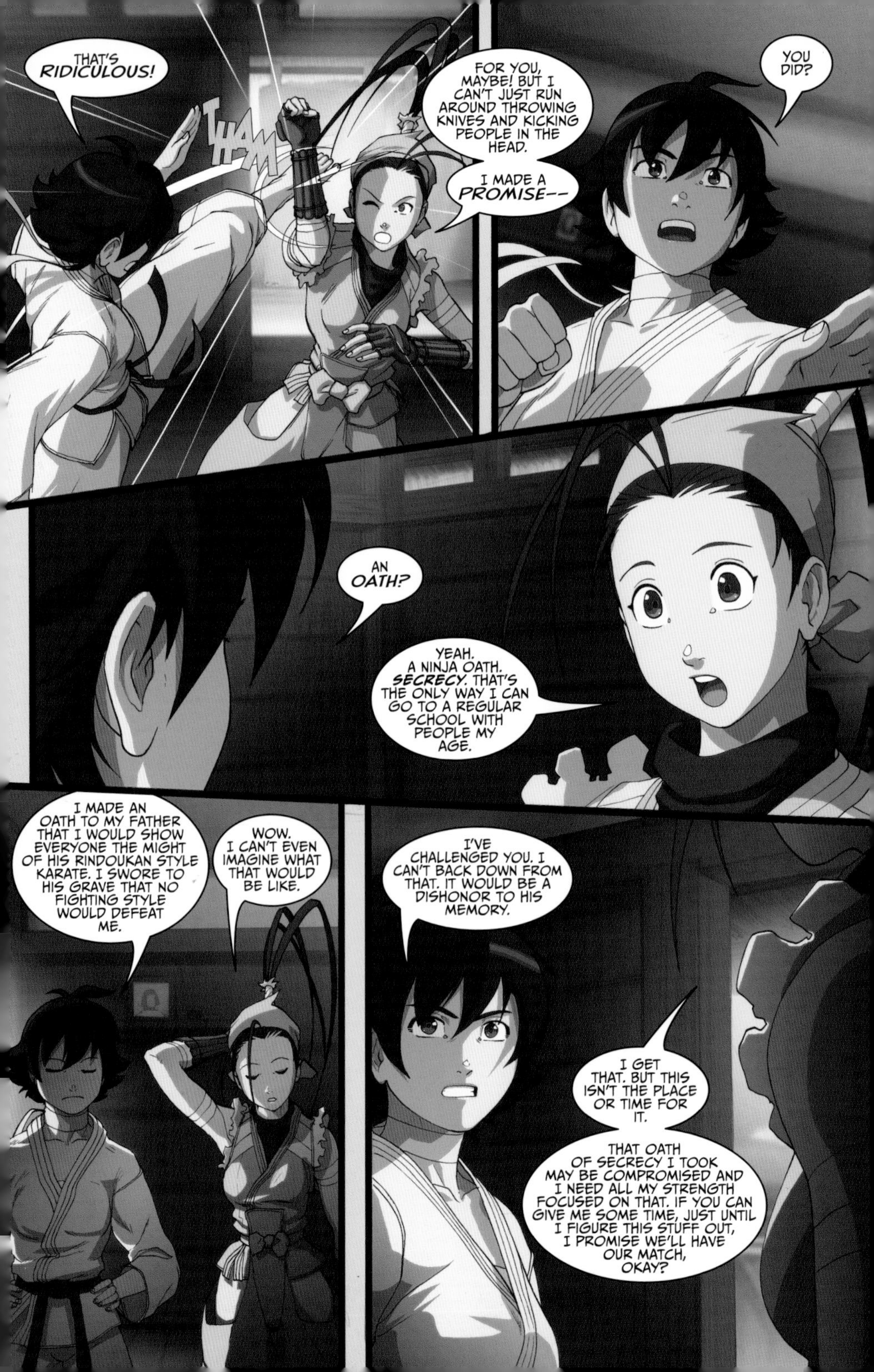
THAT'S *RIDICULOUS!*
THAM
FOR YOU, MAYBE! BUT I CAN'T JUST RUN AROUND THROWING KNIVES AND KICKING PEOPLE IN THE HEAD.
I MADE A *PROMISE*--
YOU DID?
AN *OATH?*
YEAH. A NINJA OATH. *SECRECY*. THAT'S THE ONLY WAY I CAN GO TO A REGULAR SCHOOL WITH PEOPLE MY AGE.
I MADE AN OATH TO MY FATHER THAT I WOULD SHOW EVERYONE THE MIGHT OF HIS RINDOUKAN STYLE KARATE. I SWORE TO HIS GRAVE THAT NO FIGHTING STYLE WOULD DEFEAT ME.
WOW. I CAN'T EVEN IMAGINE WHAT THAT WOULD BE LIKE.
I'VE CHALLENGED YOU. I CAN'T BACK DOWN FROM THAT. IT WOULD BE A DISHONOR TO HIS MEMORY.
I GET THAT. BUT THIS ISN'T THE PLACE OR TIME FOR IT.
THAT OATH OF SECRECY I TOOK MAY BE COMPROMISED AND I NEED ALL MY STRENGTH FOCUSED ON THAT. IF YOU CAN GIVE ME SOME TIME, JUST UNTIL I FIGURE THIS STUFF OUT, I PROMISE WE'LL HAVE OUR MATCH, OKAY?

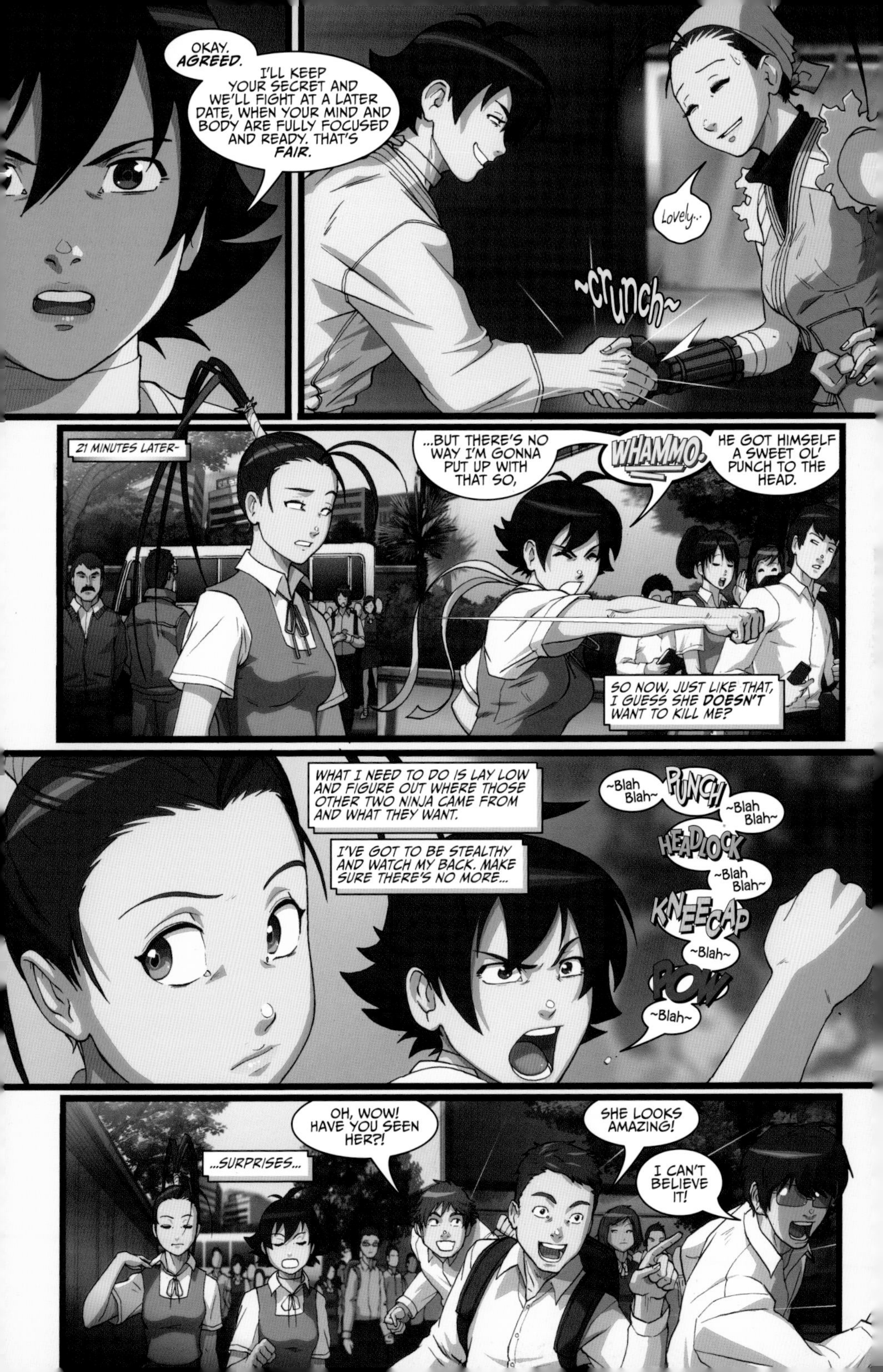
OKAY. AGREED. I'LL KEEP YOUR SECRET AND WE'LL FIGHT AT A LATER DATE, WHEN YOUR MIND AND BODY ARE FULLY FOCUSED AND READY. THAT'S FAIR.
Lovely...
~crunch~
21 MINUTES LATER-
...BUT THERE'S NO WAY I'M GONNA PUT UP WITH THAT SO,
WHAMMO.
HE GOT HIMSELF A SWEET OL' PUNCH TO THE HEAD.
SO NOW, JUST LIKE THAT, I GUESS SHE DOESN'T WANT TO KILL ME?
WHAT I NEED TO DO IS LAY LOW AND FIGURE OUT WHERE THOSE OTHER TWO NINJA CAME FROM AND WHAT THEY WANT.
I'VE GOT TO BE STEALTHY AND WATCH MY BACK. MAKE SURE THERE'S NO MORE...
~Blah Blah~
PUNCH
~Blah Blah~
HEADLOCK
~Blah Blah~
KNEECAP
~Blah~
POW
~Blah~
...SURPRISES...
OH, WOW! HAVE YOU SEEN HER?!
SHE LOOKS AMAZING!
I CAN'T BELIEVE IT!

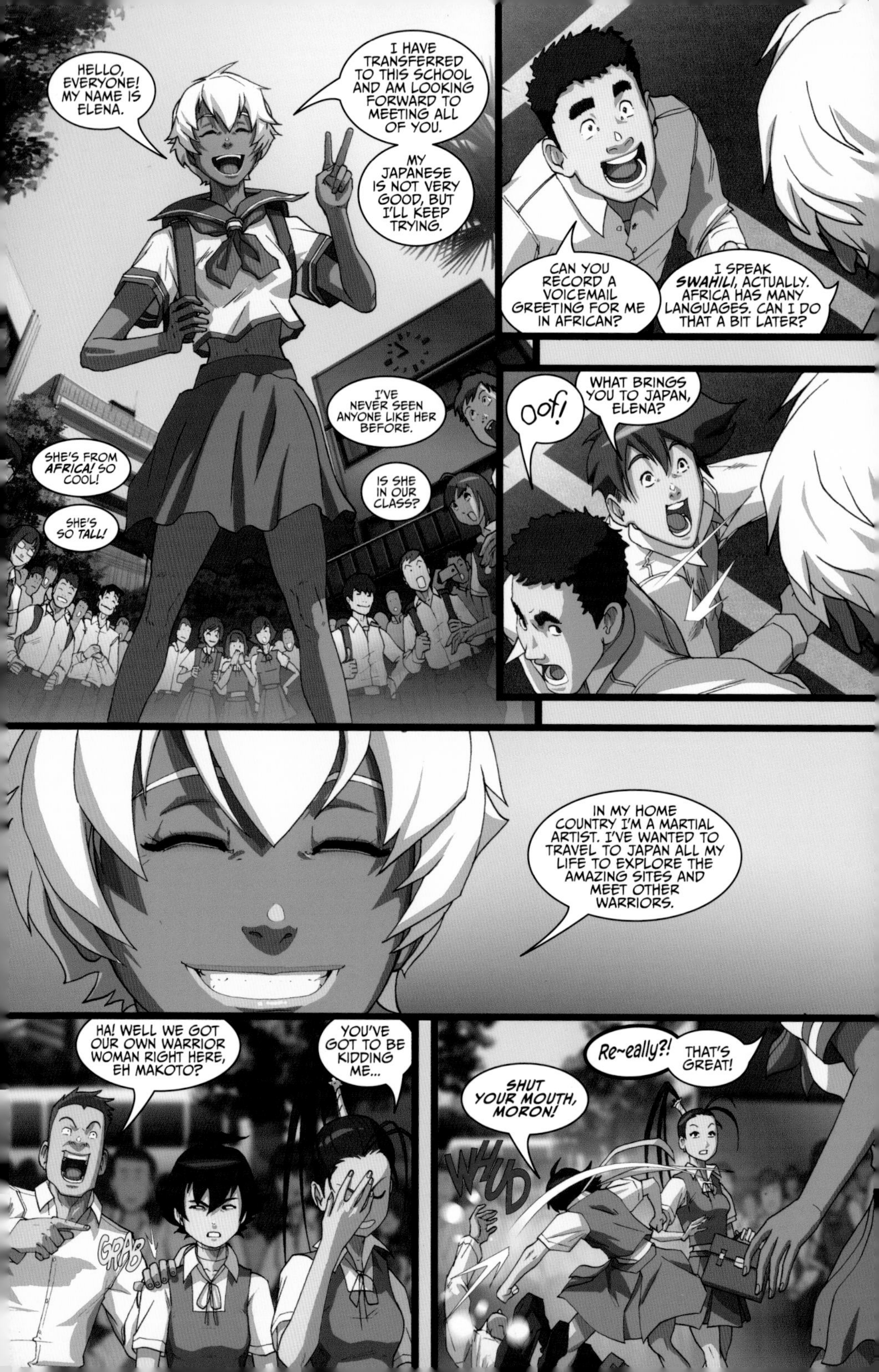
HELLO, EVERYONE! MY NAME IS ELENA.
I HAVE TRANSFERRED TO THIS SCHOOL AND AM LOOKING FORWARD TO MEETING ALL OF YOU.
MY JAPANESE IS NOT VERY GOOD, BUT I'LL KEEP TRYING.
I'VE NEVER SEEN ANYONE LIKE HER BEFORE.
SHE'S FROM AFRICA! SO COOL!
IS SHE IN OUR CLASS?
SHE'S SO TALL!
CAN YOU RECORD A VOICEMAIL GREETING FOR ME IN AFRICAN?
I SPEAK SWAHILI, ACTUALLY. AFRICA HAS MANY LANGUAGES. CAN I DO THAT A BIT LATER?
OOF!
WHAT BRINGS YOU TO JAPAN, ELENA?
IN MY HOME COUNTRY I'M A MARTIAL ARTIST. I'VE WANTED TO TRAVEL TO JAPAN ALL MY LIFE TO EXPLORE THE AMAZING SITES AND MEET OTHER WARRIORS.
HA! WELL WE GOT OUR OWN WARRIOR WOMAN RIGHT HERE, EH MAKOTO?
YOU'VE GOT TO BE KIDDING ME...
GRAB
Re~eally?!
THAT'S GREAT!
SHUT YOUR MOUTH, MORON!
WHUD

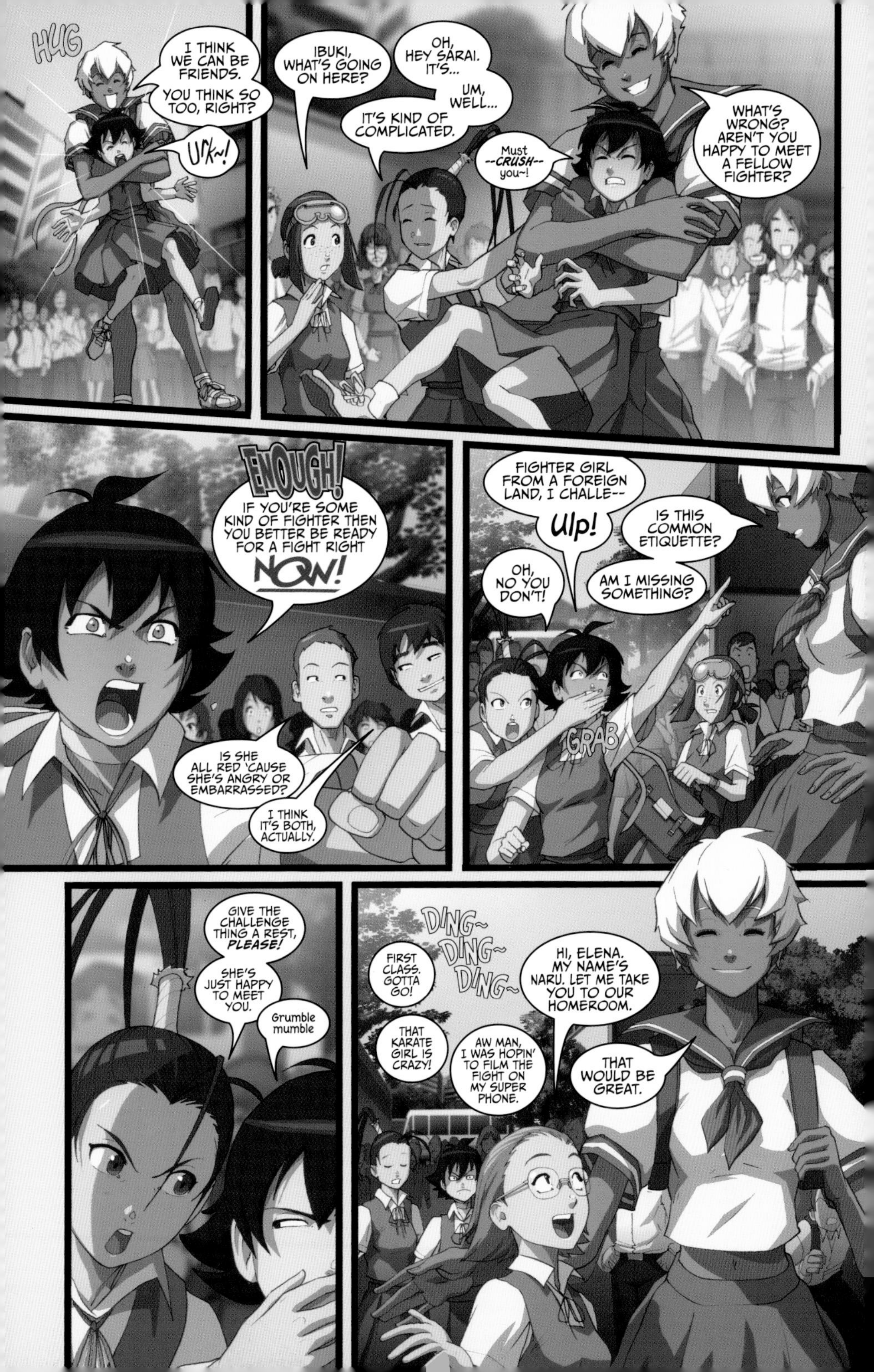
HUG
I THINK WE CAN BE FRIENDS.
YOU THINK SO TOO, RIGHT?
Urk~!
IBUKI, WHAT'S GOING ON HERE?
OH, HEY SARAI. IT'S...
UM, WELL...
IT'S KIND OF COMPLICATED.
Must --CRUSH-- you~!
WHAT'S WRONG? AREN'T YOU HAPPY TO MEET A FELLOW FIGHTER?
ENOUGH!
IF YOU'RE SOME KIND OF FIGHTER THEN YOU BETTER BE READY FOR A FIGHT RIGHT NOW!
IS SHE ALL RED 'CAUSE SHE'S ANGRY OR EMBARRASSED?
I THINK IT'S BOTH, ACTUALLY.
FIGHTER GIRL FROM A FOREIGN LAND, I CHALLE--
Ulp!
OH, NO YOU DON'T!
IS THIS COMMON ETIQUETTE?
AM I MISSING SOMETHING?
GRAB
GIVE THE CHALLENGE THING A REST, PLEASE!
SHE'S JUST HAPPY TO MEET YOU.
Grumble mumble
DING~ DING~ DING~
FIRST CLASS. GOTTA GO!
THAT KARATE GIRL IS CRAZY!
AW MAN, I WAS HOPIN' TO FILM THE FIGHT ON MY SUPER PHONE.
HI, ELENA. MY NAME'S NARU. LET ME TAKE YOU TO OUR HOMEROOM.
THAT WOULD BE GREAT.

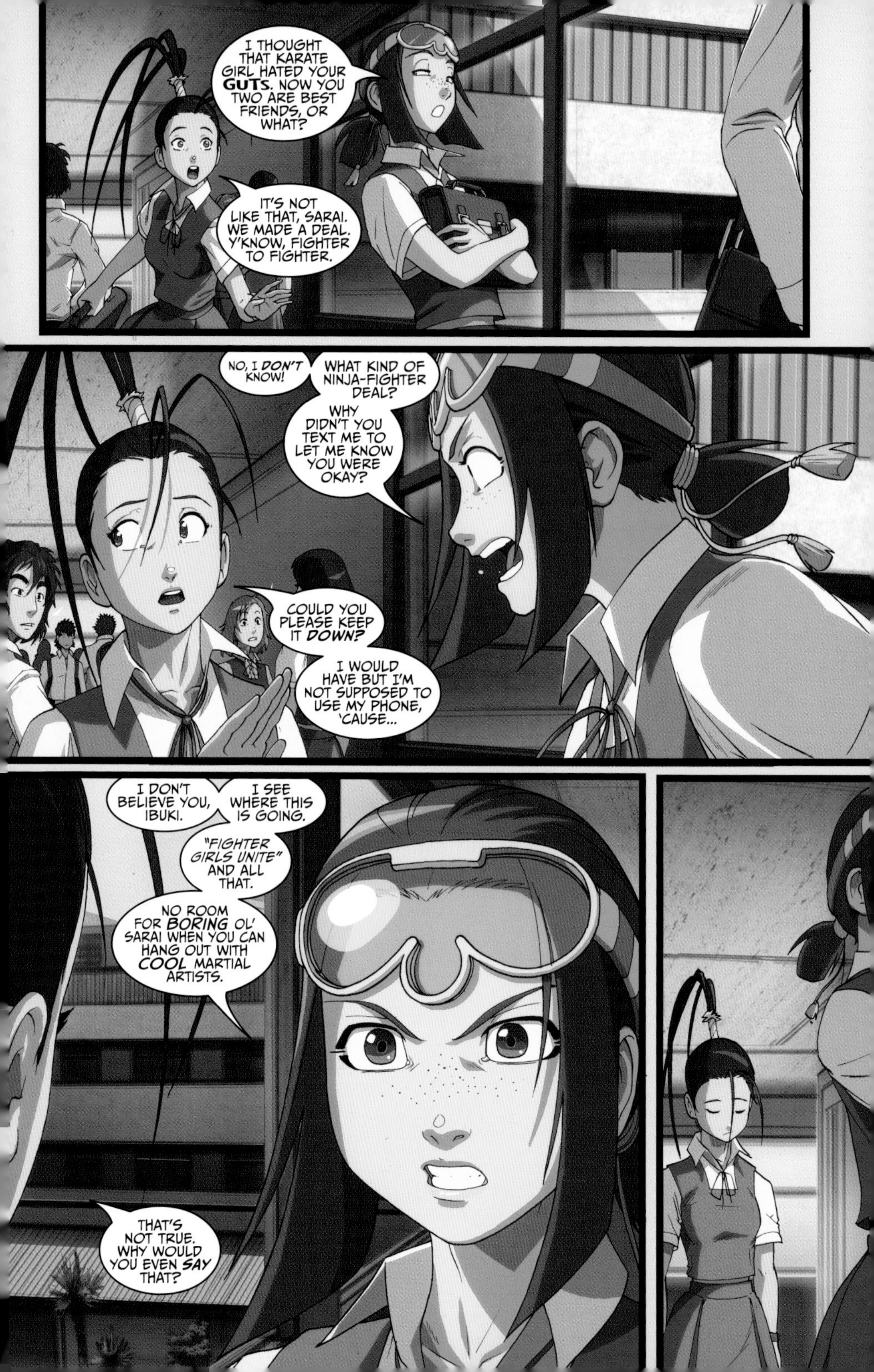
I THOUGHT THAT KARATE GIRL HATED YOUR **GUTS**. NOW YOU TWO ARE BEST FRIENDS, OR WHAT?
IT'S NOT LIKE THAT, SARAI. WE MADE A DEAL. Y'KNOW, FIGHTER TO FIGHTER.
NO, I *DON'T* KNOW!
WHAT KIND OF NINJA-FIGHTER DEAL?
WHY DIDN'T YOU TEXT ME TO LET ME KNOW YOU WERE OKAY?
COULD YOU PLEASE KEEP IT *DOWN?*
I WOULD HAVE BUT I'M NOT SUPPOSED TO USE MY PHONE, 'CAUSE...
I DON'T BELIEVE YOU, IBUKI.
I SEE WHERE THIS IS GOING.
"FIGHTER GIRLS UNITE" AND ALL THAT.
NO ROOM FOR ***BORING*** OL' SARAI WHEN YOU CAN HANG OUT WITH **COOL** MARTIAL ARTISTS.
THAT'S NOT TRUE. WHY WOULD YOU EVEN ***SAY*** THAT?

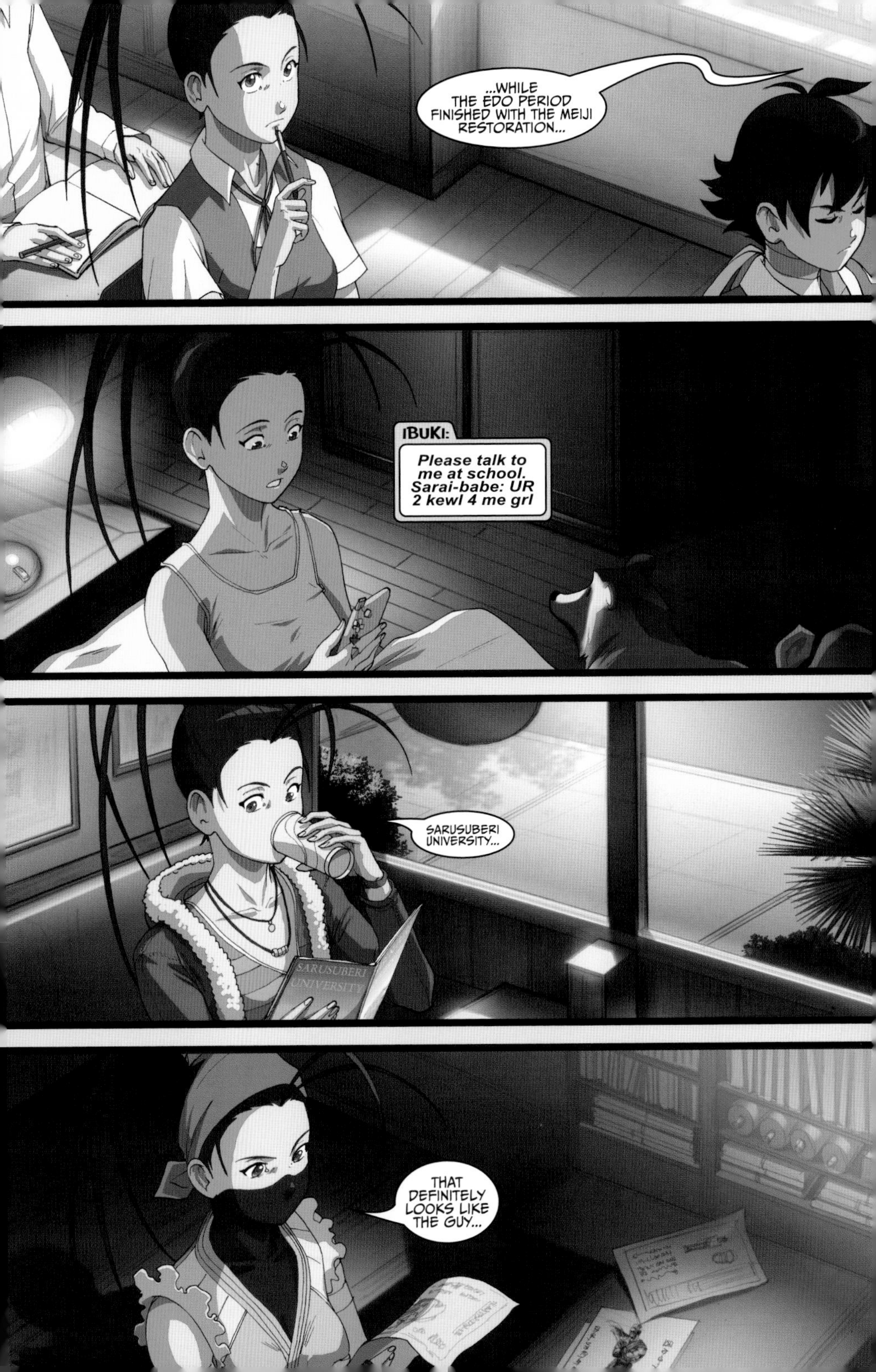
...WHILE THE EDO PERIOD FINISHED WITH THE MEIJI RESTORATION...
IBUKI:
Please talk to me at school. Sarai-babe: UR 2 kewl 4 me grl
SARUSUBERI UNIVERSITY...
SARUSUBERI UNIVERSITY
THAT DEFINITELY LOOKS LIKE THE GUY...

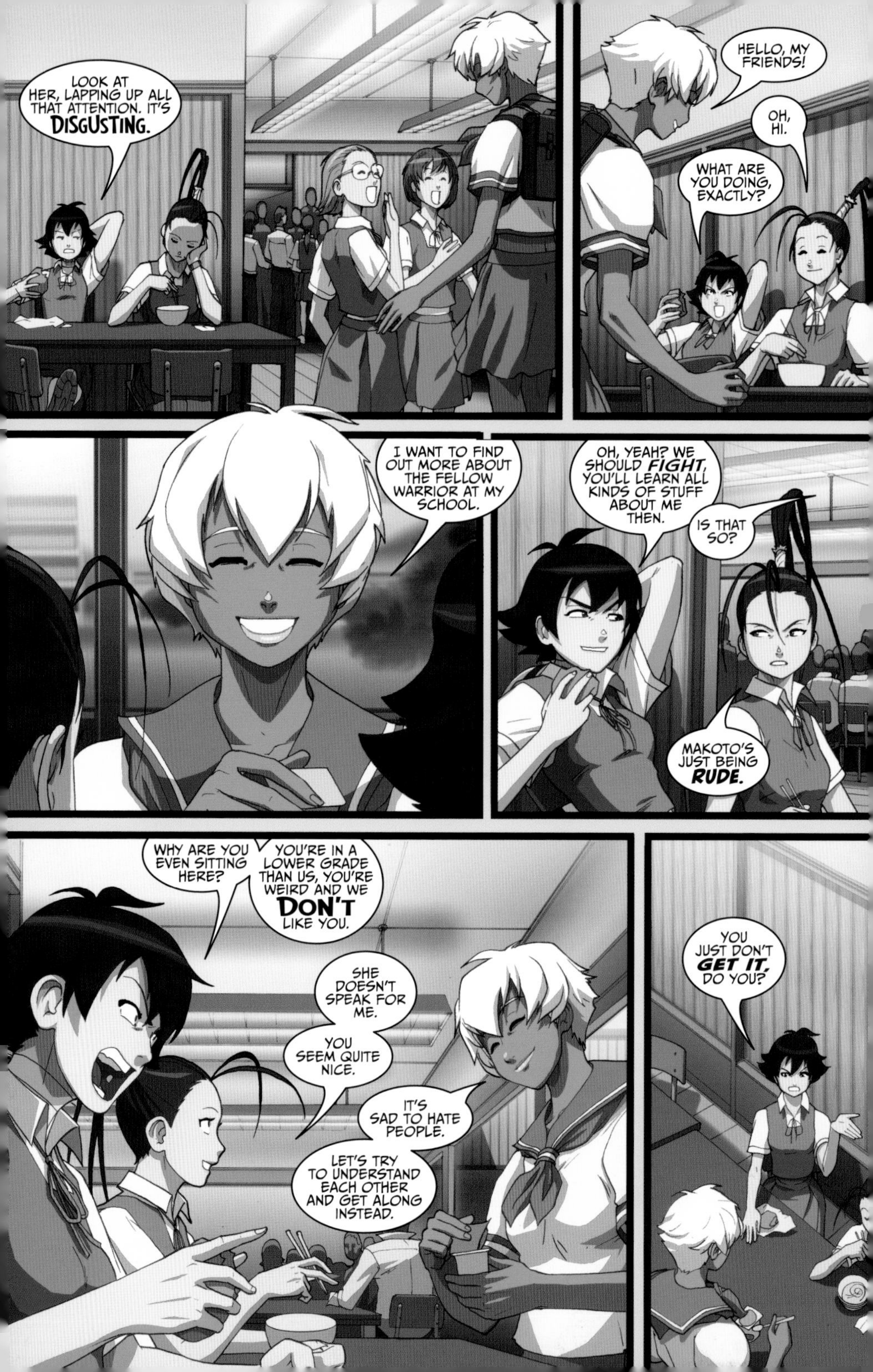
LOOK AT HER, LAPPING UP ALL THAT ATTENTION. IT'S DISGUSTING.
HELLO, MY FRIENDS!
OH, HI.
WHAT ARE YOU DOING, EXACTLY?
I WANT TO FIND OUT MORE ABOUT THE FELLOW WARRIOR AT MY SCHOOL.
OH, YEAH? WE SHOULD FIGHT, YOU'LL LEARN ALL KINDS OF STUFF ABOUT ME THEN.
IS THAT SO?
MAKOTO'S JUST BEING RUDE.
WHY ARE YOU EVEN SITTING HERE?
YOU'RE IN A LOWER GRADE THAN US, YOU'RE WEIRD AND WE DON'T LIKE YOU.
SHE DOESN'T SPEAK FOR ME.
YOU SEEM QUITE NICE.
IT'S SAD TO HATE PEOPLE.
LET'S TRY TO UNDERSTAND EACH OTHER AND GET ALONG INSTEAD.
YOU JUST DON'T GET IT, DO YOU?

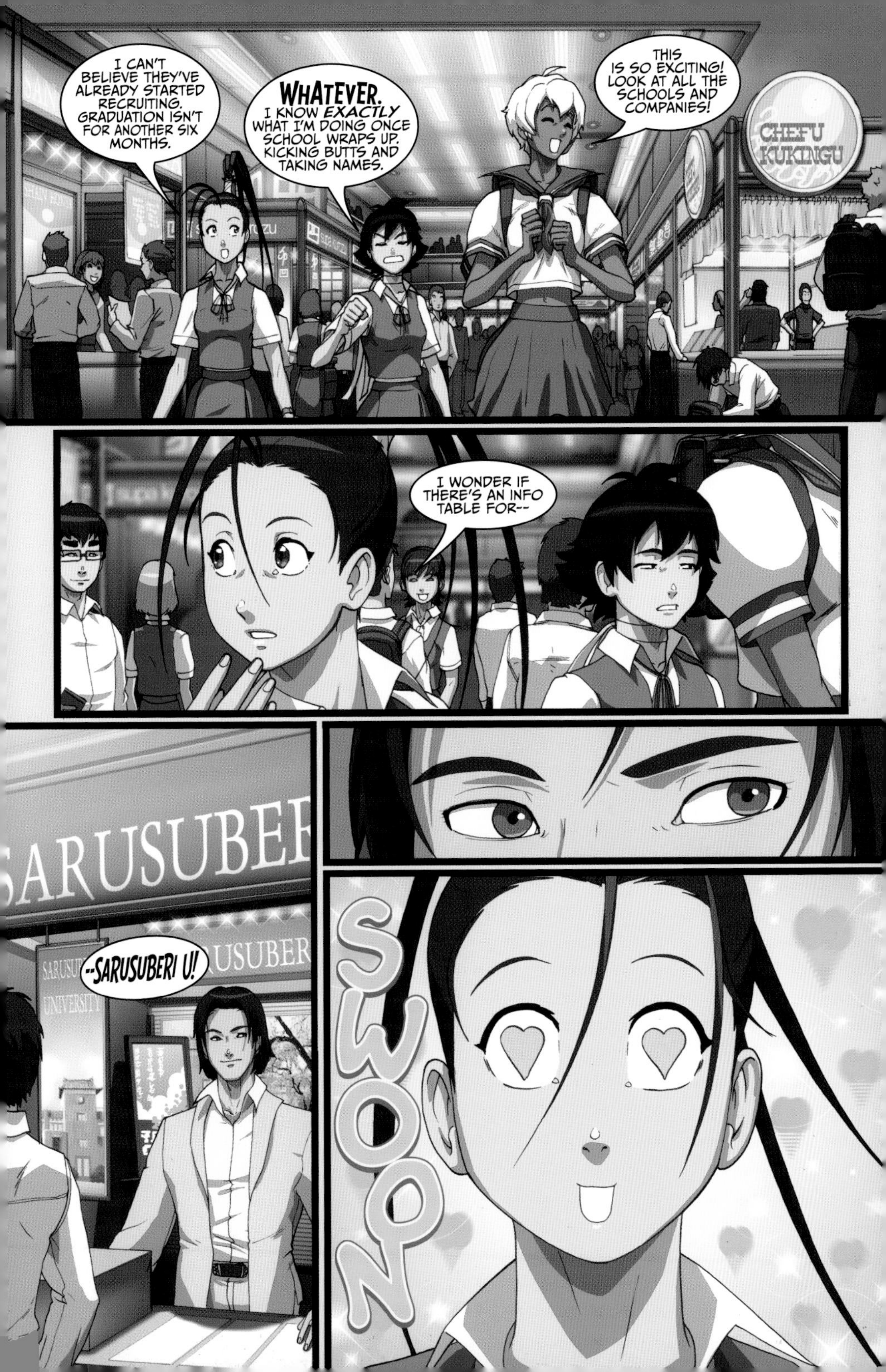
I CAN'T BELIEVE THEY'VE ALREADY STARTED RECRUITING. GRADUATION ISN'T FOR ANOTHER SIX MONTHS.
WHATEVER. I KNOW EXACTLY WHAT I'M DOING ONCE SCHOOL WRAPS UP. KICKING BUTTS AND TAKING NAMES.
THIS IS SO EXCITING! LOOK AT ALL THE SCHOOLS AND COMPANIES!
CHEFU KUKINGU
I WONDER IF THERE'S AN INFO TABLE FOR--
SARUSUBER
--SARUSUBERI U!
SARUSUBER
SWOON

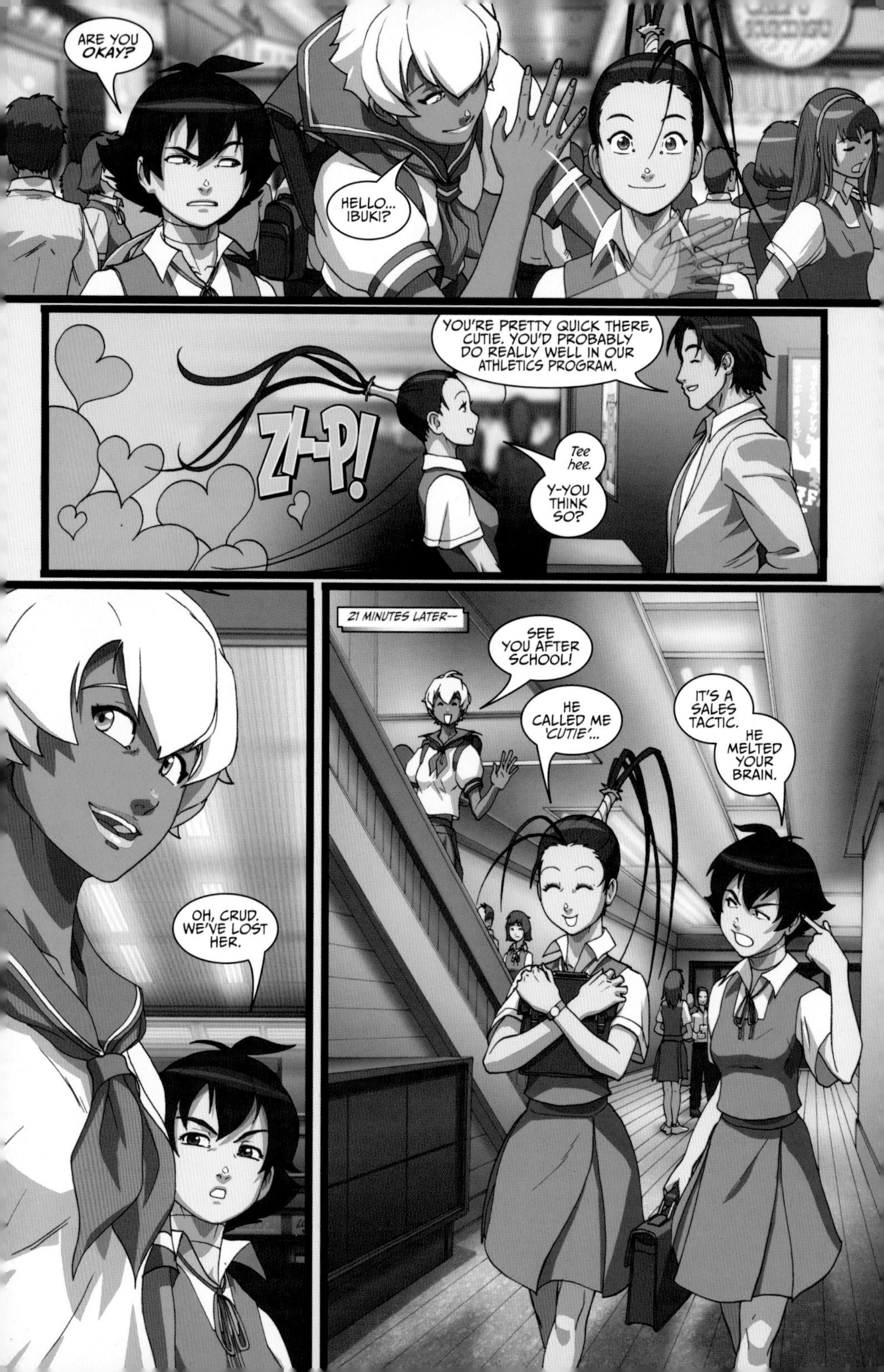
ARE YOU OKAY?
HELLO... IBUKI?
YOU'RE PRETTY QUICK THERE, CUTIE. YOU'D PROBABLY DO REALLY WELL IN OUR ATHLETICS PROGRAM.
ZI--P!
Tee hee.
Y-YOU THINK SO?
OH, CRUD. WE'VE LOST HER.
21 MINUTES LATER--
SEE YOU AFTER SCHOOL!
HE CALLED ME 'CUTIE'...
IT'S A SALES TACTIC.
HE MELTED YOUR BRAIN.

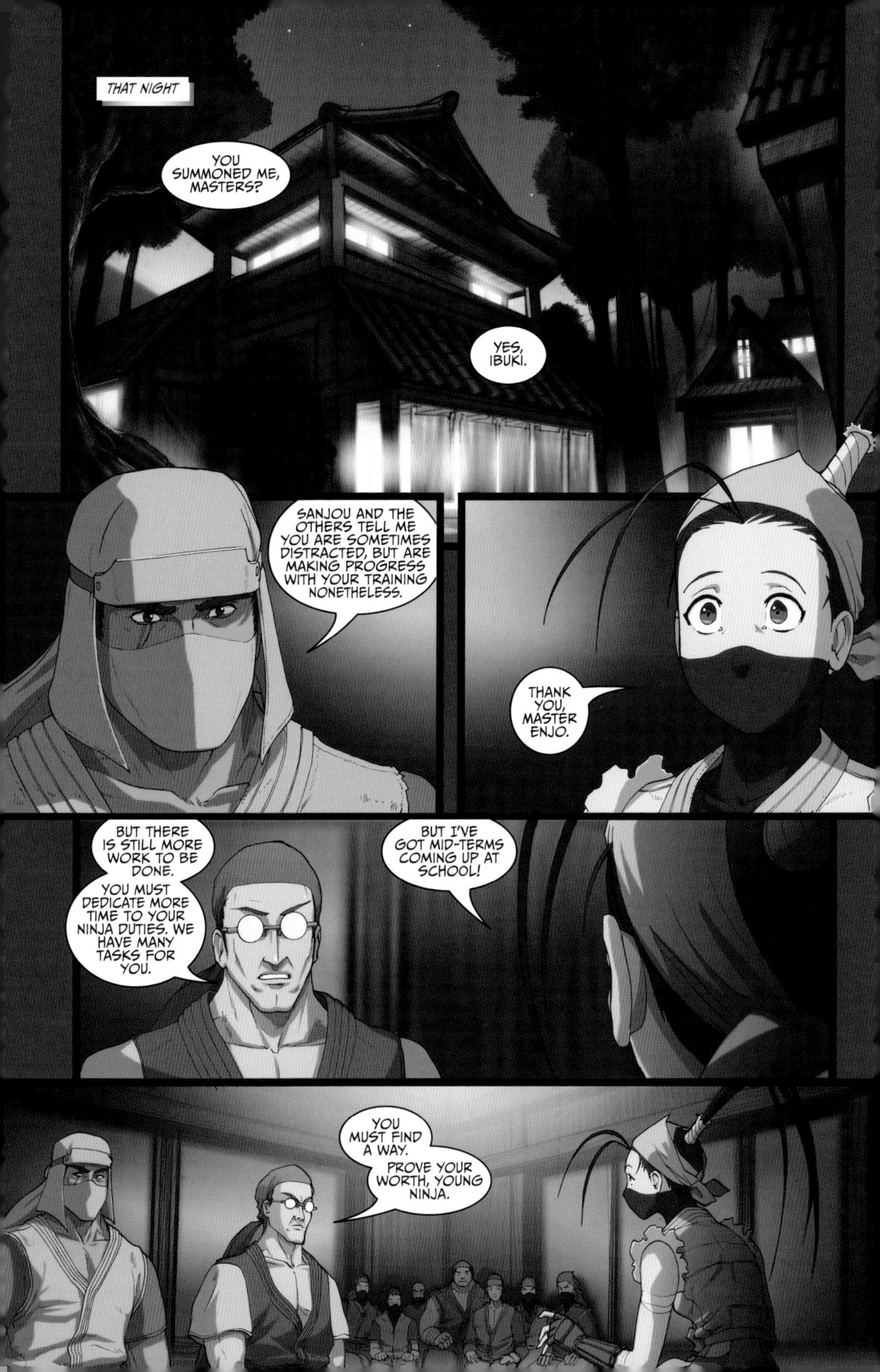
THAT NIGHT
YOU SUMMONED ME, MASTERS?
YES, IBUKI.
SANJOU AND THE OTHERS TELL ME YOU ARE SOMETIMES DISTRACTED, BUT ARE MAKING PROGRESS WITH YOUR TRAINING NONETHELESS.
THANK YOU, MASTER ENJO.
BUT THERE IS STILL MORE WORK TO BE DONE.
YOU MUST DEDICATE MORE TIME TO YOUR NINJA DUTIES. WE HAVE MANY TASKS FOR YOU.
BUT I'VE GOT MID-TERMS COMING UP AT SCHOOL!
YOU MUST FIND A WAY.
PROVE YOUR WORTH, YOUNG NINJA.

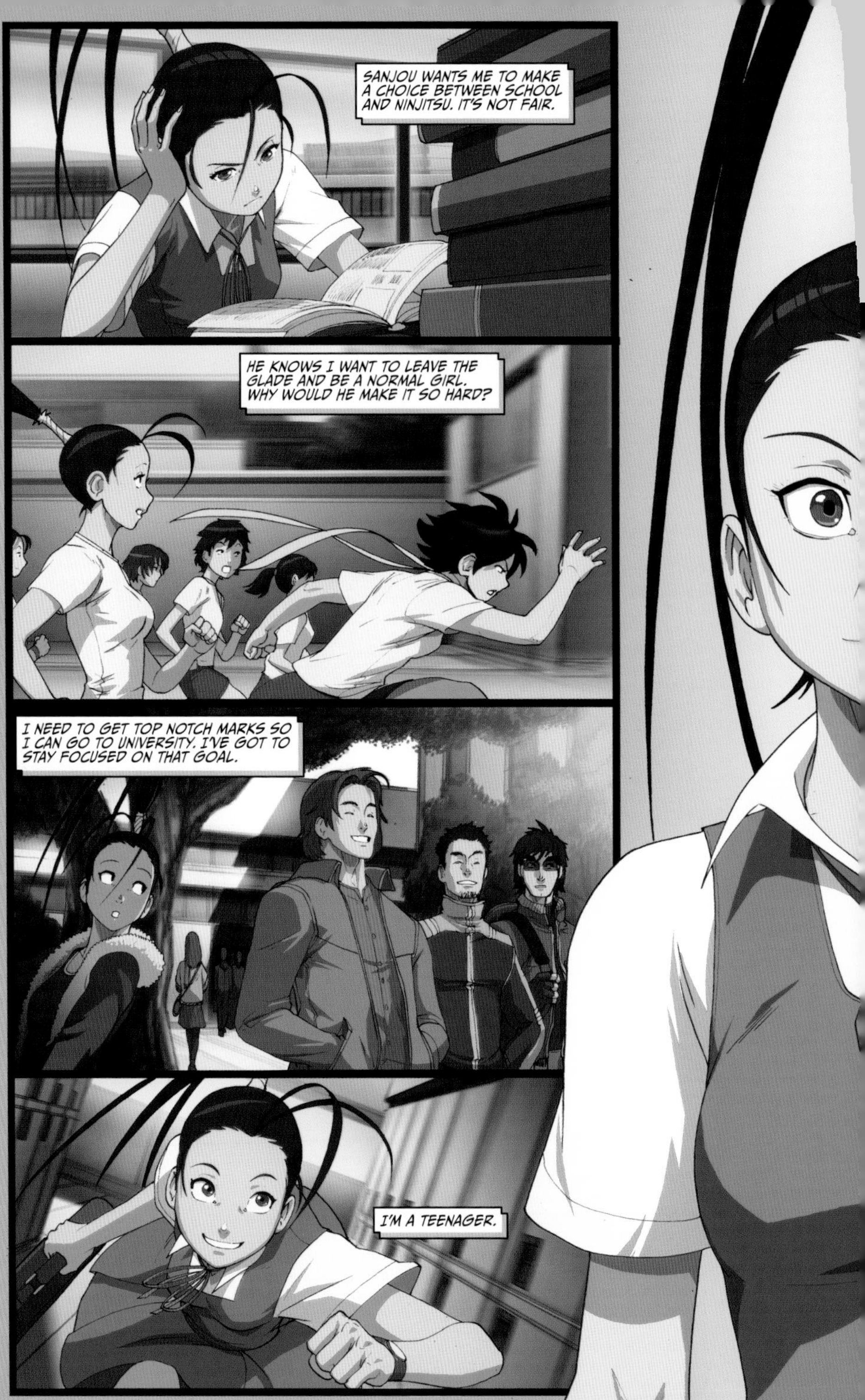
SANJOU WANTS ME TO MAKE A CHOICE BETWEEN SCHOOL AND NINJITSU. IT'S NOT FAIR.
HE KNOWS I WANT TO LEAVE THE GLADE AND BE A NORMAL GIRL. WHY WOULD HE MAKE IT SO HARD?
I NEED TO GET TOP NOTCH MARKS SO I CAN GO TO UNIVERSITY. I'VE GOT TO STAY FOCUSED ON THAT GOAL.
I'M A TEENAGER.

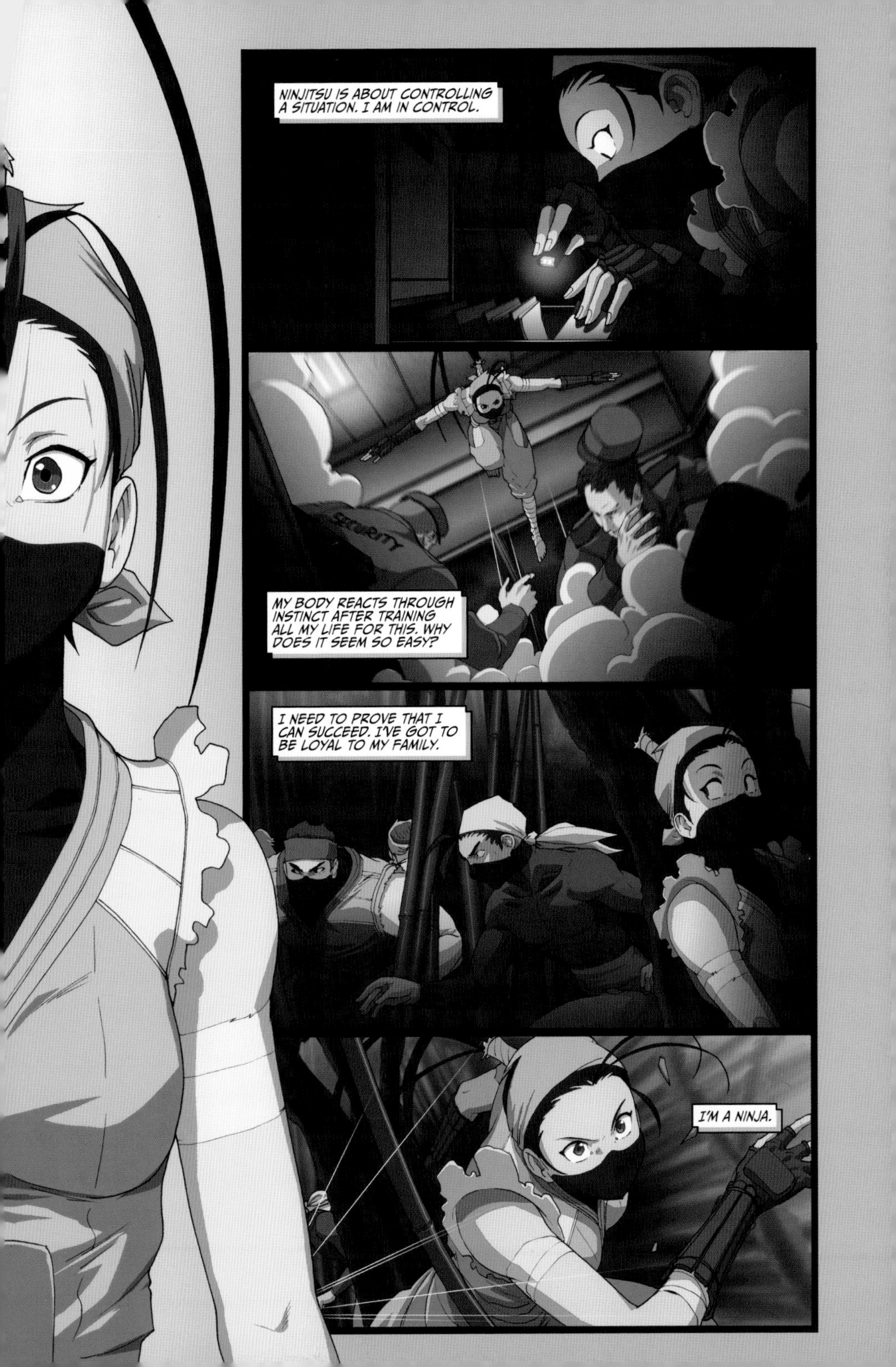
NINJITSU IS ABOUT CONTROLLING A SITUATION. I AM IN CONTROL.
SECURITY
MY BODY REACTS THROUGH INSTINCT AFTER TRAINING ALL MY LIFE FOR THIS. WHY DOES IT SEEM SO EASY?
I NEED TO PROVE THAT I CAN SUCCEED. I'VE GOT TO BE LOYAL TO MY FAMILY.
I'M A NINJA.

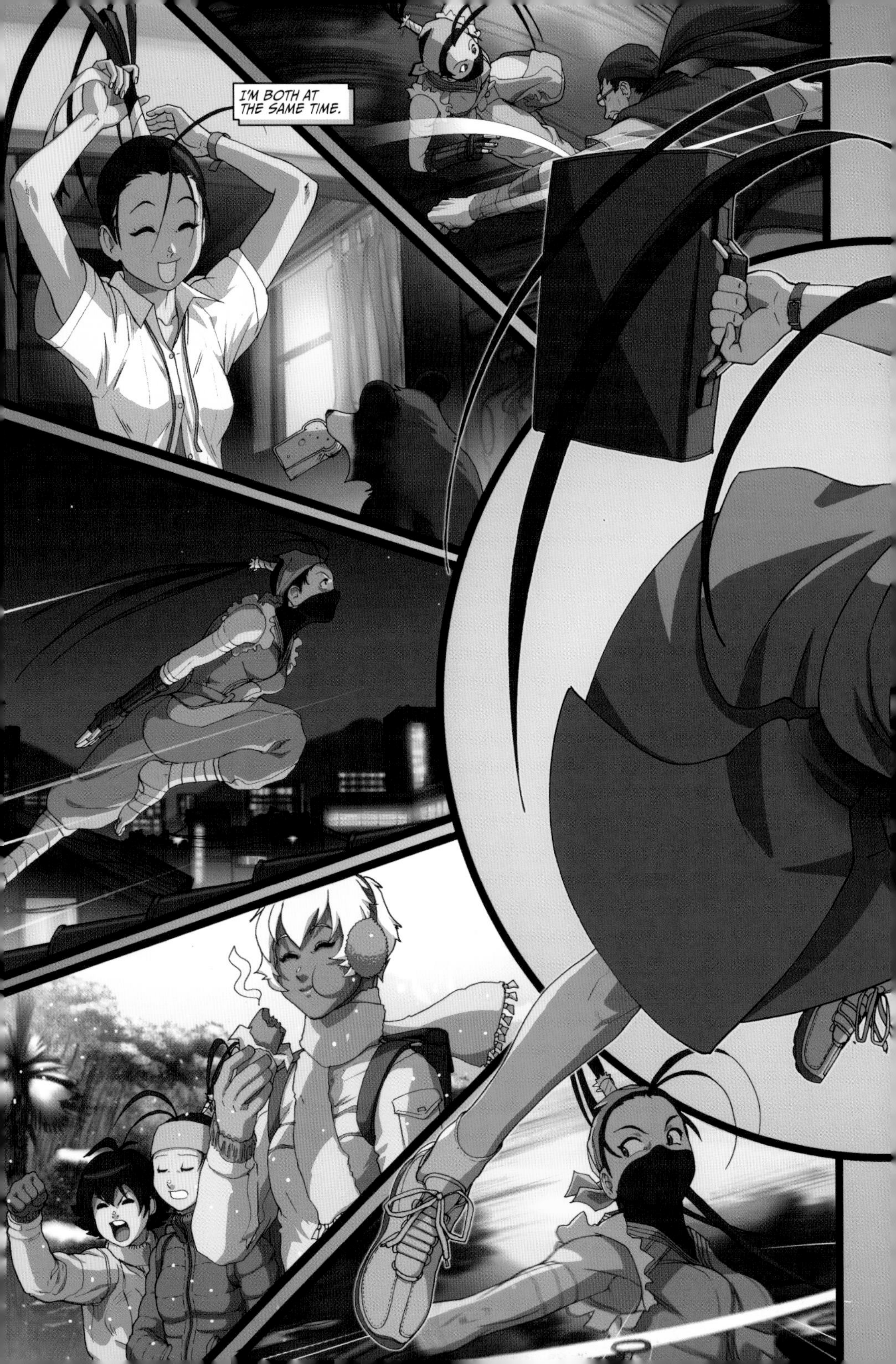
I'M BOTH AT THE SAME TIME.

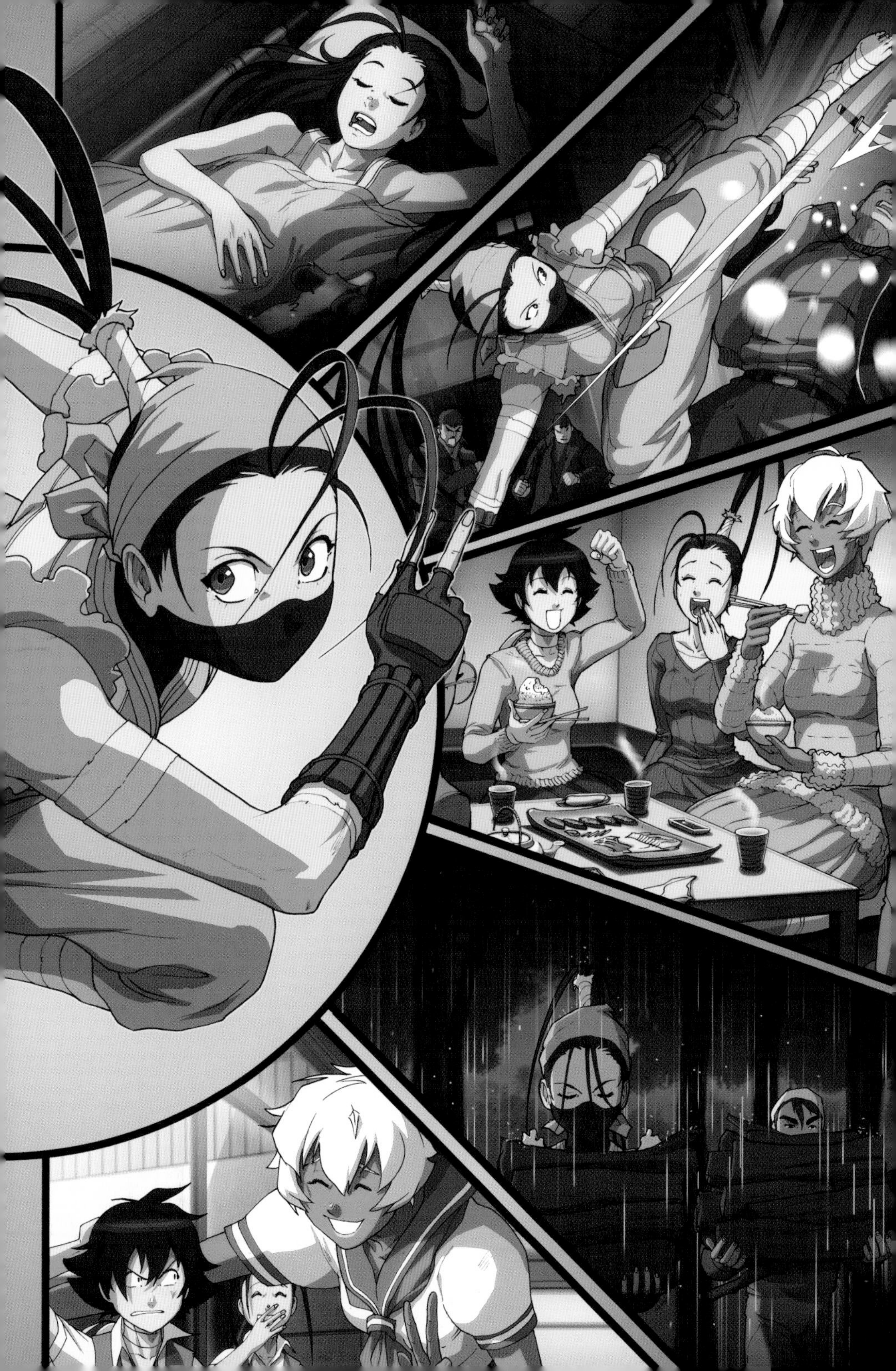

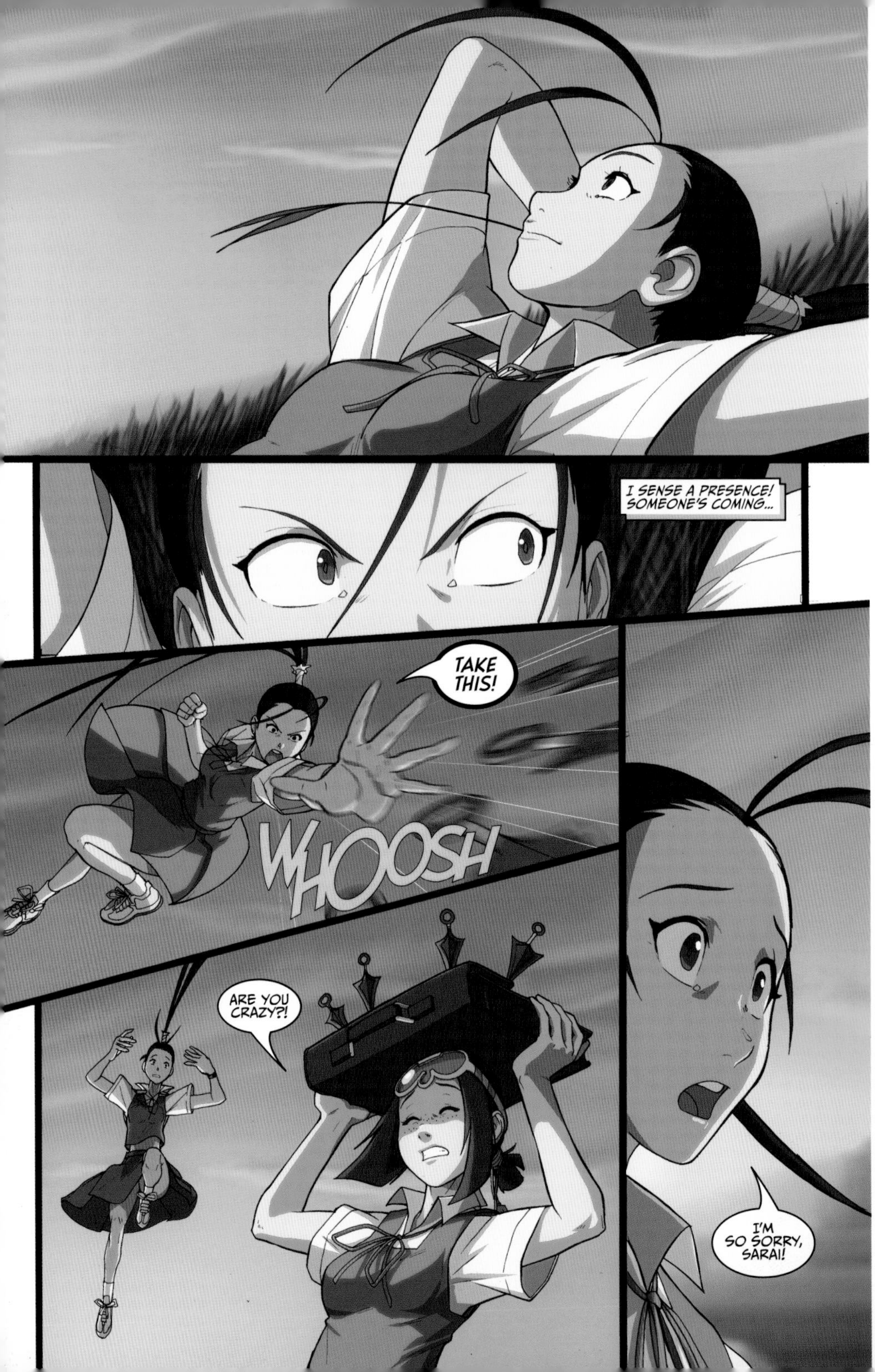
I SENSE A PRESENCE! SOMEONE'S COMING...
TAKE THIS!
WHOOSH
ARE YOU CRAZY?!
I'M SO SORRY, SARAI!

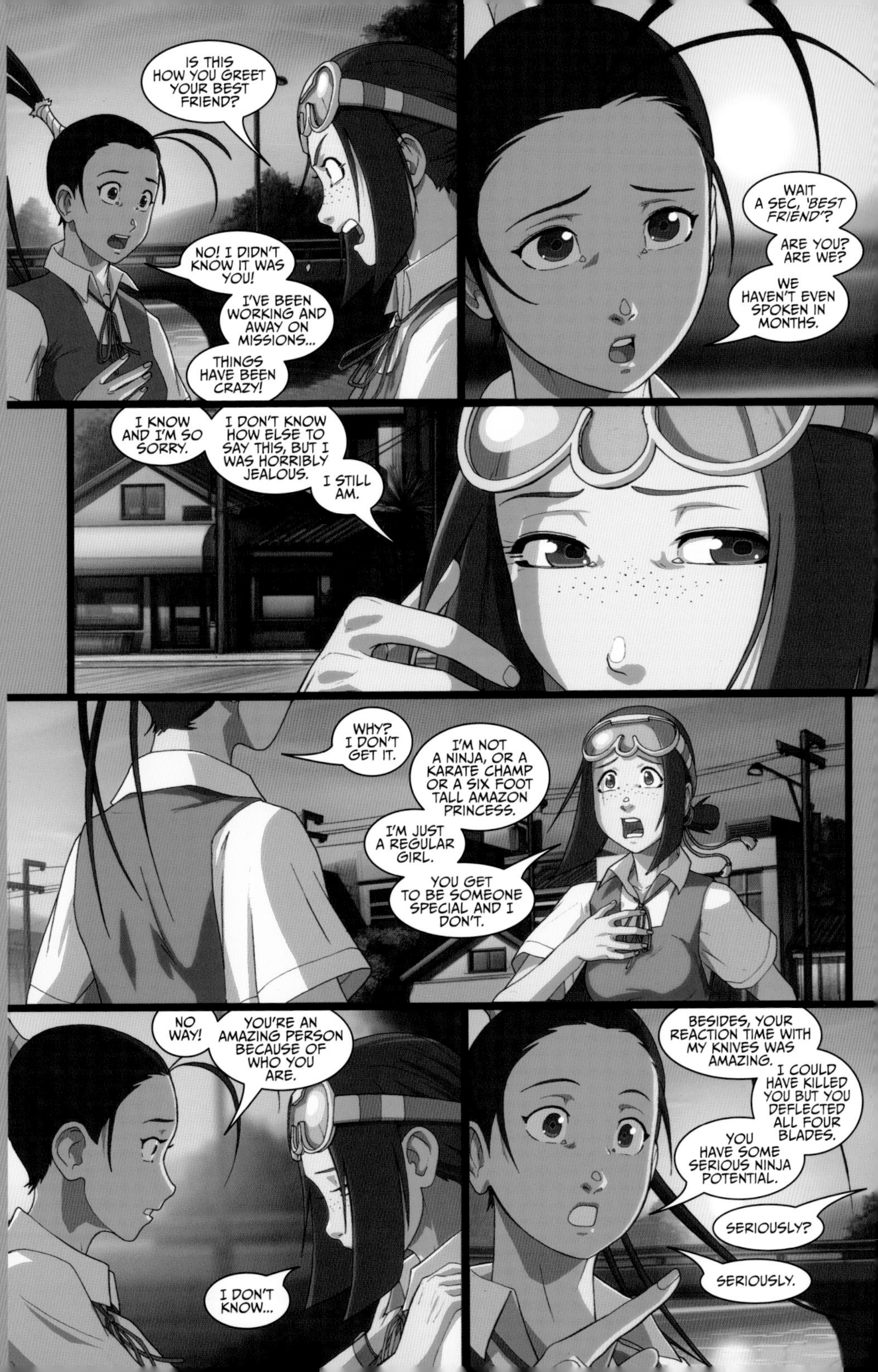
IS THIS HOW YOU GREET YOUR BEST FRIEND?
NO! I DIDN'T KNOW IT WAS YOU!
I'VE BEEN WORKING AND AWAY ON MISSIONS...
THINGS HAVE BEEN CRAZY!
WAIT A SEC, 'BEST FRIEND'?
ARE YOU? ARE WE?
WE HAVEN'T EVEN SPOKEN IN MONTHS.
I KNOW AND I'M SO SORRY.
I DON'T KNOW HOW ELSE TO SAY THIS, BUT I WAS HORRIBLY JEALOUS.
I STILL AM.
WHY? I DON'T GET IT.
I'M NOT A NINJA, OR A KARATE CHAMP OR A SIX FOOT TALL AMAZON PRINCESS.
I'M JUST A REGULAR GIRL.
YOU GET TO BE SOMEONE SPECIAL AND I DON'T.
NO WAY!
YOU'RE AN AMAZING PERSON BECAUSE OF WHO YOU ARE.
I DON'T KNOW...
BESIDES, YOUR REACTION TIME WITH MY KNIVES WAS AMAZING.
I COULD HAVE KILLED YOU BUT YOU DEFLECTED ALL FOUR BLADES.
YOU HAVE SOME SERIOUS NINJA POTENTIAL.
SERIOUSLY?
SERIOUSLY.

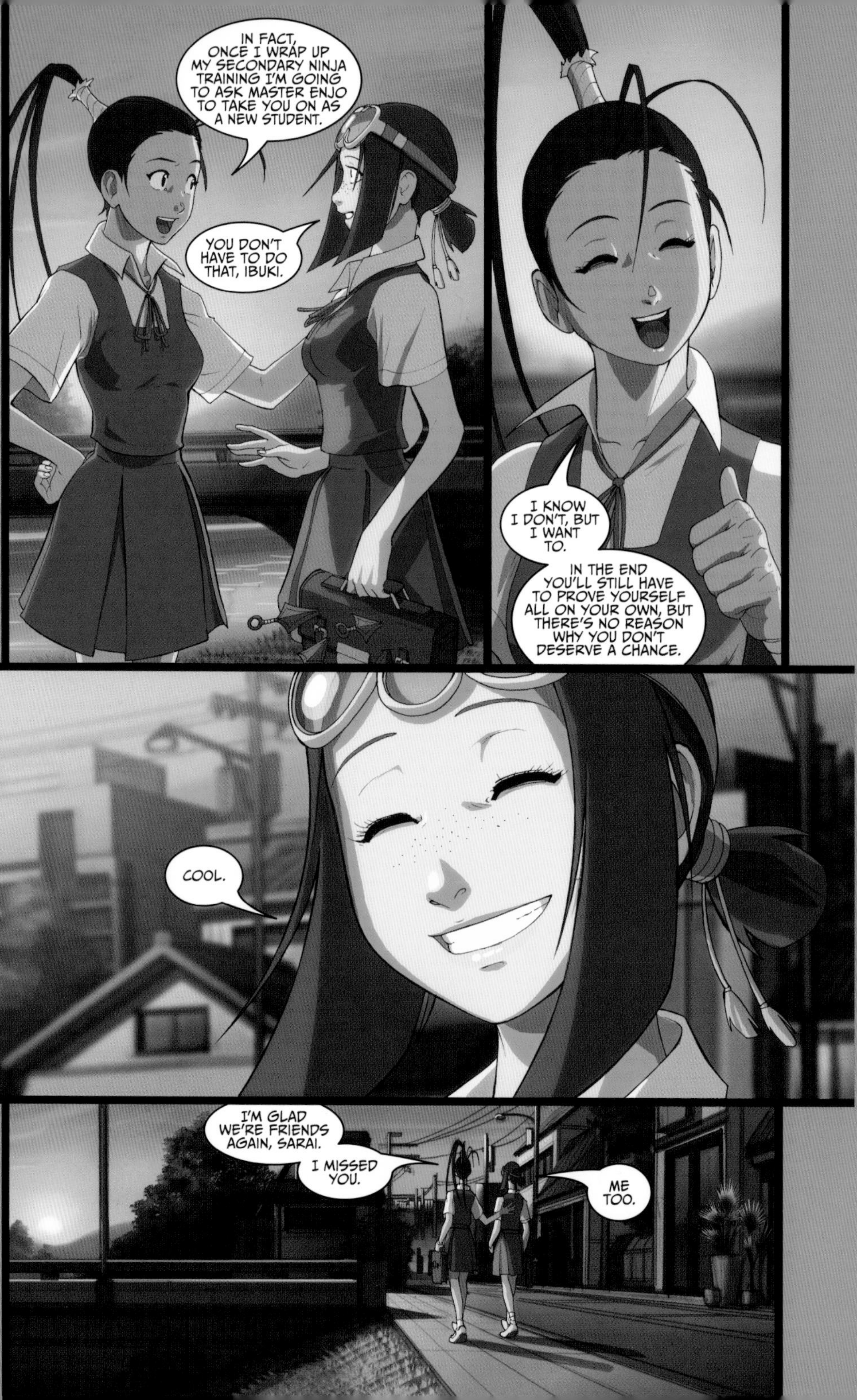
IN FACT, ONCE I WRAP UP MY SECONDARY NINJA TRAINING I'M GOING TO ASK MASTER ENJO TO TAKE YOU ON AS A NEW STUDENT.
YOU DON'T HAVE TO DO THAT, IBUKI.
I KNOW I DON'T, BUT I WANT TO.
IN THE END YOU'LL STILL HAVE TO PROVE YOURSELF ALL ON YOUR OWN, BUT THERE'S NO REASON WHY YOU DON'T DESERVE A CHANCE.
COOL.
I'M GLAD WE'RE FRIENDS AGAIN, SARAI.
I MISSED YOU.
ME TOO.

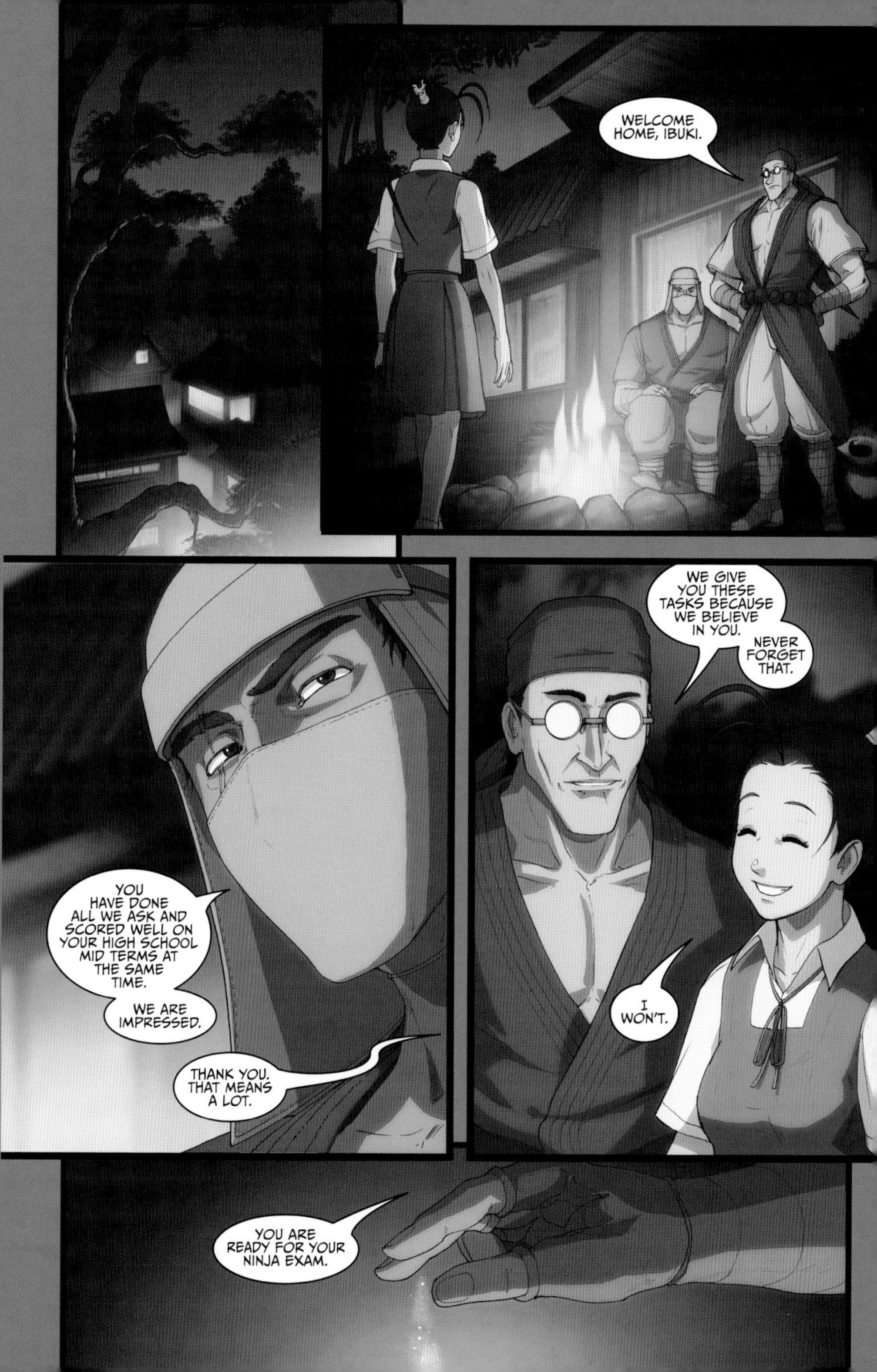
WELCOME HOME, IBUKI.
YOU HAVE DONE ALL WE ASK AND SCORED WELL ON YOUR HIGH SCHOOL MID TERMS AT THE SAME TIME.
WE ARE IMPRESSED.
THANK YOU. THAT MEANS A LOT.
WE GIVE YOU THESE TASKS BECAUSE WE BELIEVE IN YOU.
NEVER FORGET THAT.
I WON'T.
YOU ARE READY FOR YOUR NINJA EXAM.

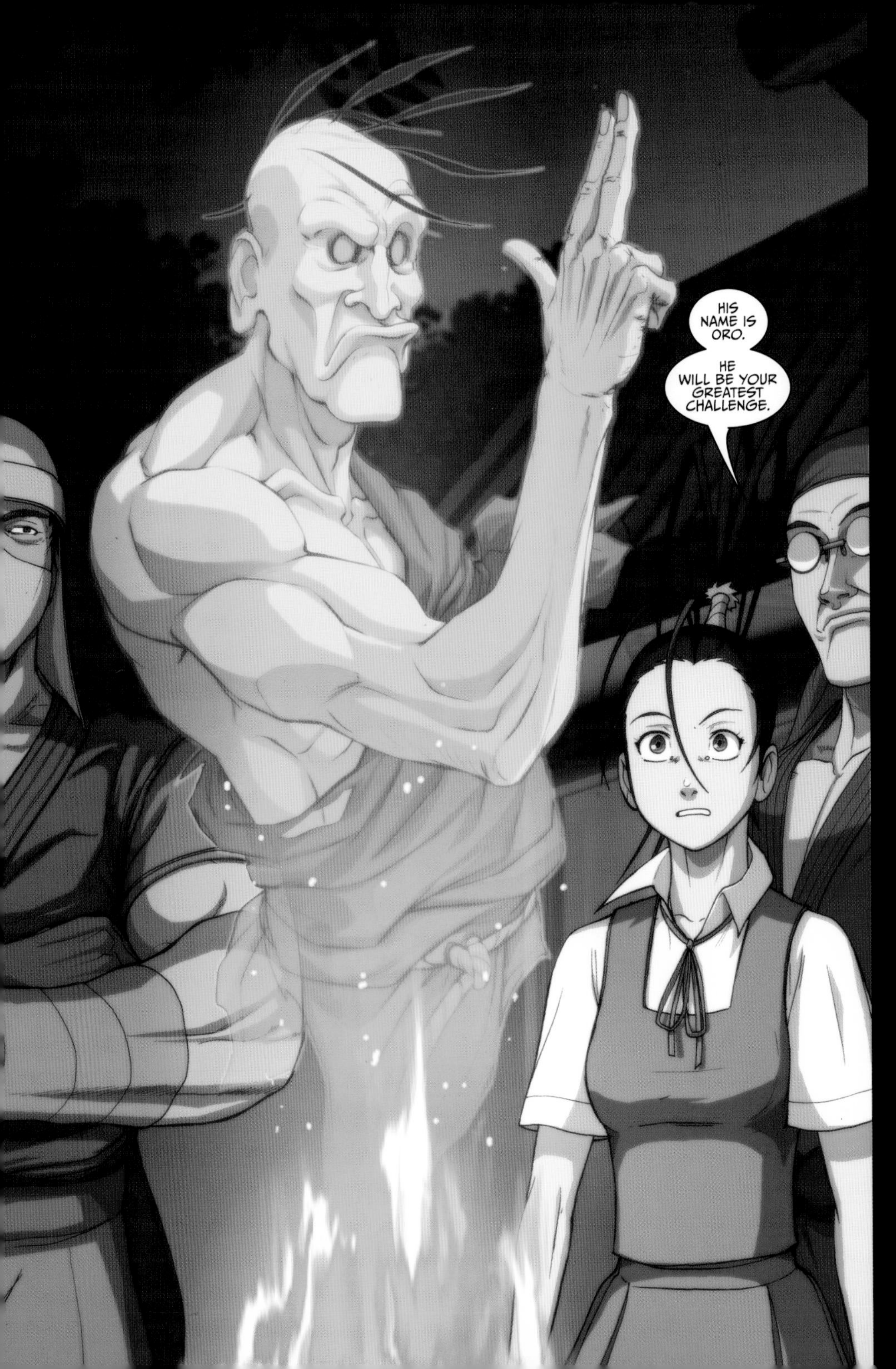
HIS NAME IS ORO.
HE WILL BE YOUR GREATEST CHALLENGE.

Art by: Joe Vriens

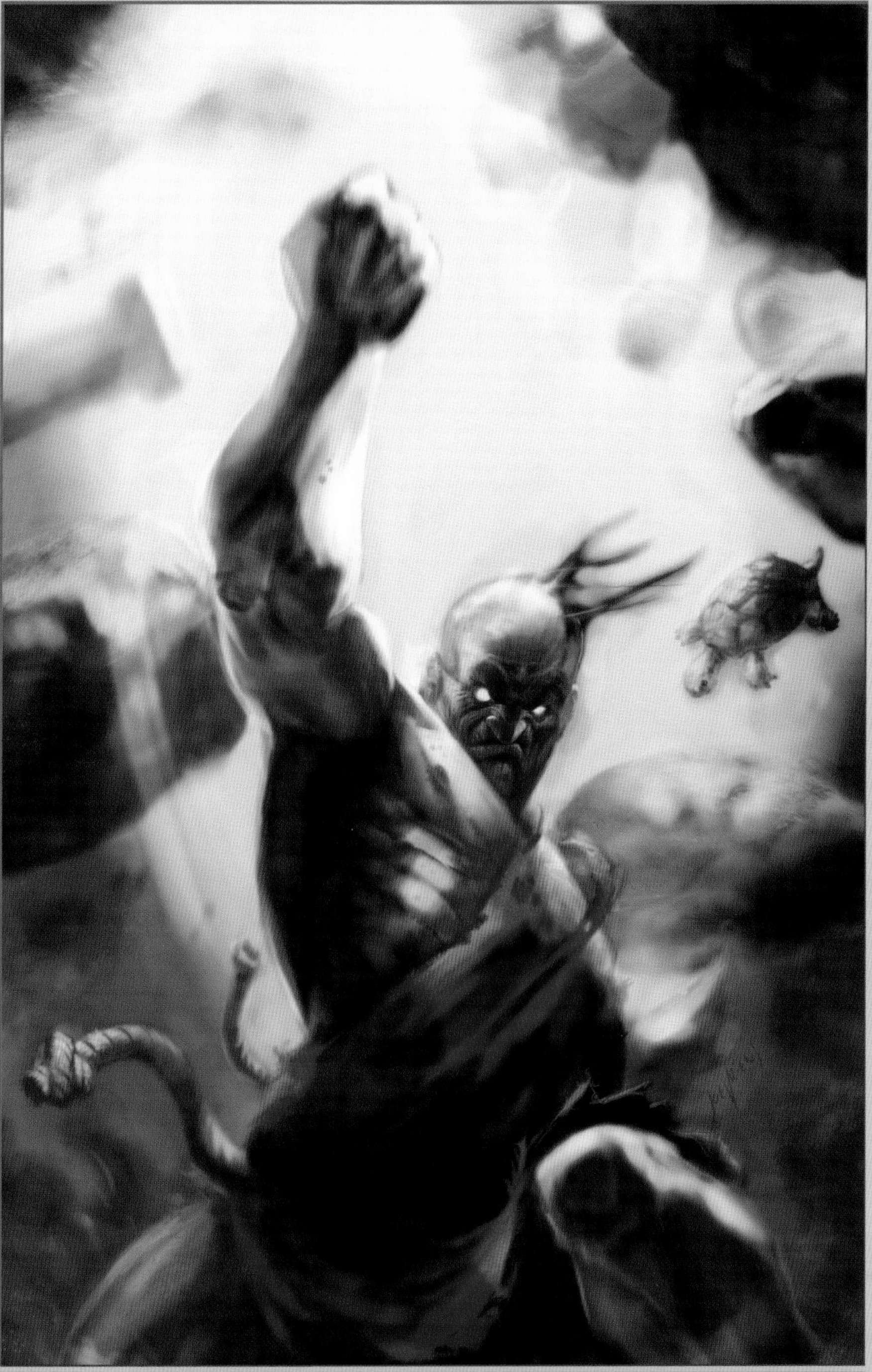

Bonus Story: ORO

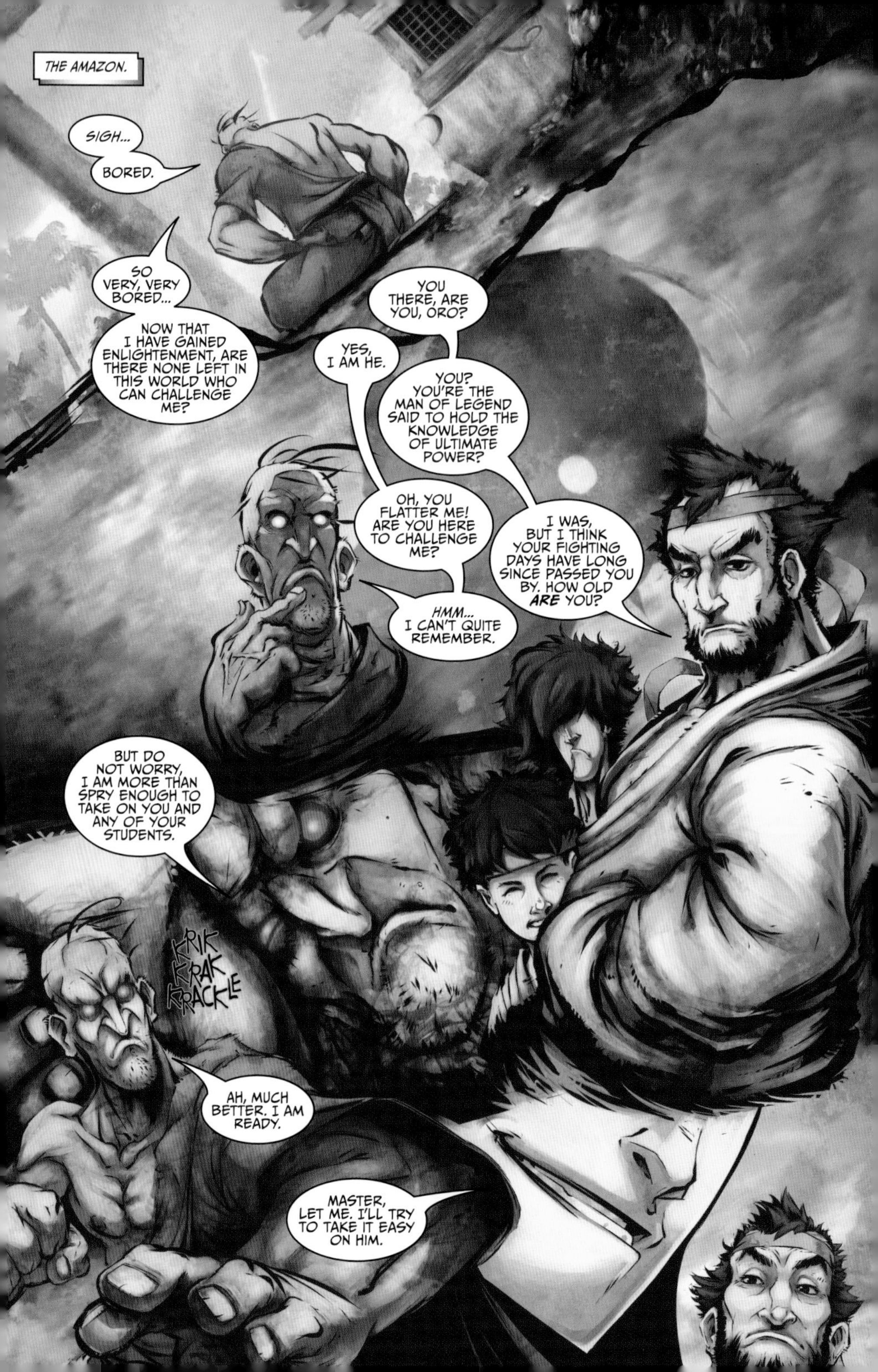

THE AMAZON.
SIGH...
BORED.
SO VERY, VERY BORED...
NOW THAT I HAVE GAINED ENLIGHTENMENT, ARE THERE NONE LEFT IN THIS WORLD WHO CAN CHALLENGE ME?
YOU THERE, ARE YOU, ORO?
YES, I AM HE.
YOU? YOU'RE THE MAN OF LEGEND SAID TO HOLD THE KNOWLEDGE OF ULTIMATE POWER?
OH, YOU FLATTER ME! ARE YOU HERE TO CHALLENGE ME?
I WAS, BUT I THINK YOUR FIGHTING DAYS HAVE LONG SINCE PASSED YOU BY. HOW OLD ARE YOU?
HMM... I CAN'T QUITE REMEMBER.
BUT DO NOT WORRY, I AM MORE THAN SPRY ENOUGH TO TAKE ON YOU AND ANY OF YOUR STUDENTS.
KRIK KRAK KRACKLE
AH, MUCH BETTER. I AM READY.
MASTER, LET ME. I'LL TRY TO TAKE IT EASY ON HIM.

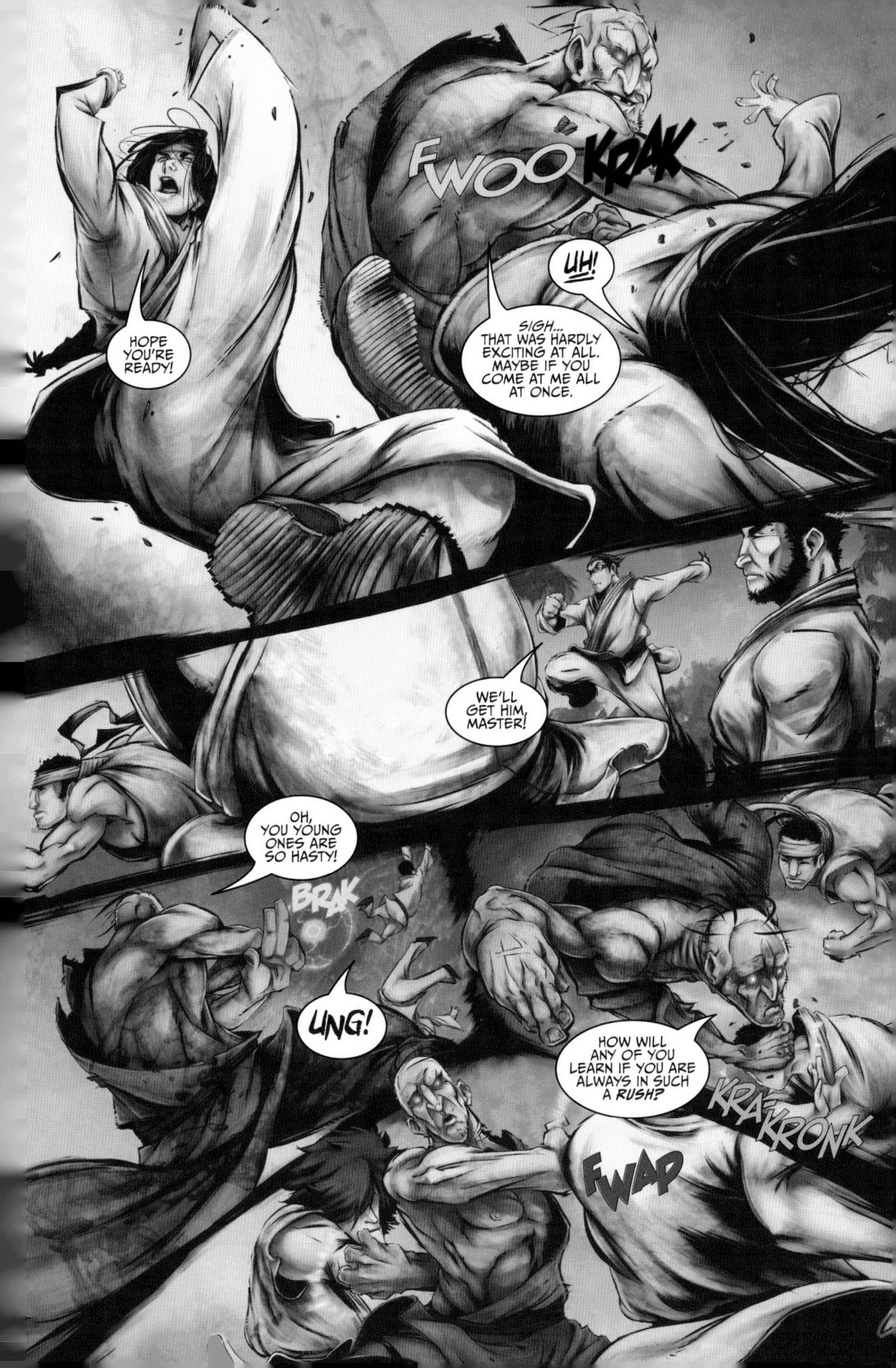
HOPE YOU'RE READY!
FWOO
KRAK
UH!
SIGH... THAT WAS HARDLY EXCITING AT ALL. MAYBE IF YOU COME AT ME ALL AT ONCE.
WE'LL GET HIM, MASTER!
OH, YOU YOUNG ONES ARE SO HASTY!
BRAK
UNG!
HOW WILL ANY OF YOU LEARN IF YOU ARE ALWAYS IN SUCH A RUSH?
KRA-KRONK
FWAP

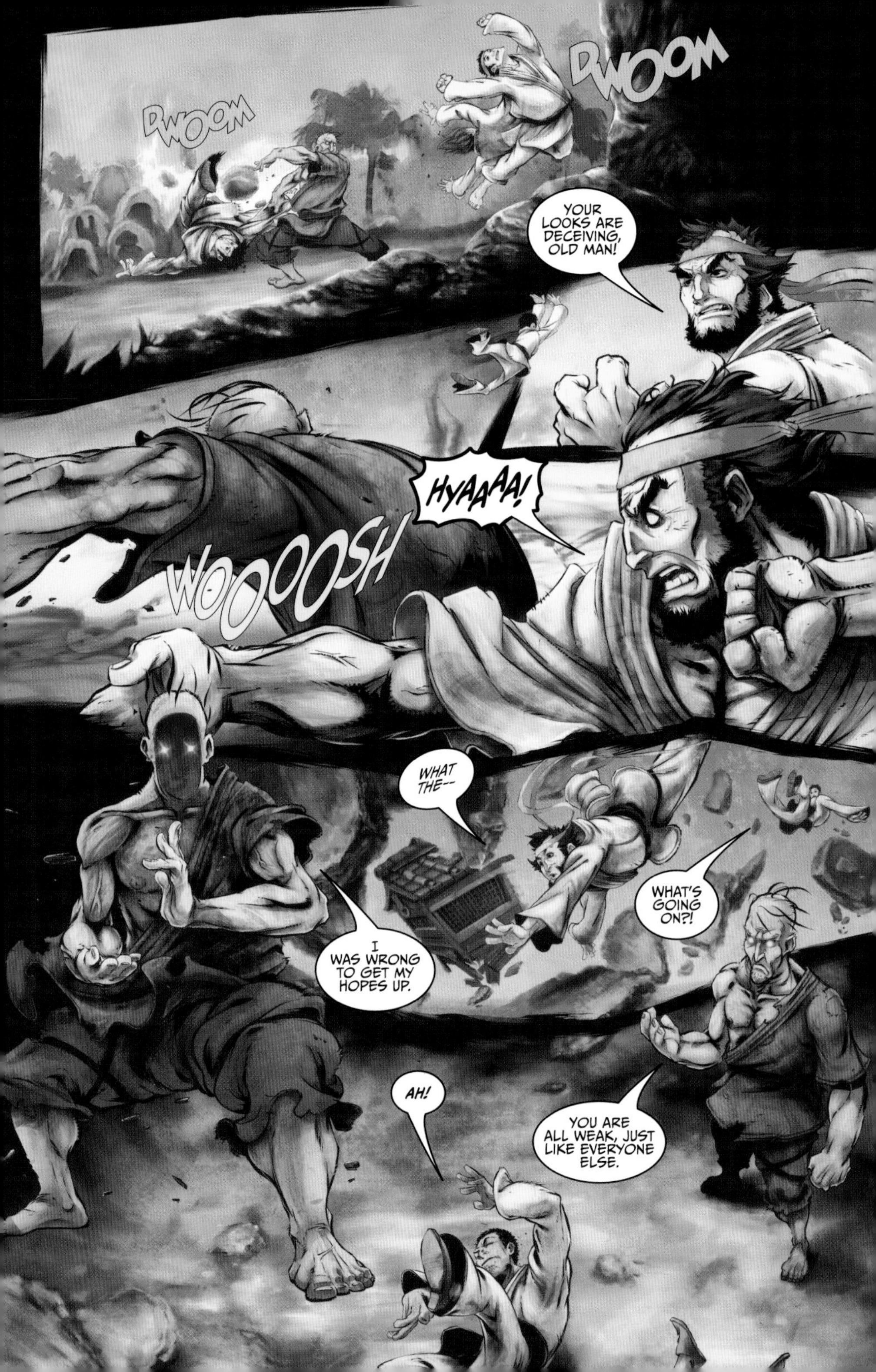
DWOOM
DWOOM
YOUR LOOKS ARE DECEIVING, OLD MAN!
HYAAAA!
WOOOOSH
WHAT THE--
I WAS WRONG TO GET MY HOPES UP.
WHAT'S GOING ON?!
AH!
YOU ARE ALL WEAK, JUST LIKE EVERYONE ELSE.

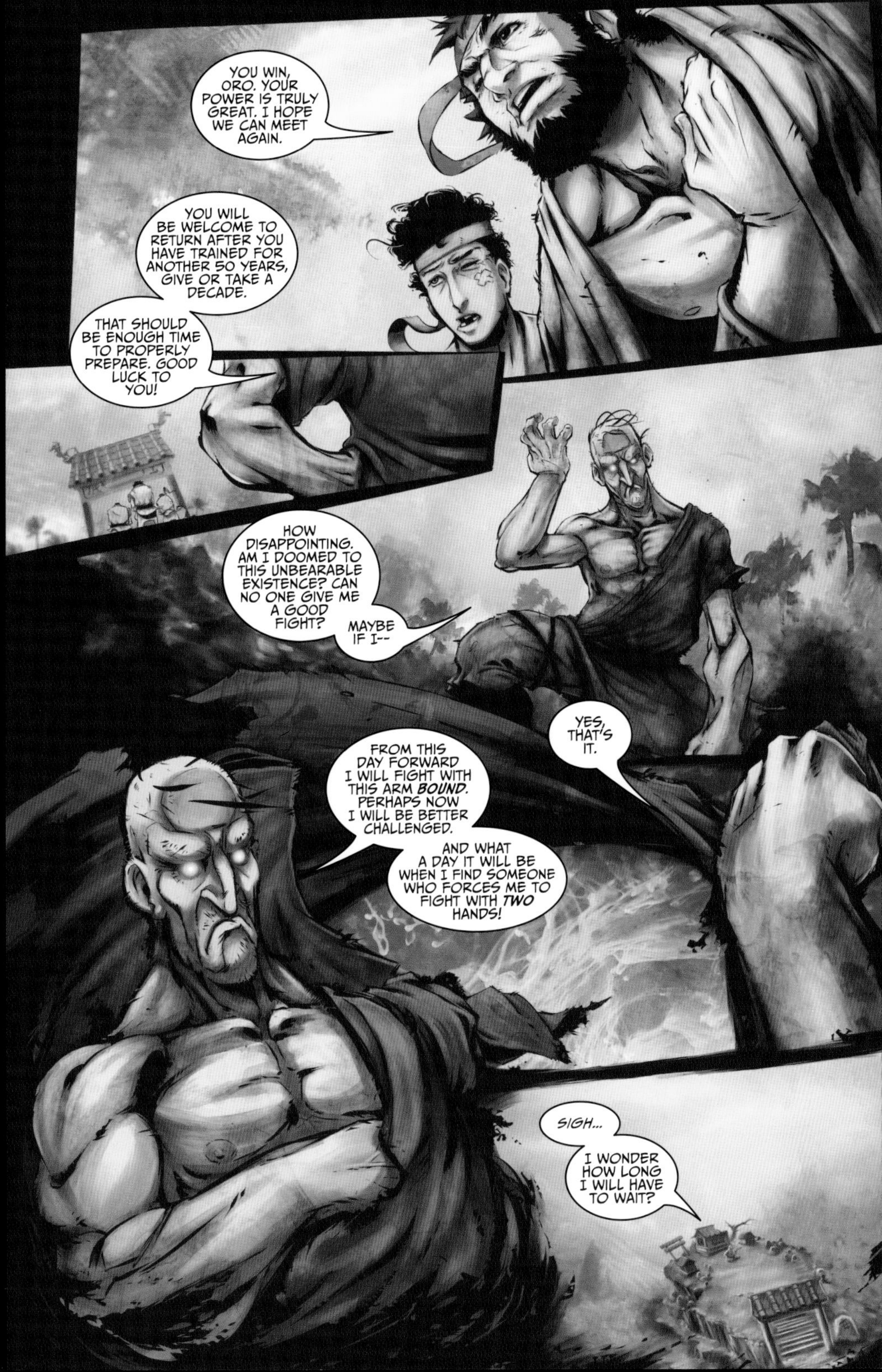
YOU WIN, ORO. YOUR POWER IS TRULY GREAT. I HOPE WE CAN MEET AGAIN.
YOU WILL BE WELCOME TO RETURN AFTER YOU HAVE TRAINED FOR ANOTHER 50 YEARS, GIVE OR TAKE A DECADE.
THAT SHOULD BE ENOUGH TIME TO PROPERLY PREPARE. GOOD LUCK TO YOU!
HOW DISAPPOINTING. AM I DOOMED TO THIS UNBEARABLE EXISTENCE? CAN NO ONE GIVE ME A GOOD FIGHT?
MAYBE IF I--
YES, THAT'S IT.
FROM THIS DAY FORWARD I WILL FIGHT WITH THIS ARM *BOUND*. PERHAPS NOW I WILL BE BETTER CHALLENGED.
AND WHAT A DAY IT WILL BE WHEN I FIND SOMEONE WHO FORCES ME TO FIGHT WITH *TWO* HANDS!
SIGH...
I WONDER HOW LONG I WILL HAVE TO WAIT?

Chapter 3: THE CHOSEN PATH

Art by: Omar Dogan

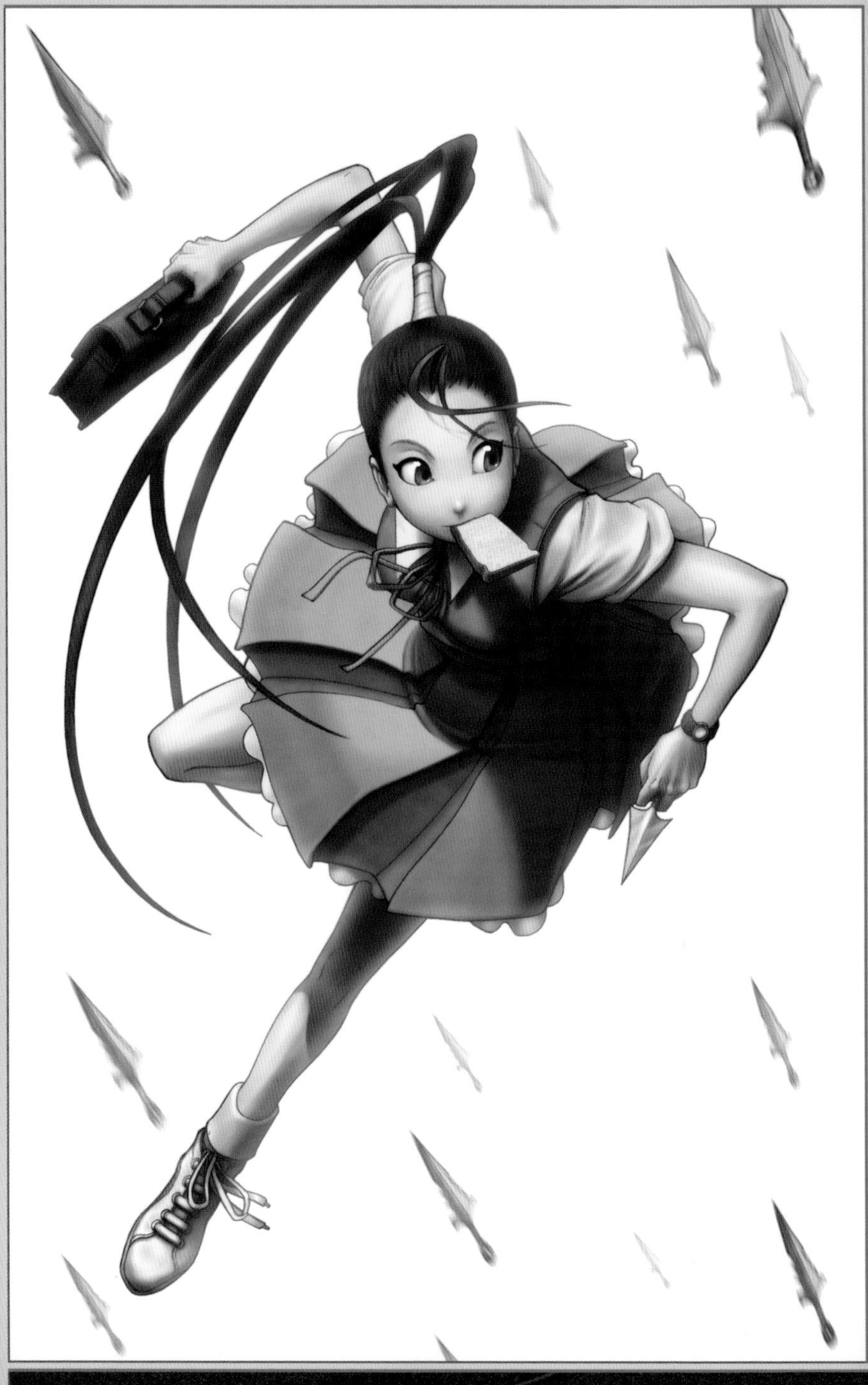

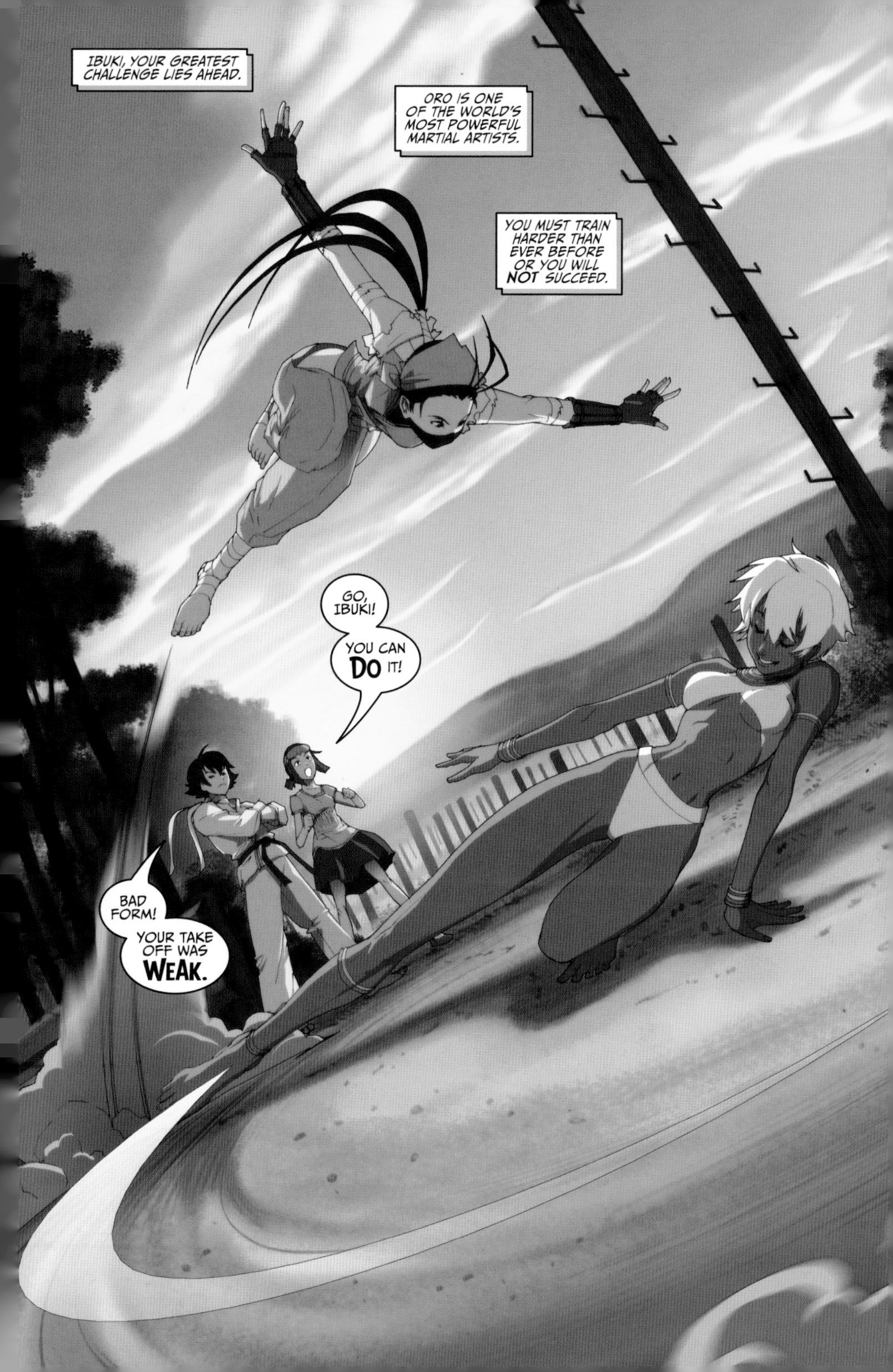
IBUKI, YOUR GREATEST CHALLENGE LIES AHEAD.
ORO IS ONE OF THE WORLD'S MOST POWERFUL MARTIAL ARTISTS.
YOU MUST TRAIN HARDER THAN EVER BEFORE OR YOU WILL NOT SUCCEED.
GO, IBUKI!
YOU CAN DO IT!
BAD FORM!
YOUR TAKE OFF WAS WEAK.

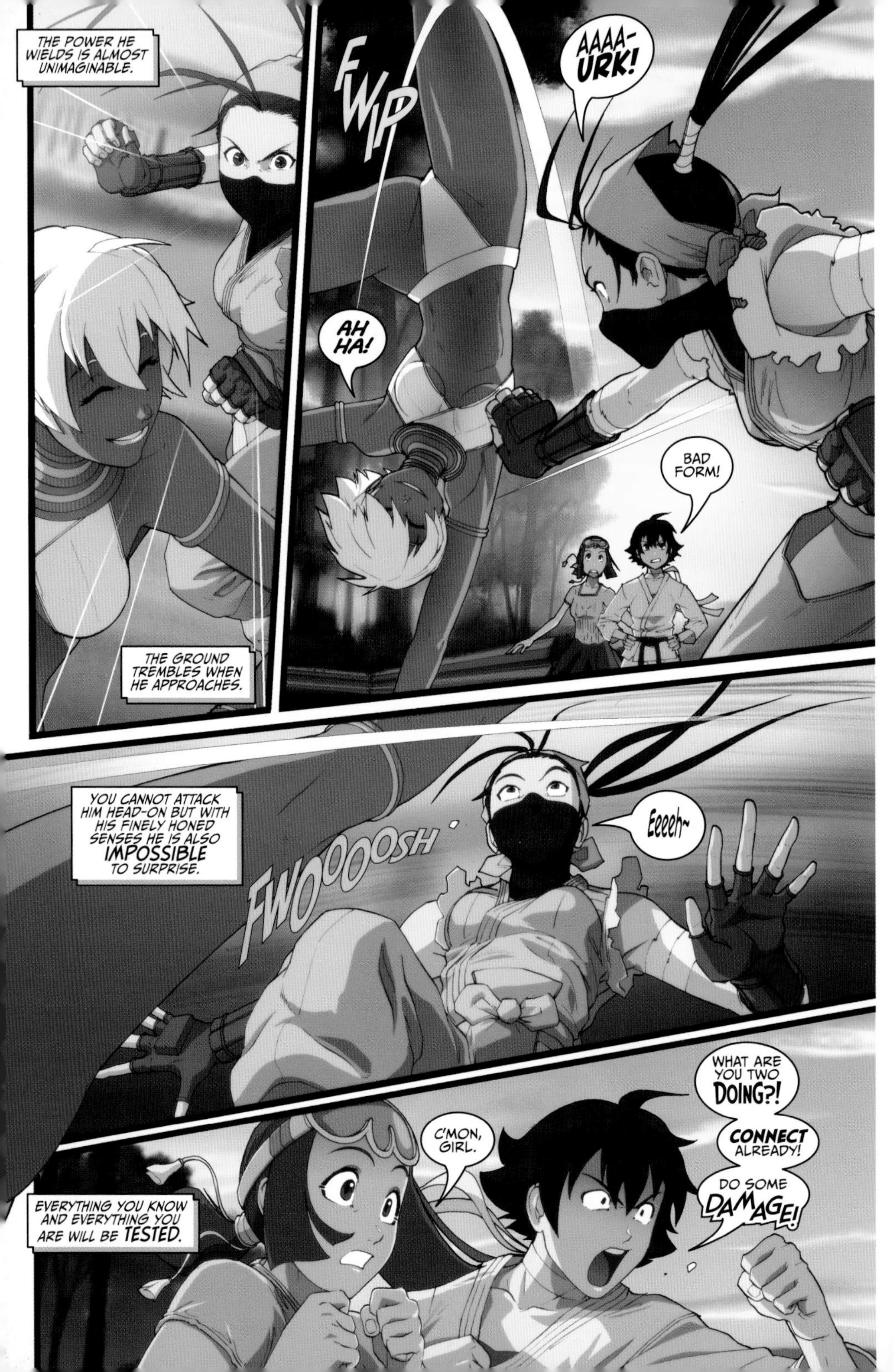
THE POWER HE WIELDS IS ALMOST UNIMAGINABLE.
THE GROUND TREMBLES WHEN HE APPROACHES.
FWIP
AH HA!
AAAA-URK!
BAD FORM!
YOU CANNOT ATTACK HIM HEAD-ON BUT WITH HIS FINELY HONED SENSES HE IS ALSO IMPOSSIBLE TO SURPRISE.
FWOOOOSH
Eeeeh~
EVERYTHING YOU KNOW AND EVERYTHING YOU ARE WILL BE TESTED.
C'MON, GIRL.
WHAT ARE YOU TWO DOING?!
CONNECT ALREADY!
DO SOME DAMAGE!

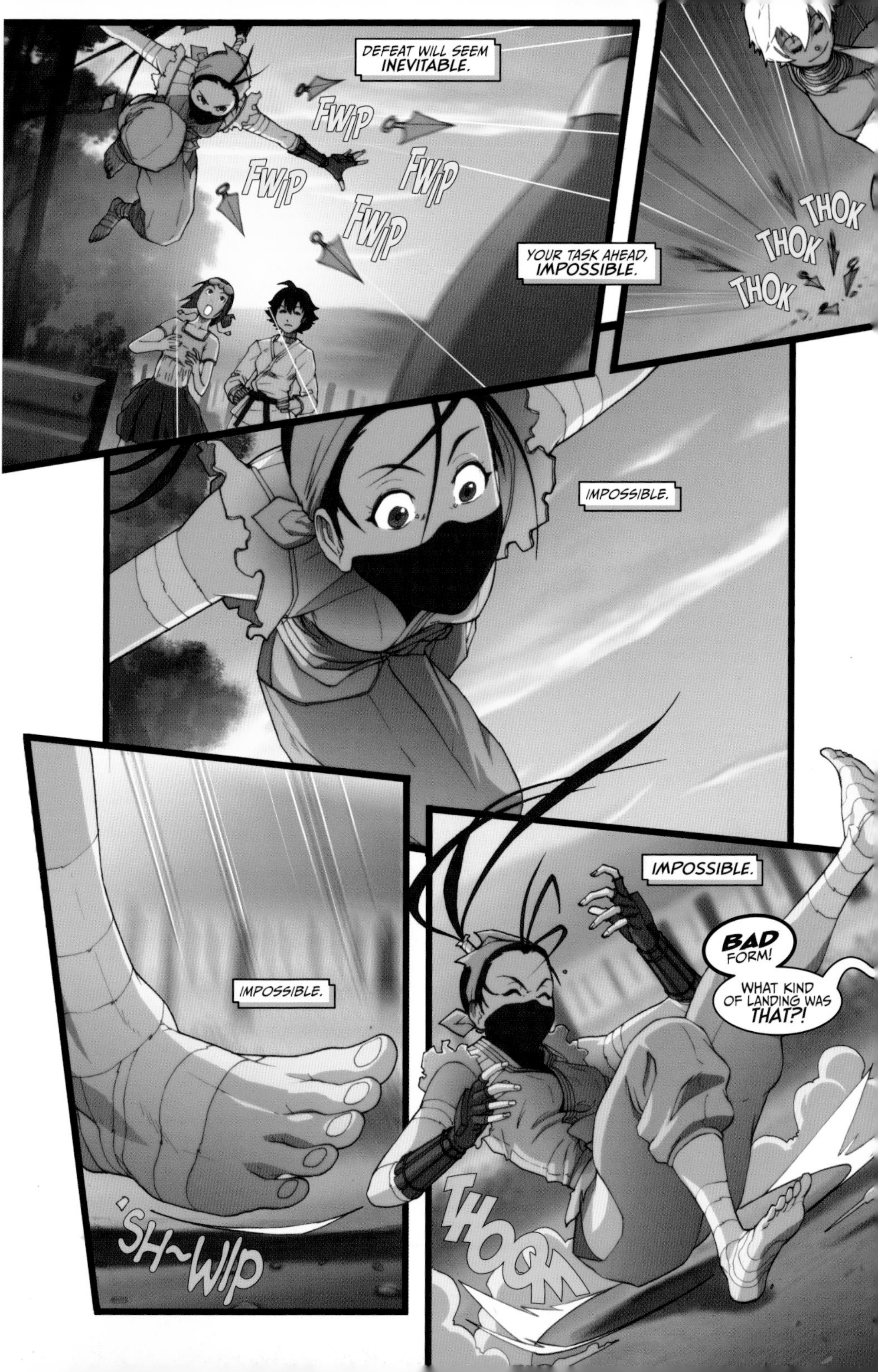
DEFEAT WILL SEEM INEVITABLE.
FWIP
FWIP
FWIP
FWIP
YOUR TASK AHEAD, IMPOSSIBLE.
THOK
THOK
THOK
IMPOSSIBLE.
IMPOSSIBLE.
'SH~WIP
IMPOSSIBLE.
BAD FORM!
WHAT KIND OF LANDING WAS THAT?!
THOOM

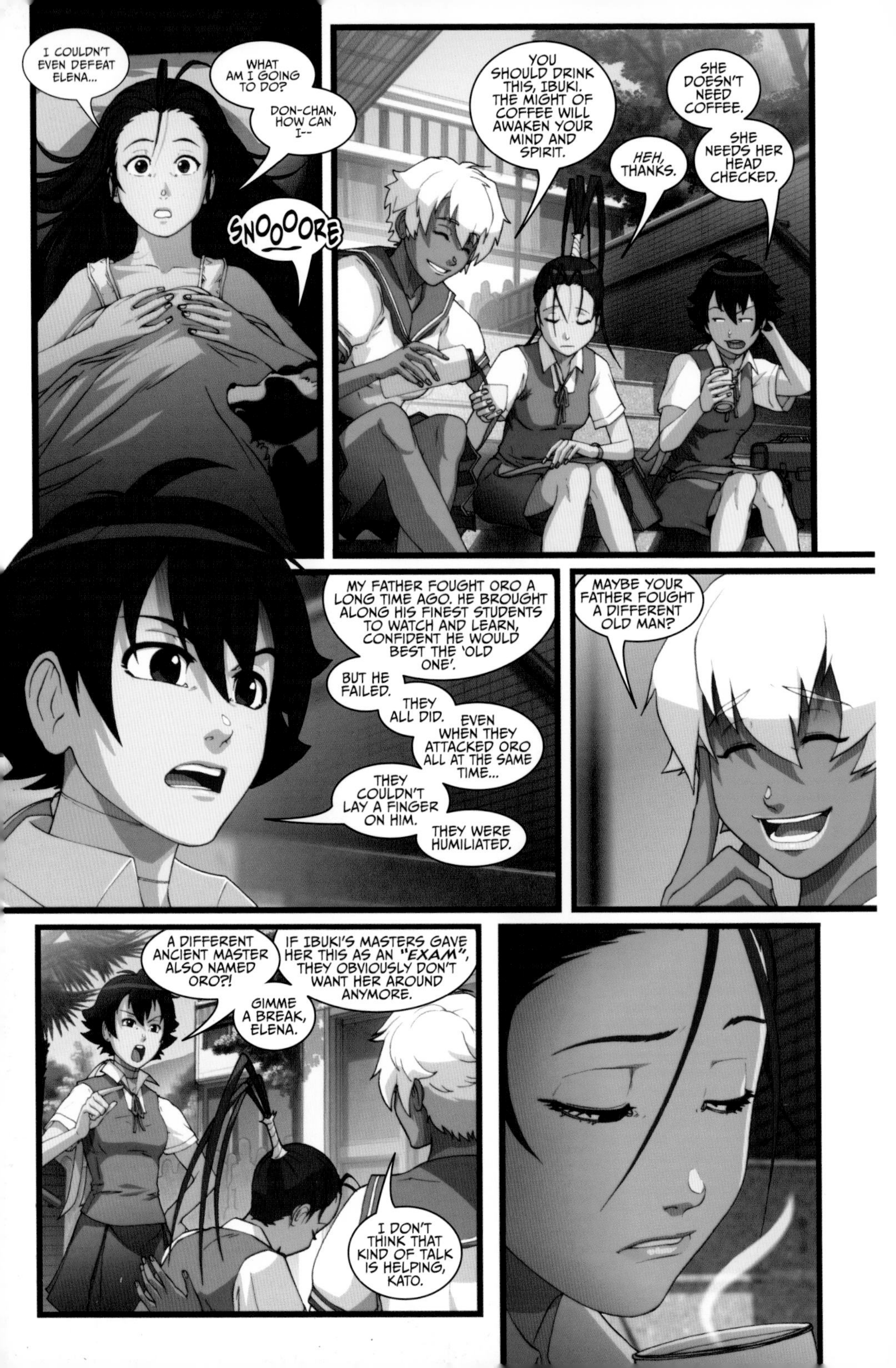
I COULDN'T EVEN DEFEAT ELENA...
WHAT AM I GOING TO DO?
DON-CHAN, HOW CAN I--
SNOOOORE
YOU SHOULD DRINK THIS, IBUKI. THE MIGHT OF COFFEE WILL AWAKEN YOUR MIND AND SPIRIT.
HEH, THANKS.
SHE DOESN'T NEED COFFEE.
SHE NEEDS HER HEAD CHECKED.
MY FATHER FOUGHT ORO A LONG TIME AGO. HE BROUGHT ALONG HIS FINEST STUDENTS TO WATCH AND LEARN, CONFIDENT HE WOULD BEST THE 'OLD ONE'.
BUT HE FAILED.
THEY ALL DID.
EVEN WHEN THEY ATTACKED ORO ALL AT THE SAME TIME...
THEY COULDN'T LAY A FINGER ON HIM.
THEY WERE HUMILIATED.
MAYBE YOUR FATHER FOUGHT A DIFFERENT OLD MAN?
A DIFFERENT ANCIENT MASTER ALSO NAMED ORO?!
GIMME A BREAK, ELENA.
IF IBUKI'S MASTERS GAVE HER THIS AS AN "EXAM", THEY OBVIOUSLY DON'T WANT HER AROUND ANYMORE.
I DON'T THINK THAT KIND OF TALK IS HELPING, KATO.

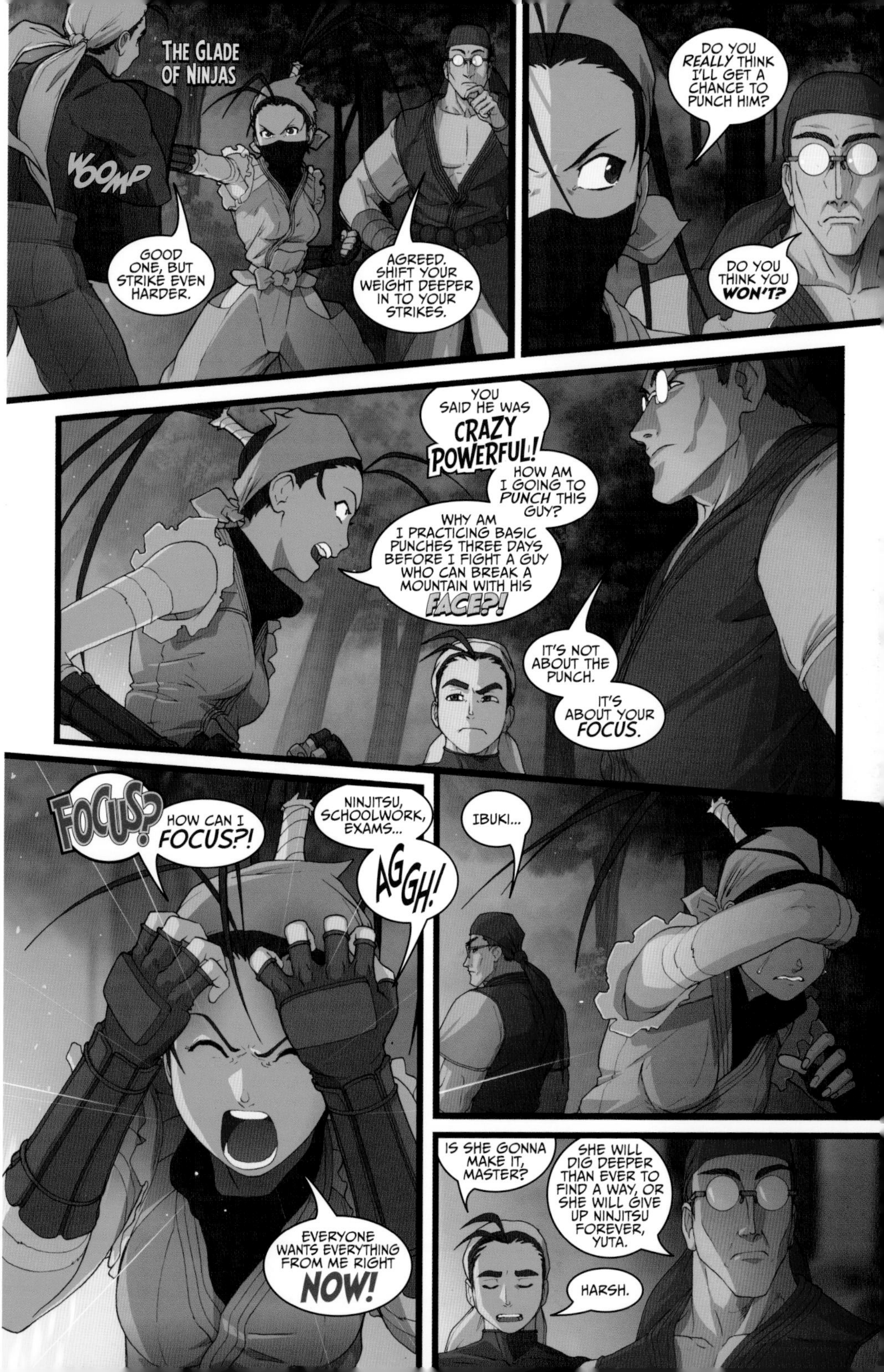
THE GLADE OF NINJAS
WOOMP
GOOD ONE, BUT STRIKE EVEN HARDER.
AGREED. SHIFT YOUR WEIGHT DEEPER IN TO YOUR STRIKES.
DO YOU *REALLY* THINK I'LL GET A CHANCE TO PUNCH HIM?
DO YOU THINK YOU **WON'T?**
YOU SAID HE WAS **CRAZY POWERFUL!**
HOW AM I GOING TO *PUNCH* THIS GUY?
WHY AM I PRACTICING BASIC PUNCHES THREE DAYS BEFORE I FIGHT A GUY WHO CAN BREAK A MOUNTAIN WITH HIS **FACE?!**
IT'S NOT ABOUT THE PUNCH.
IT'S ABOUT YOUR **FOCUS**.
FOCUS?
HOW CAN I **FOCUS?!**
NINJITSU, SCHOOLWORK, EXAMS...
AGGH!
EVERYONE WANTS EVERYTHING FROM ME RIGHT **NOW!**
IBUKI...
IS SHE GONNA MAKE IT, MASTER?
SHE WILL DIG DEEPER THAN EVER TO FIND A WAY, OR SHE WILL GIVE UP NINJITSU FOREVER, YUTA.
HARSH.

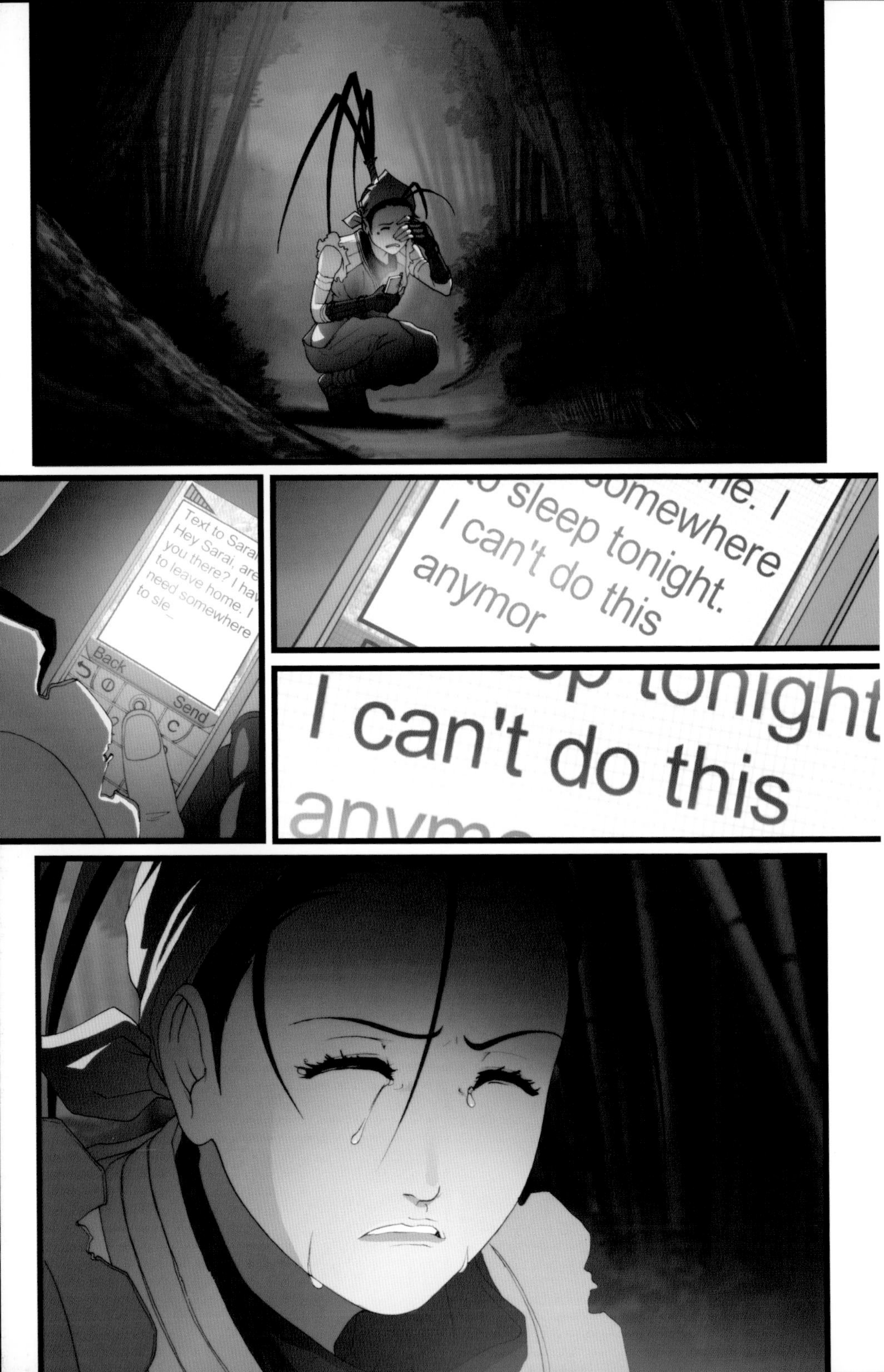
Text to Sara
Hey Sarai, are
you there? I hav
to leave home. I
need somewhere
to sle_
Back
Send
somewhere
sleep tonight.
I can't do this
anymor
tonight
I can't do this

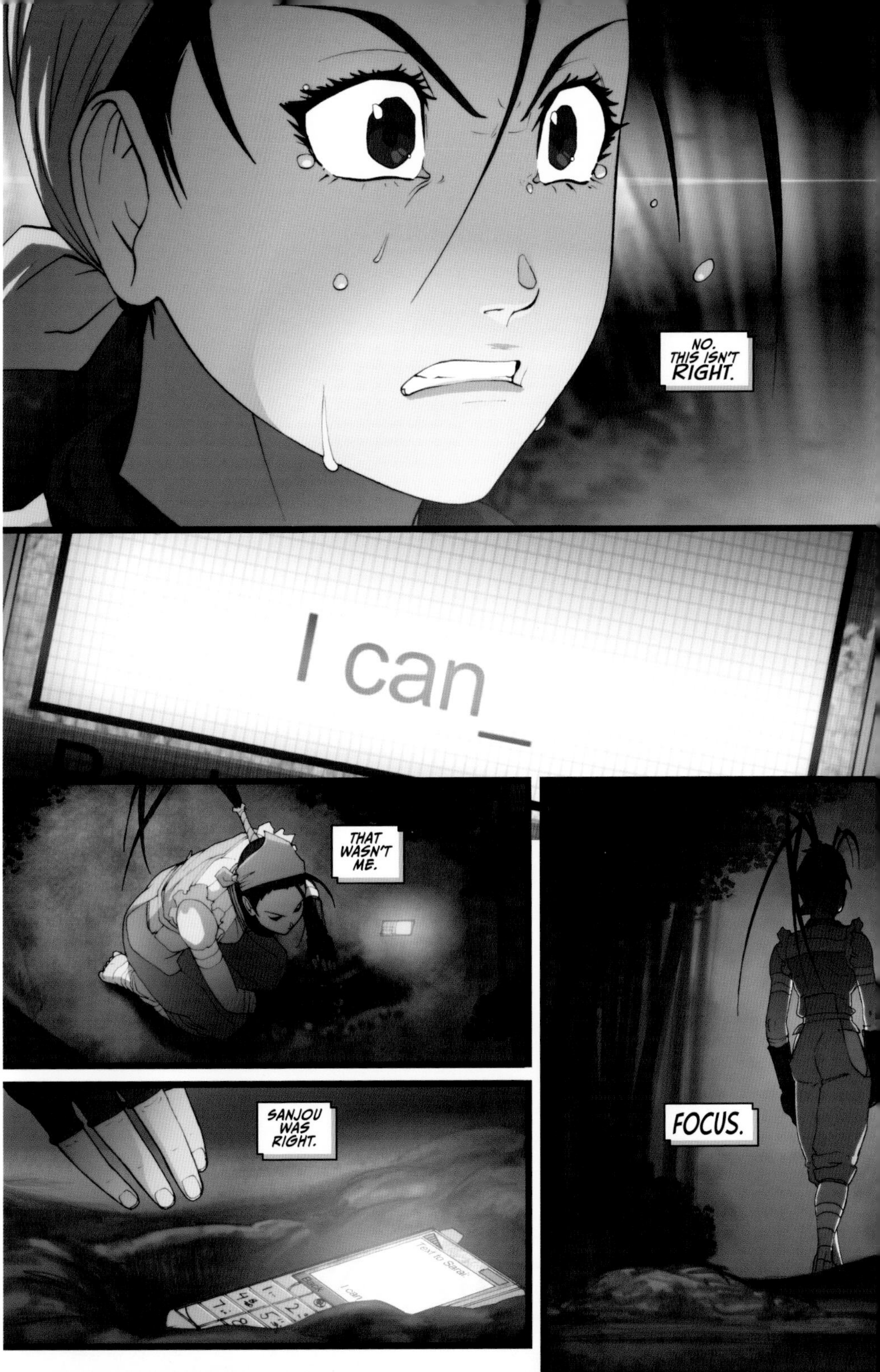
NO. THIS ISN'T RIGHT.
I can_
THAT WASN'T ME.
SANJOU WAS RIGHT.
Text to Sarai:
I can
FOCUS.

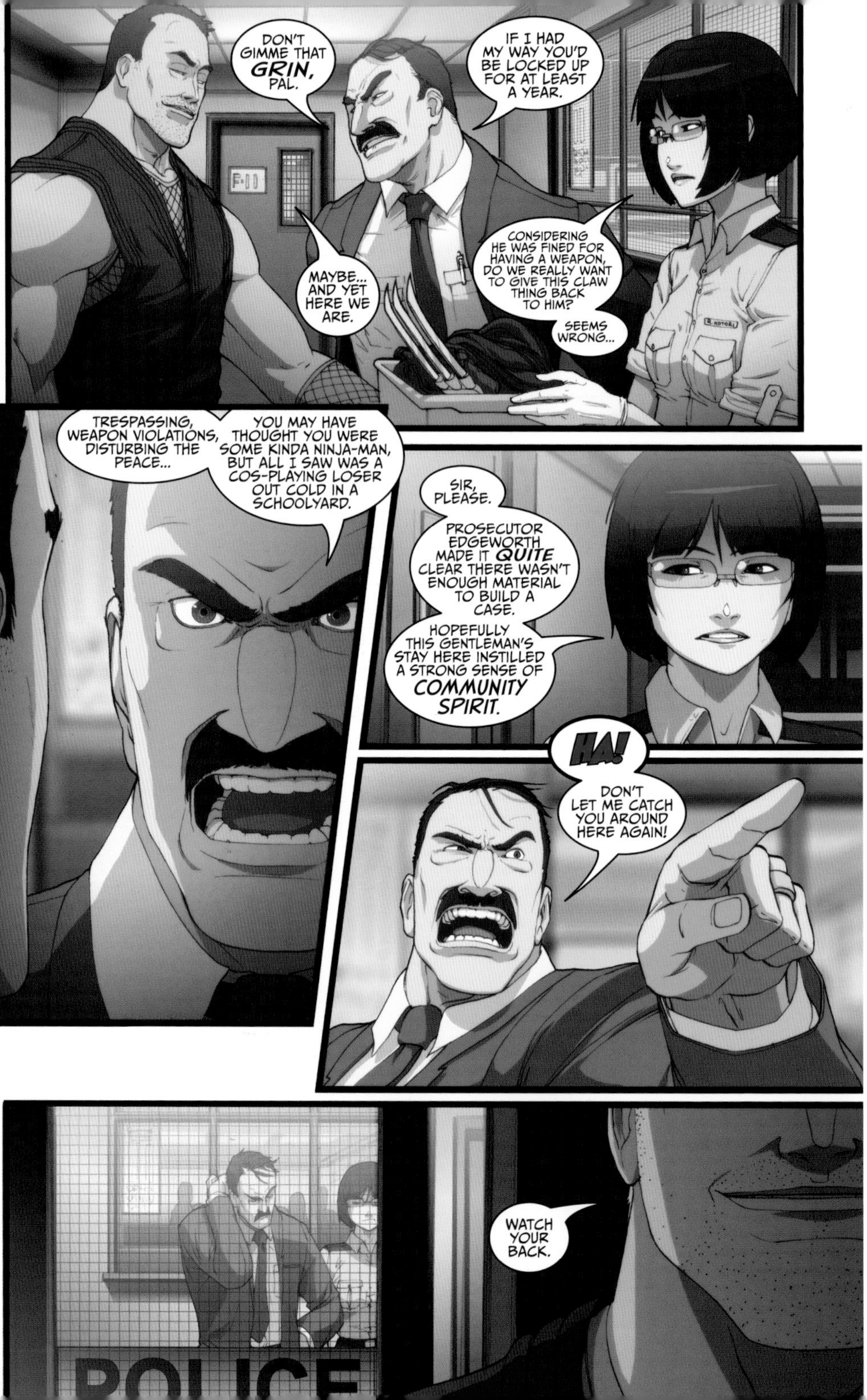
DON'T GIMME THAT **GRIN,** PAL.
IF I HAD MY WAY YOU'D BE LOCKED UP FOR AT LEAST A YEAR.
MAYBE... AND YET HERE WE ARE.
CONSIDERING HE WAS FINED FOR HAVING A WEAPON, DO WE REALLY WANT TO GIVE THIS CLAW THING BACK TO HIM?
SEEMS WRONG...
TRESPASSING, WEAPON VIOLATIONS, DISTURBING THE PEACE...
YOU MAY HAVE THOUGHT YOU WERE SOME KINDA NINJA-MAN, BUT ALL I SAW WAS A COS-PLAYING LOSER OUT COLD IN A SCHOOLYARD.
SIR, PLEASE.
PROSECUTOR EDGEWORTH MADE IT **QUITE** CLEAR THERE WASN'T ENOUGH MATERIAL TO BUILD A CASE.
HOPEFULLY THIS GENTLEMAN'S STAY HERE INSTILLED A STRONG SENSE OF **COMMUNITY SPIRIT.**
HA!
DON'T LET ME CATCH YOU AROUND HERE AGAIN!
POLICE
WATCH YOUR BACK.

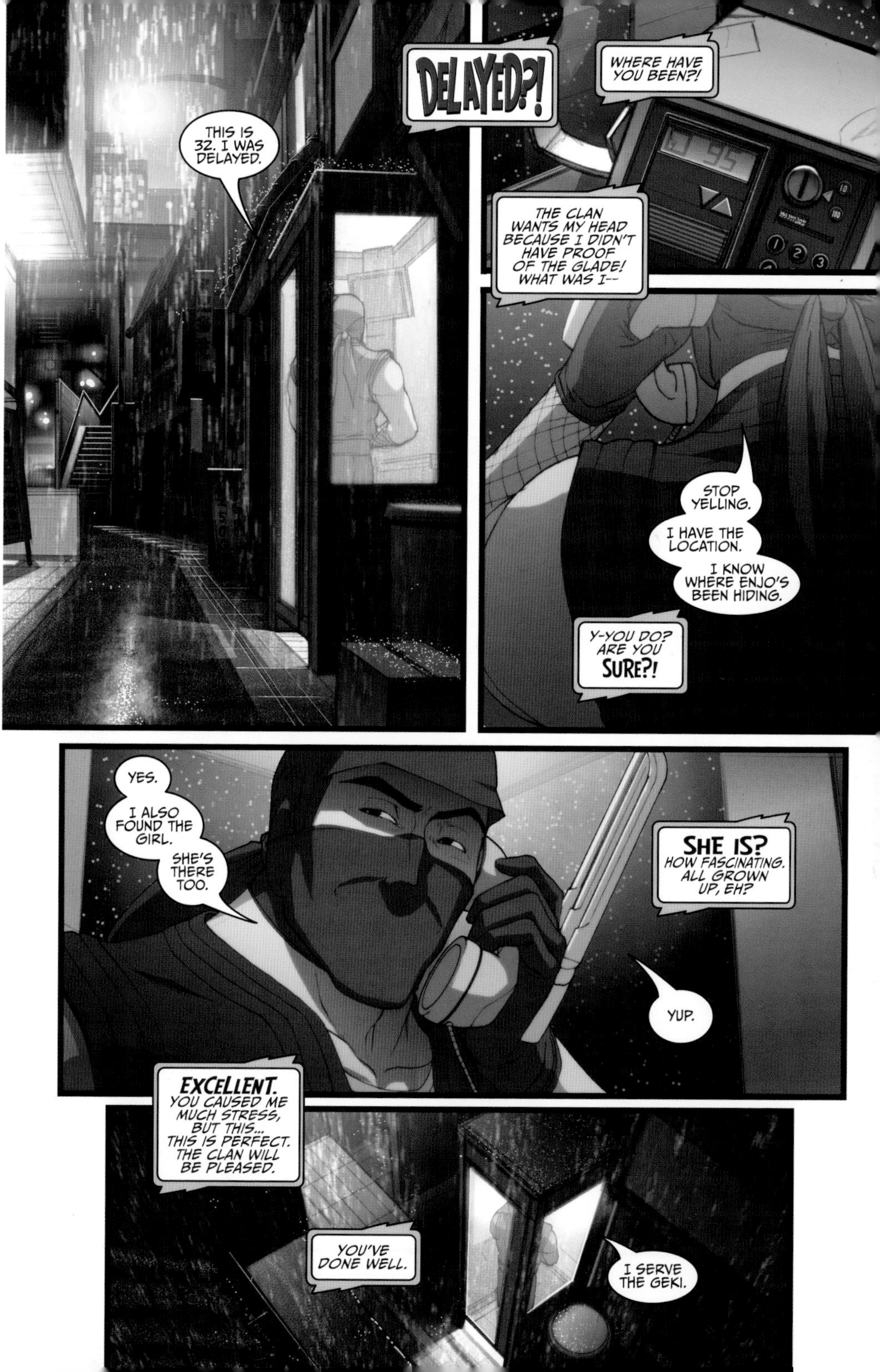
THIS IS 32. I WAS DELAYED.
DELAYED?!
WHERE HAVE YOU BEEN?!
THE CLAN WANTS MY HEAD BECAUSE I DIDN'T HAVE PROOF OF THE GLADE! WHAT WAS I--
STOP YELLING.
I HAVE THE LOCATION.
I KNOW WHERE ENJO'S BEEN HIDING.
Y-YOU DO? ARE YOU SURE?!
YES.
I ALSO FOUND THE GIRL.
SHE'S THERE TOO.
SHE IS? HOW FASCINATING. ALL GROWN UP, EH?
YUP.
EXCELLENT. YOU CAUSED ME MUCH STRESS, BUT THIS... THIS IS PERFECT. THE CLAN WILL BE PLEASED.
YOU'VE DONE WELL.
I SERVE THE GEKI.

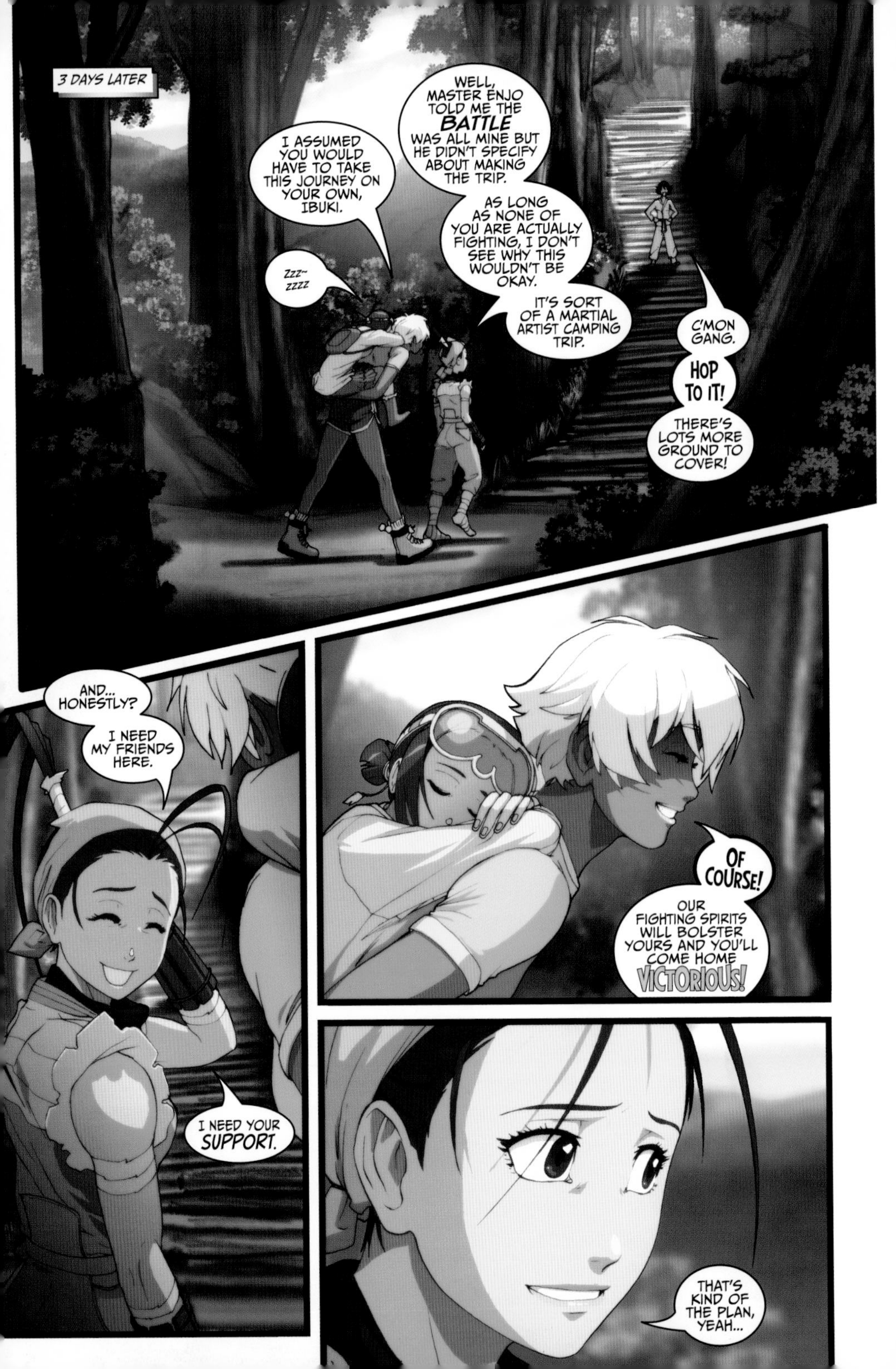
3 DAYS LATER
I ASSUMED YOU WOULD HAVE TO TAKE THIS JOURNEY ON YOUR OWN, IBUKI.
WELL, MASTER ENJO TOLD ME THE BATTLE WAS ALL MINE BUT HE DIDN'T SPECIFY ABOUT MAKING THE TRIP.
AS LONG AS NONE OF YOU ARE ACTUALLY FIGHTING, I DON'T SEE WHY THIS WOULDN'T BE OKAY.
IT'S SORT OF A MARTIAL ARTIST CAMPING TRIP.
ZZZ~ ZZZZ
C'MON GANG.
HOP TO IT!
THERE'S LOTS MORE GROUND TO COVER!
AND... HONESTLY?
I NEED MY FRIENDS HERE.
I NEED YOUR SUPPORT.
OF COURSE!
OUR FIGHTING SPIRITS WILL BOLSTER YOURS AND YOU'LL COME HOME VICTORIOUS!
THAT'S KIND OF THE PLAN, YEAH...

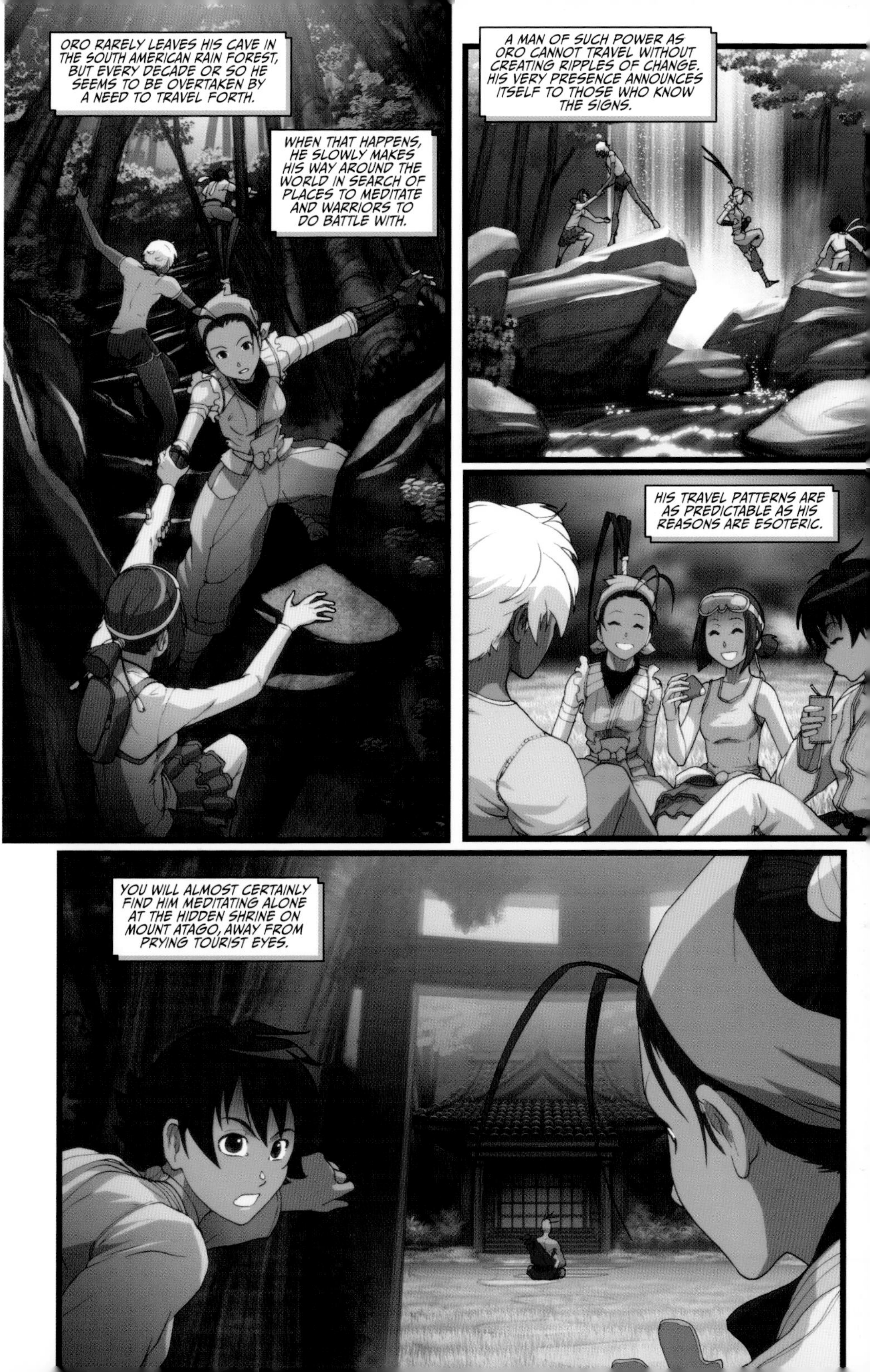
ORO RARELY LEAVES HIS CAVE IN THE SOUTH AMERICAN RAIN FOREST, BUT EVERY DECADE OR SO HE SEEMS TO BE OVERTAKEN BY A NEED TO TRAVEL FORTH.
WHEN THAT HAPPENS, HE SLOWLY MAKES HIS WAY AROUND THE WORLD IN SEARCH OF PLACES TO MEDITATE AND WARRIORS TO DO BATTLE WITH.
A MAN OF SUCH POWER AS ORO CANNOT TRAVEL WITHOUT CREATING RIPPLES OF CHANGE. HIS VERY PRESENCE ANNOUNCES ITSELF TO THOSE WHO KNOW THE SIGNS.
HIS TRAVEL PATTERNS ARE AS PREDICTABLE AS HIS REASONS ARE ESOTERIC.
YOU WILL ALMOST CERTAINLY FIND HIM MEDITATING ALONE AT THE HIDDEN SHRINE ON MOUNT ATAGO, AWAY FROM PRYING TOURIST EYES.

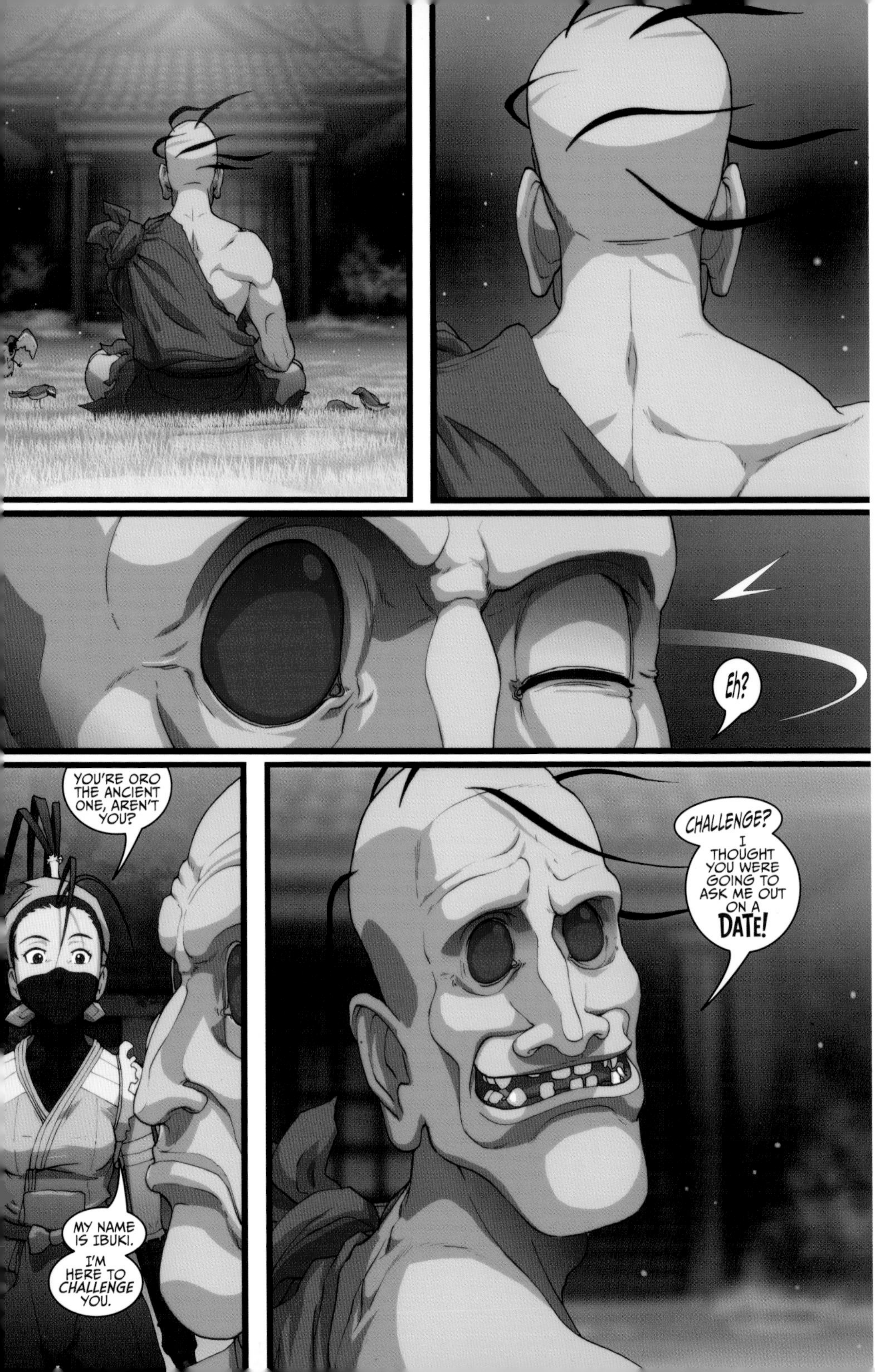
Eh?
YOU'RE ORO THE ANCIENT ONE, AREN'T YOU?
MY NAME IS IBUKI.
I'M HERE TO CHALLENGE YOU.
CHALLENGE?
I THOUGHT YOU WERE GOING TO ASK ME OUT ON A DATE!

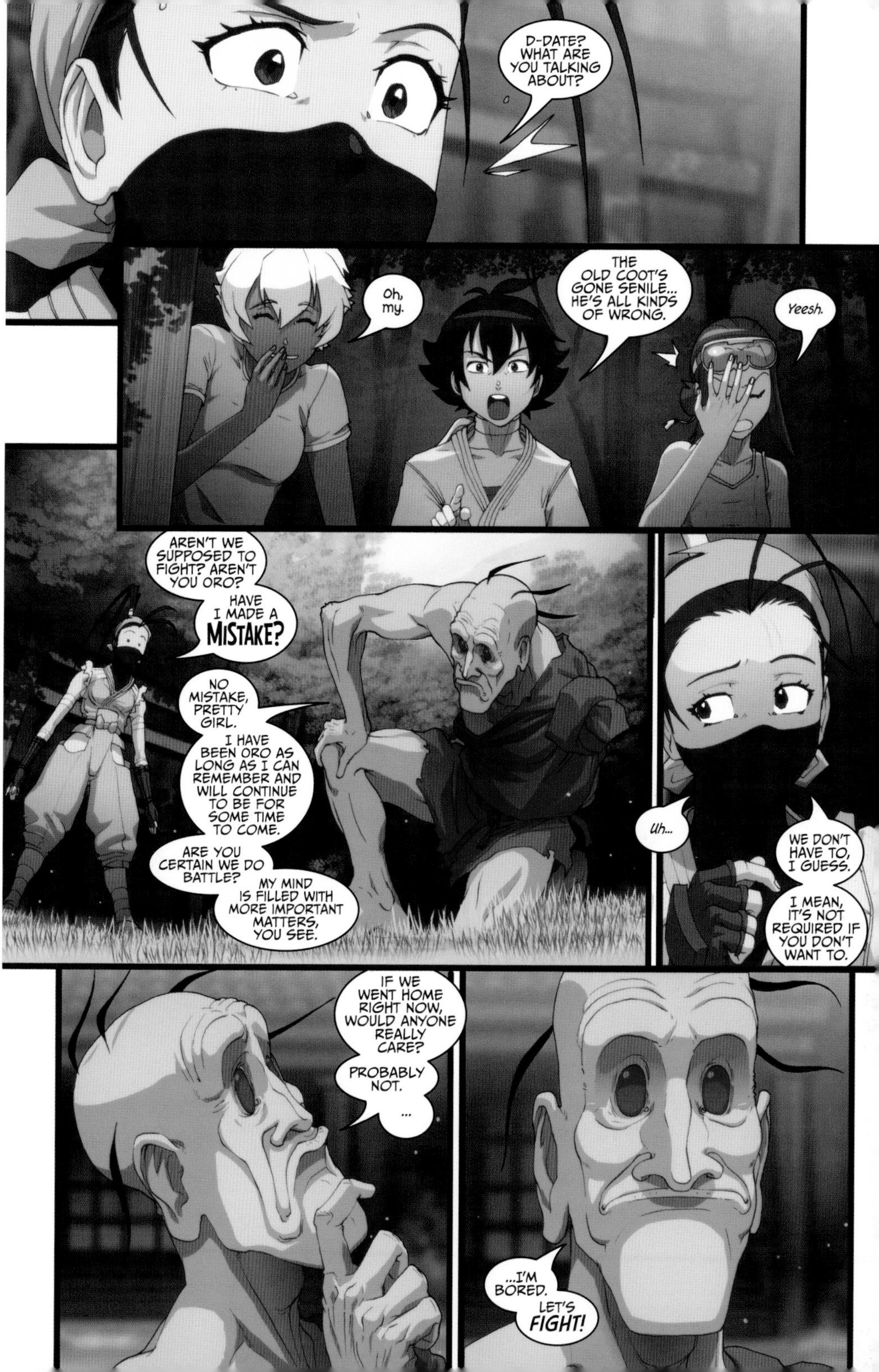
D-DATE? WHAT ARE YOU TALKING ABOUT?
Oh, my.
THE OLD COOT'S GONE SENILE... HE'S ALL KINDS OF WRONG.
Yeesh.
AREN'T WE SUPPOSED TO FIGHT? AREN'T YOU ORO?
HAVE I MADE A MISTAKE?
NO MISTAKE, PRETTY GIRL.
I HAVE BEEN ORO AS LONG AS I CAN REMEMBER AND WILL CONTINUE TO BE FOR SOME TIME TO COME.
ARE YOU CERTAIN WE DO BATTLE?
MY MIND IS FILLED WITH MORE IMPORTANT MATTERS, YOU SEE.
Uh...
WE DON'T HAVE TO, I GUESS.
I MEAN, IT'S NOT REQUIRED IF YOU DON'T WANT TO.
IF WE WENT HOME RIGHT NOW, WOULD ANYONE REALLY CARE?
PROBABLY NOT.
...
...I'M BORED.
LET'S FIGHT!

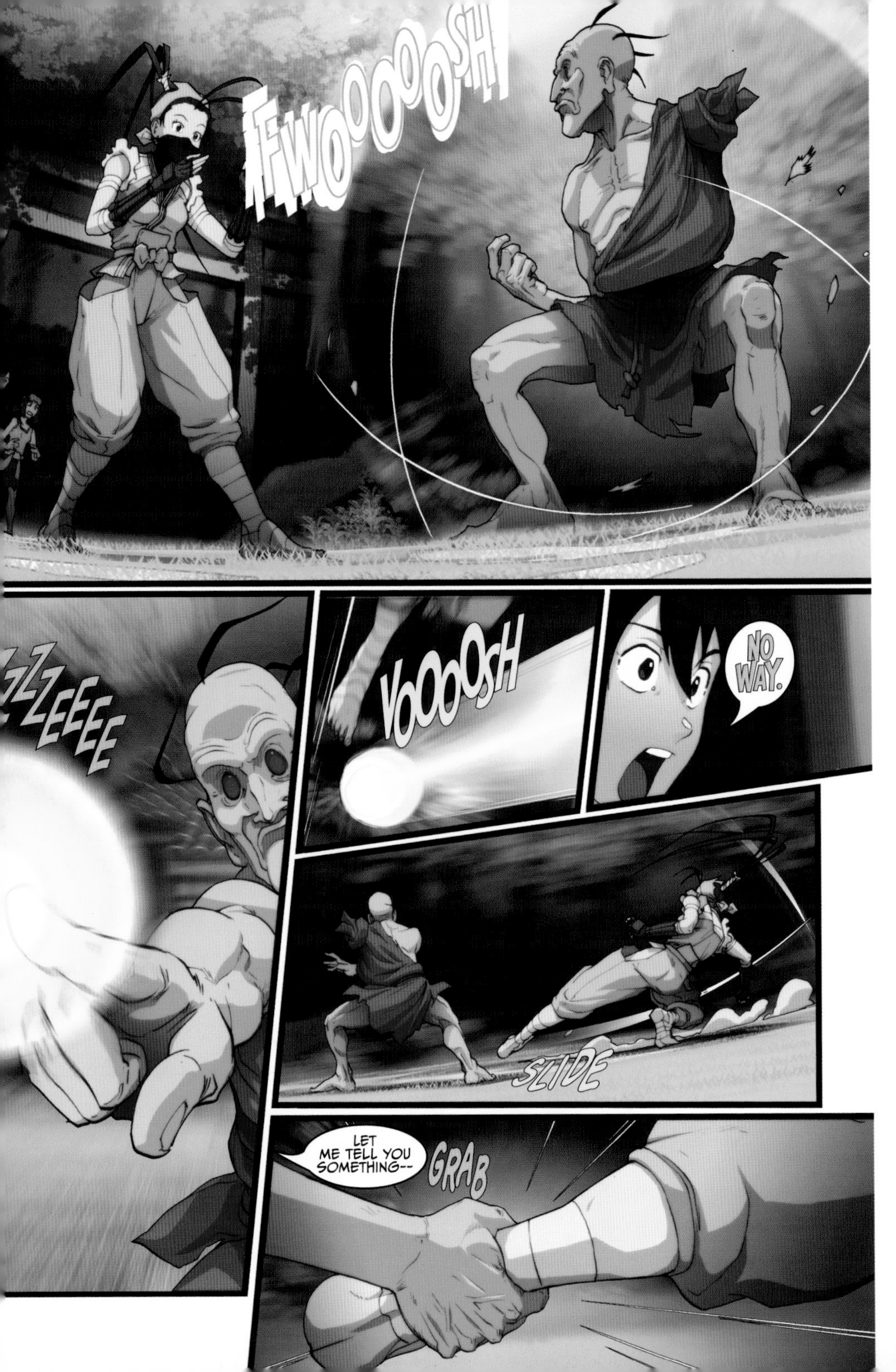
FWOOOOOOSH
ZZZEEEEE
VOOOOSH
NO WAY.
SLIDE
LET ME TELL YOU SOMETHING--
GRAB

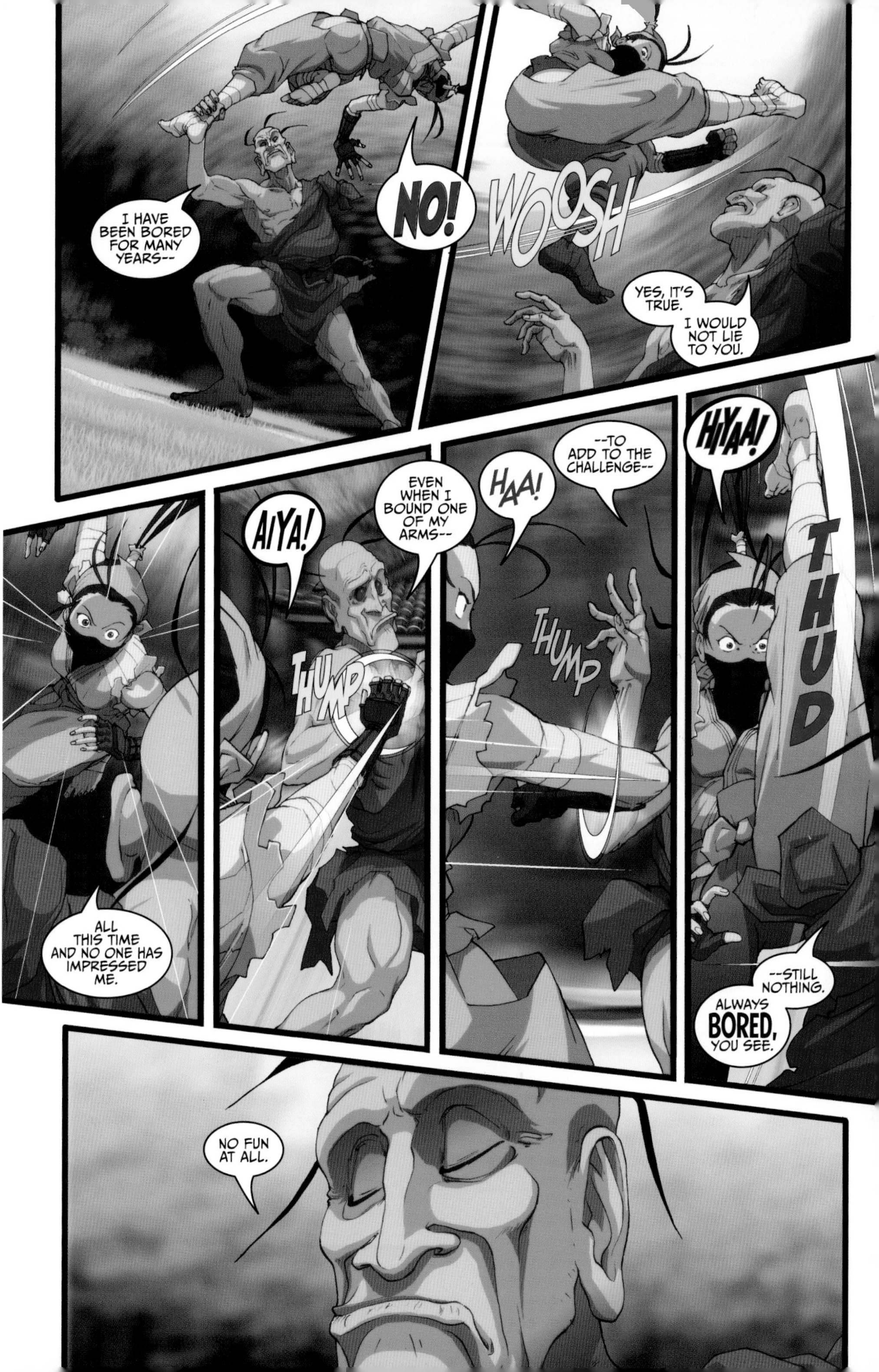
I HAVE BEEN BORED FOR MANY YEARS--
NO!
WOOSH
YES, IT'S TRUE.
I WOULD NOT LIE TO YOU.
ALL THIS TIME AND NO ONE HAS IMPRESSED ME.
AIYA!
EVEN WHEN I BOUND ONE OF MY ARMS--
THUMP
HAA!
--TO ADD TO THE CHALLENGE--
THUMP
HIYAA!
THUD
--STILL NOTHING.
ALWAYS BORED, YOU SEE.
NO FUN AT ALL.

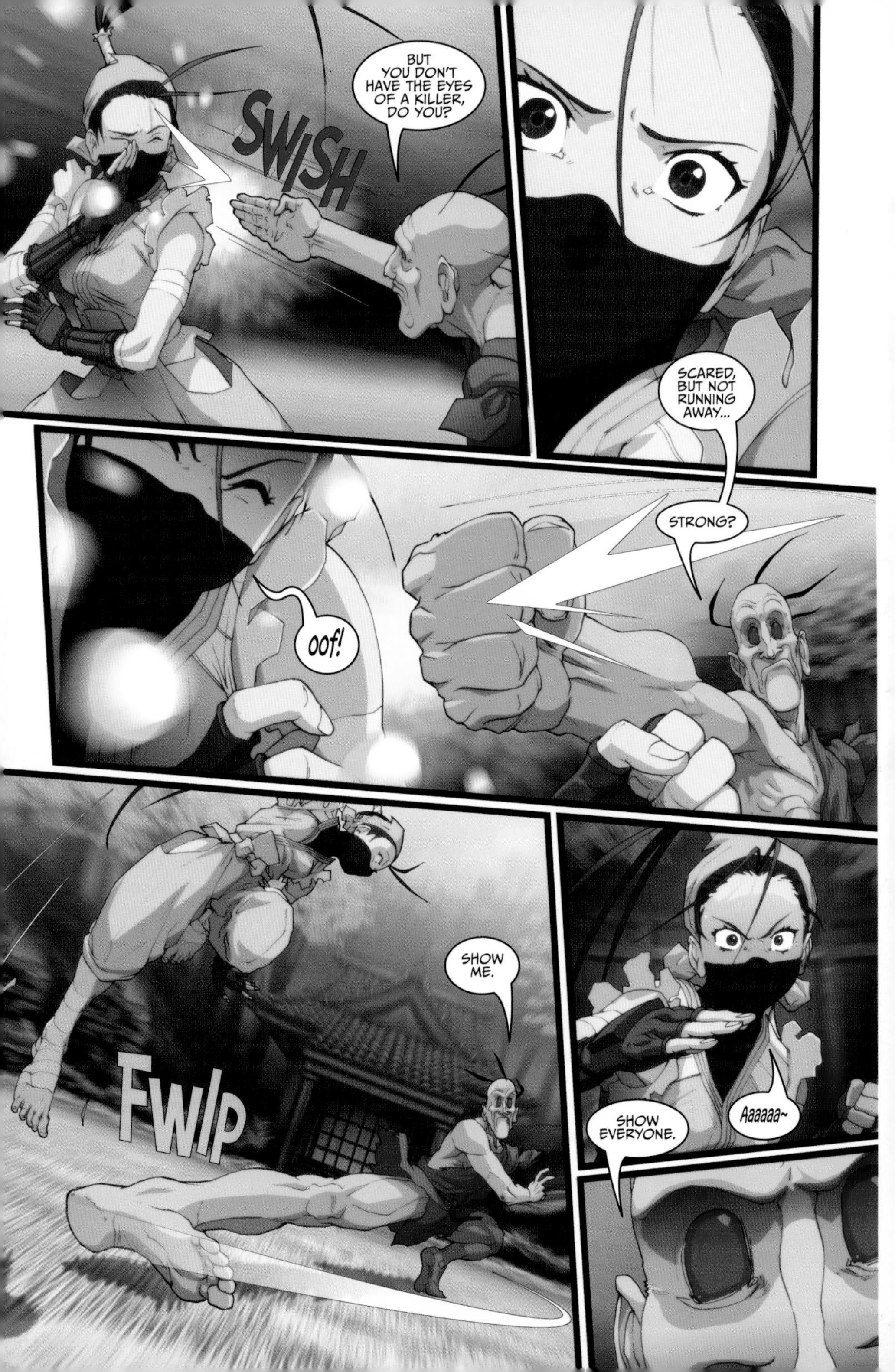
BUT YOU DON'T HAVE THE EYES OF A KILLER, DO YOU?
SWISH
SCARED, BUT NOT RUNNING AWAY...
STRONG?
oof!
SHOW ME.
FWIP
Aaaaaa~
SHOW EVERYONE.

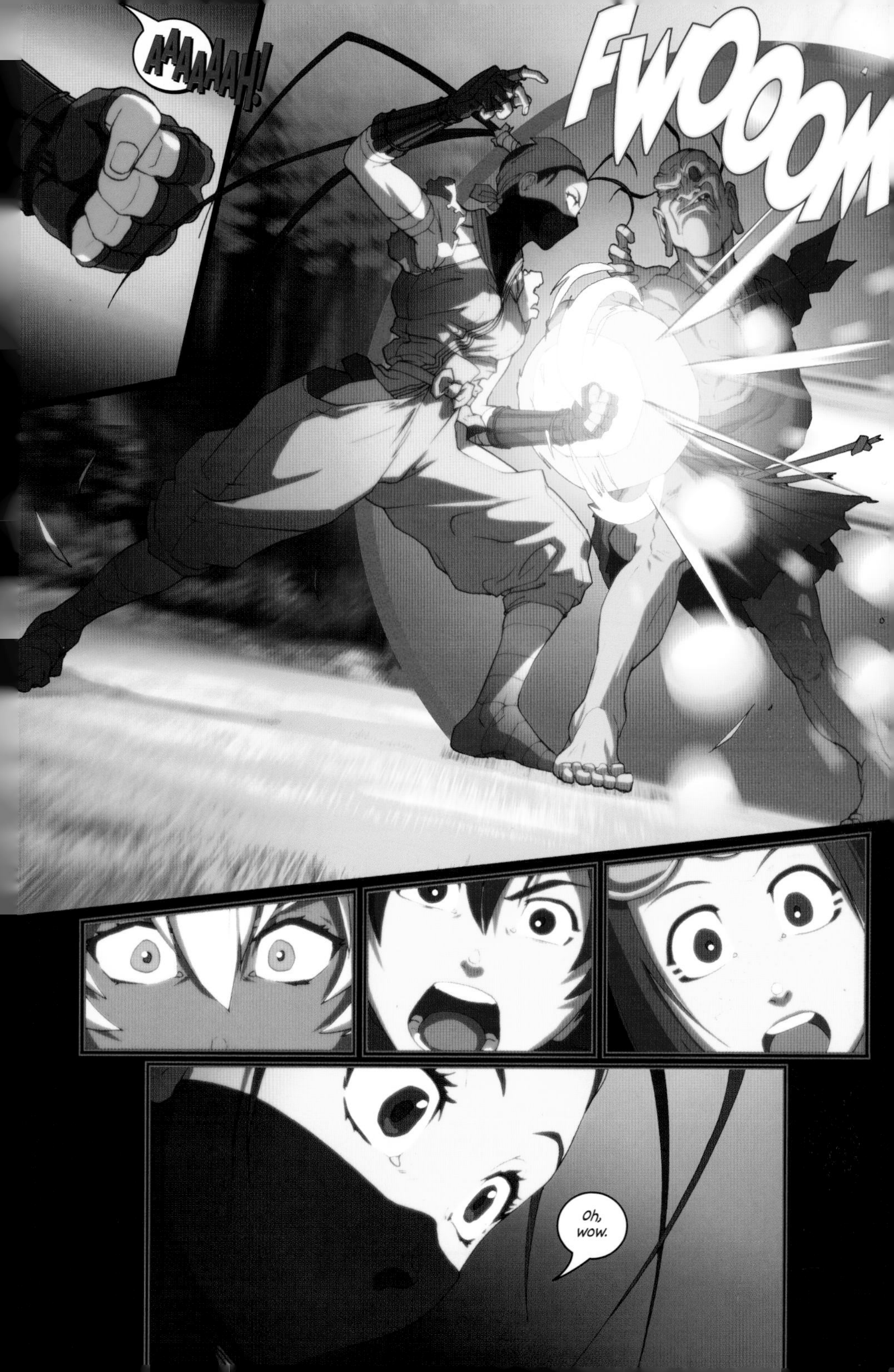
AAAAAAH!
FWOOOM
Oh, wow.

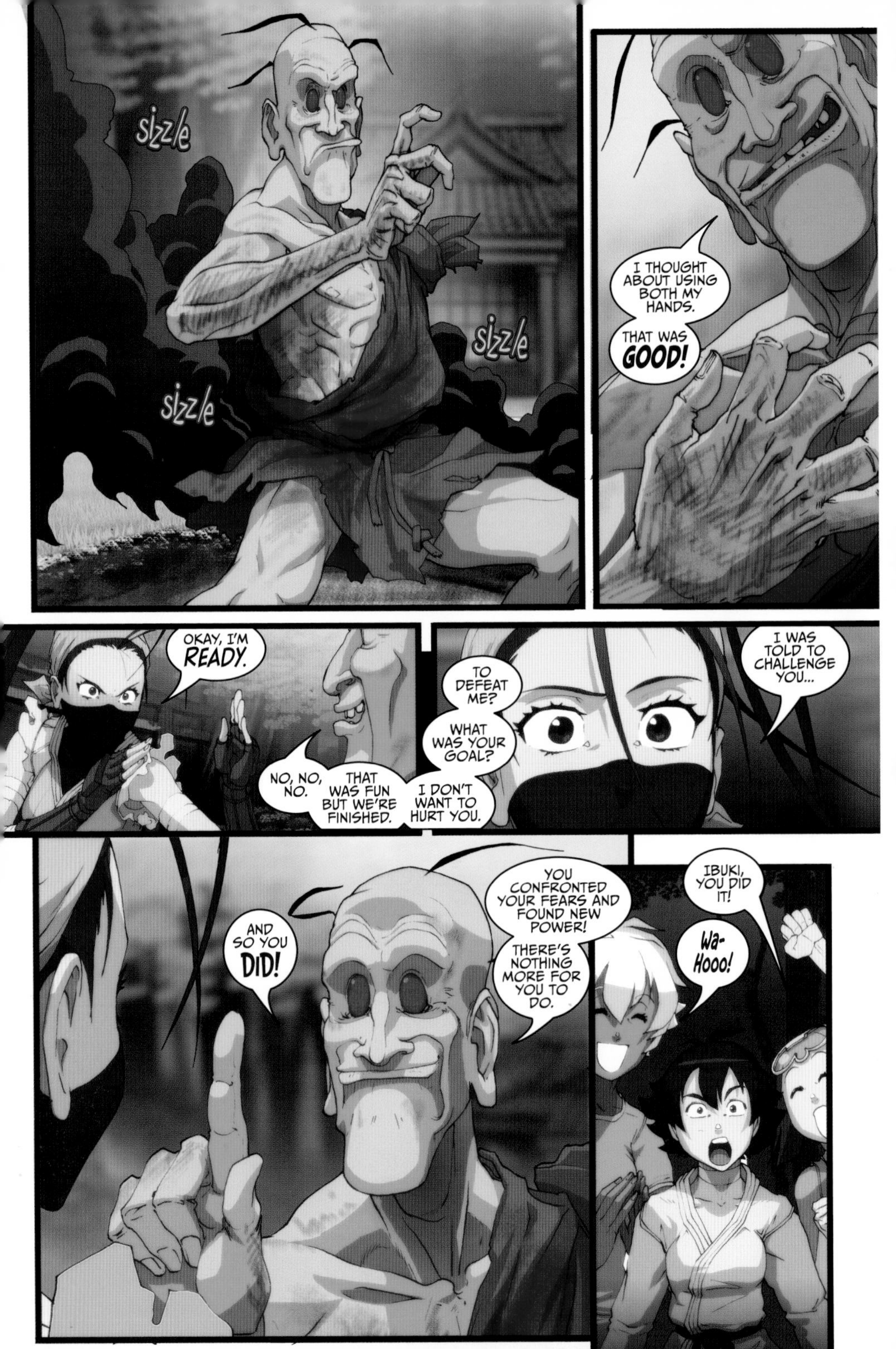
sizzle
sizzle
sizzle
I THOUGHT ABOUT USING BOTH MY HANDS.
THAT WAS GOOD!
OKAY, I'M READY.
NO, NO, NO.
THAT WAS FUN BUT WE'RE FINISHED.
I DON'T WANT TO HURT YOU.
TO DEFEAT ME?
WHAT WAS YOUR GOAL?
I WAS TOLD TO CHALLENGE YOU...
AND SO YOU DID!
YOU CONFRONTED YOUR FEARS AND FOUND NEW POWER!
THERE'S NOTHING MORE FOR YOU TO DO.
IBUKI, YOU DID IT!
Wa-Hooo!

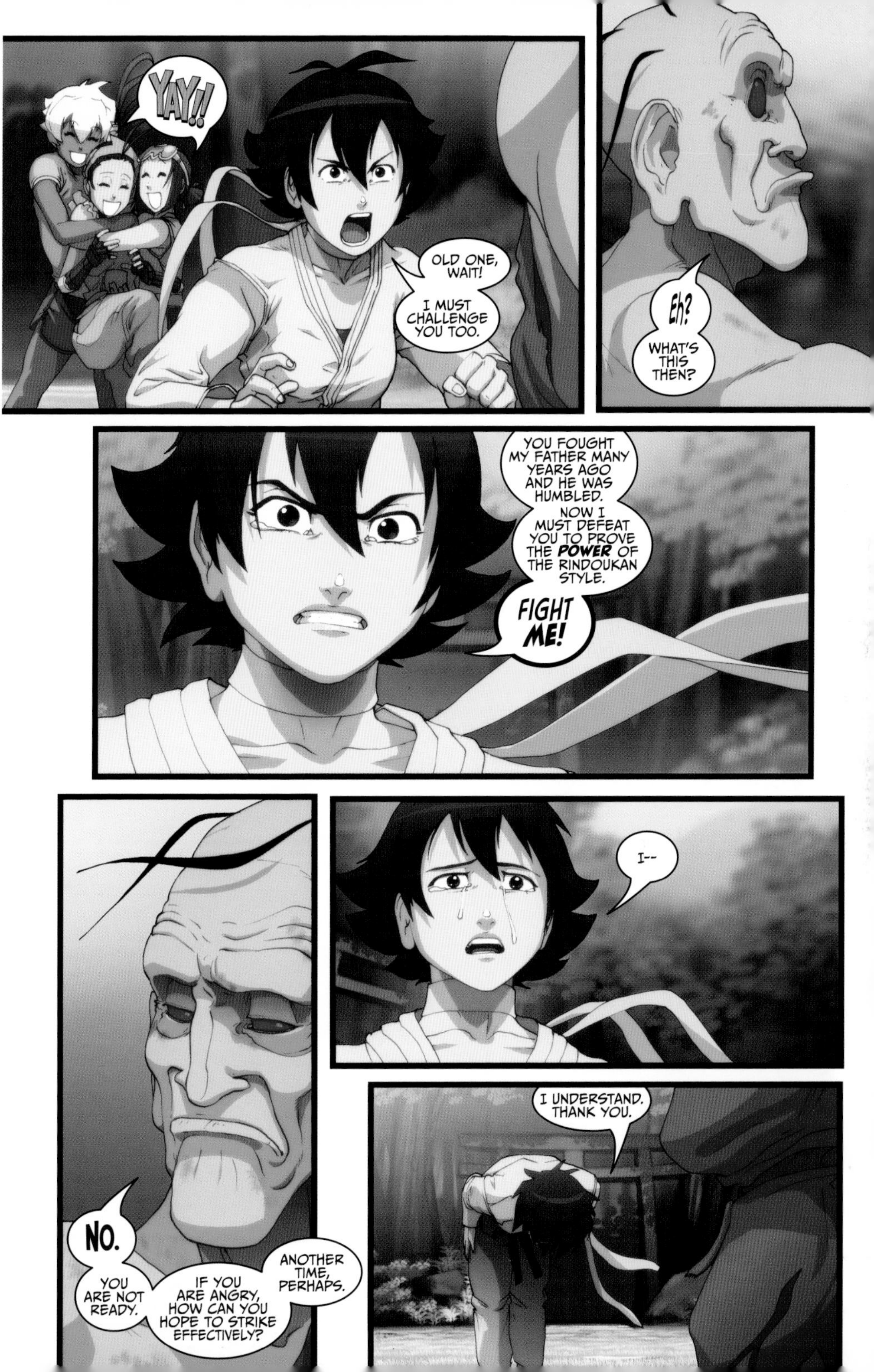
YAY!!
OLD ONE, WAIT!
I MUST CHALLENGE YOU TOO.
Eh?
WHAT'S THIS THEN?
YOU FOUGHT MY FATHER MANY YEARS AGO AND HE WAS HUMBLED.
NOW I MUST DEFEAT YOU TO PROVE THE POWER OF THE RINDOUKAN STYLE.
FIGHT ME!
NO.
YOU ARE NOT READY.
IF YOU ARE ANGRY, HOW CAN YOU HOPE TO STRIKE EFFECTIVELY?
ANOTHER TIME, PERHAPS.
I--
I UNDERSTAND. THANK YOU.

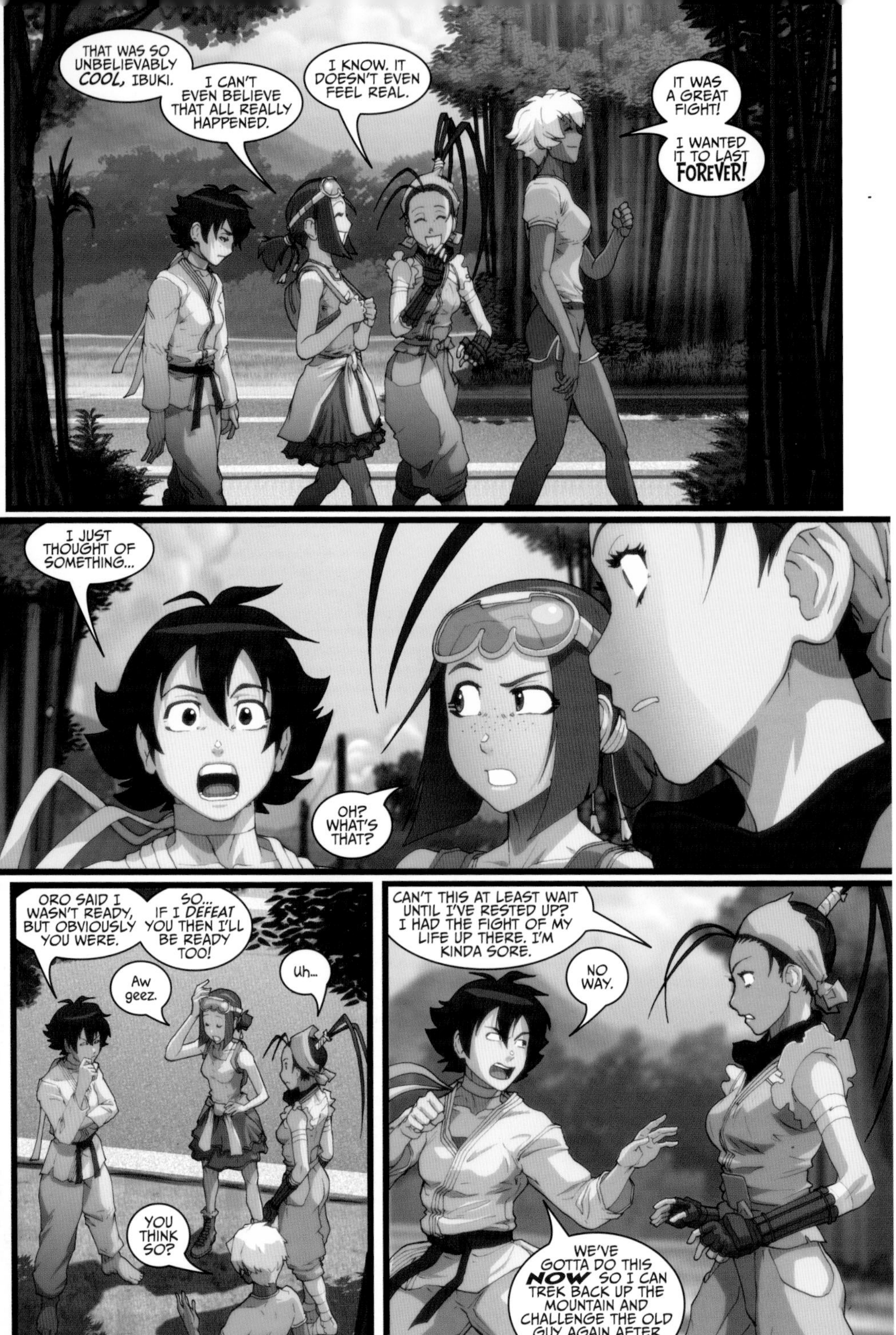
THAT WAS SO UNBELIEVABLY COOL, IBUKI.
I CAN'T EVEN BELIEVE THAT ALL REALLY HAPPENED.
I KNOW. IT DOESN'T EVEN FEEL REAL.
IT WAS A GREAT FIGHT!
I WANTED IT TO LAST FOREVER!
I JUST THOUGHT OF SOMETHING...
OH? WHAT'S THAT?
ORO SAID I WASN'T READY, BUT OBVIOUSLY YOU WERE.
SO... IF I DEFEAT YOU THEN I'LL BE READY TOO!
Aw geez.
Uh...
YOU THINK SO?
CAN'T THIS AT LEAST WAIT UNTIL I'VE RESTED UP? I HAD THE FIGHT OF MY LIFE UP THERE. I'M KINDA SORE.
NO WAY.
WE'VE GOTTA DO THIS NOW SO I CAN TREK BACK UP THE MOUNTAIN AND CHALLENGE THE OLD GUY AGAIN AFTER I KICK YOUR BUTT.

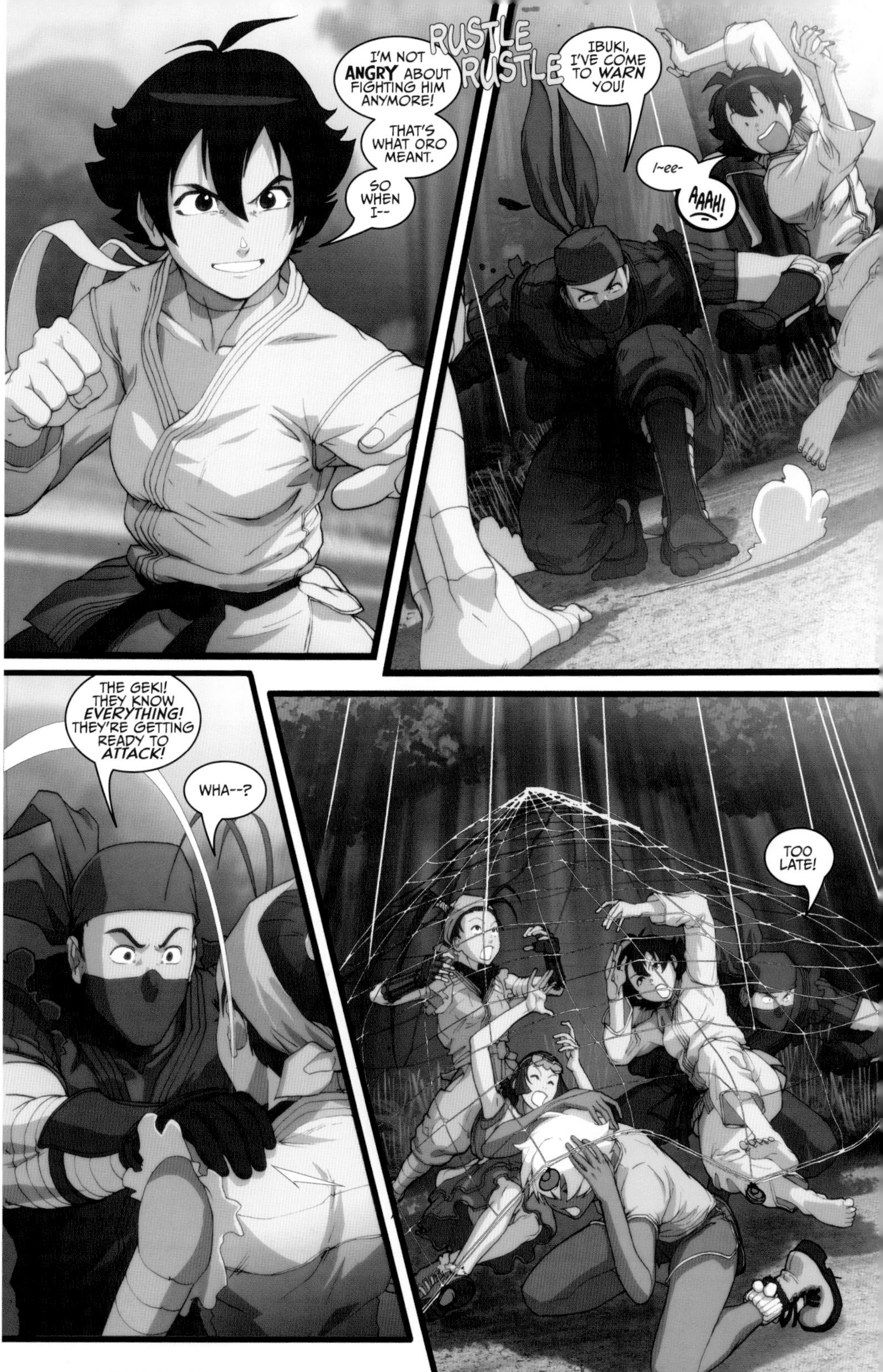
I'M NOT **ANGRY** ABOUT FIGHTING HIM ANYMORE!
THAT'S WHAT ORO MEANT.
SO WHEN I--
RUSTLE RUSTLE
IBUKI, I'VE COME TO **WARN** YOU!
I~ee-
AAAH!
THE GEKI! THEY KNOW ***EVERYTHING!*** THEY'RE GETTING READY TO ***ATTACK!***
WHA--?
TOO LATE!

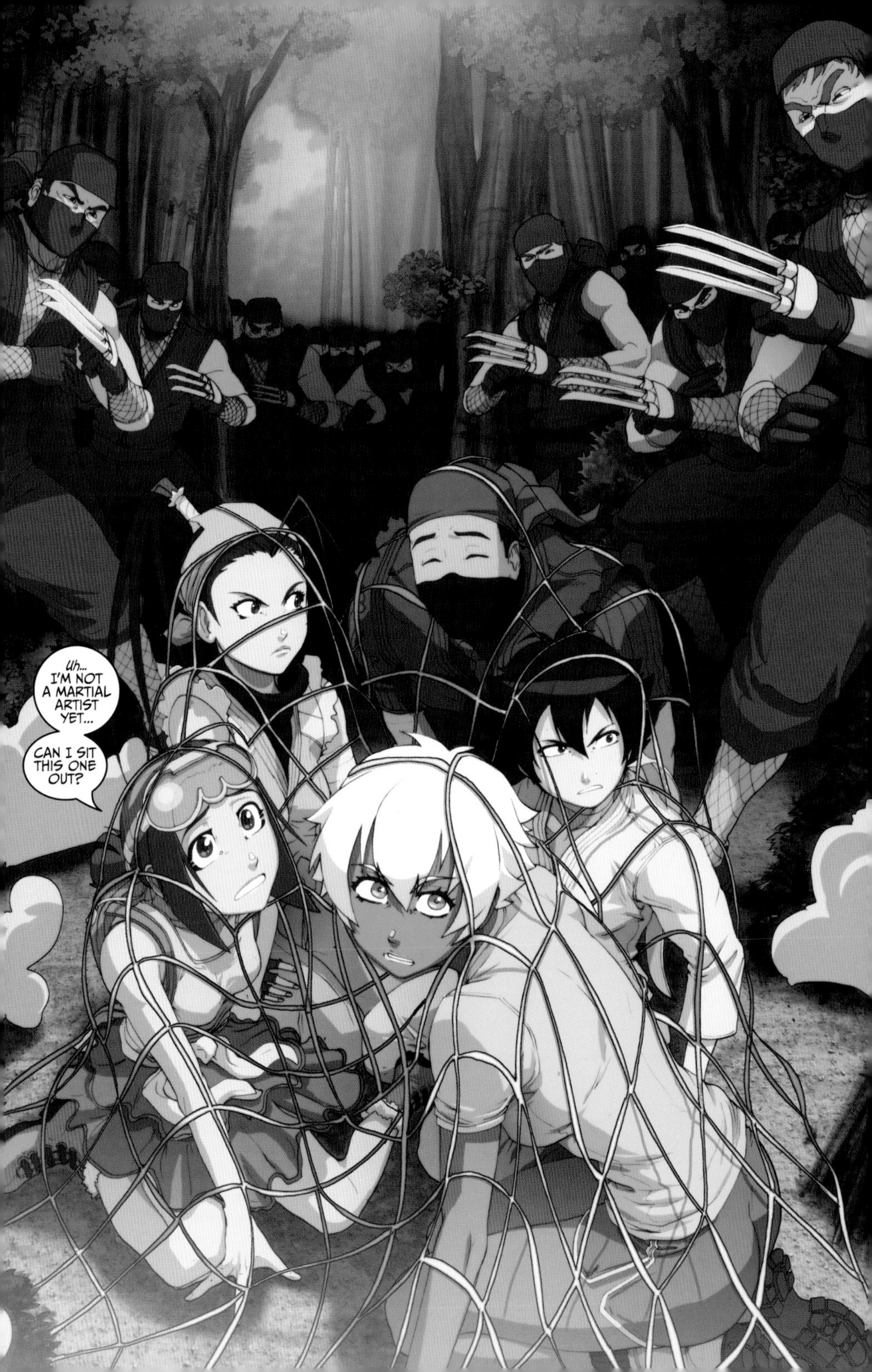
Uh... I'M NOT A MARTIAL ARTIST YET...
CAN I SIT THIS ONE OUT?

Chapter 4: CLASH OF NINJAS

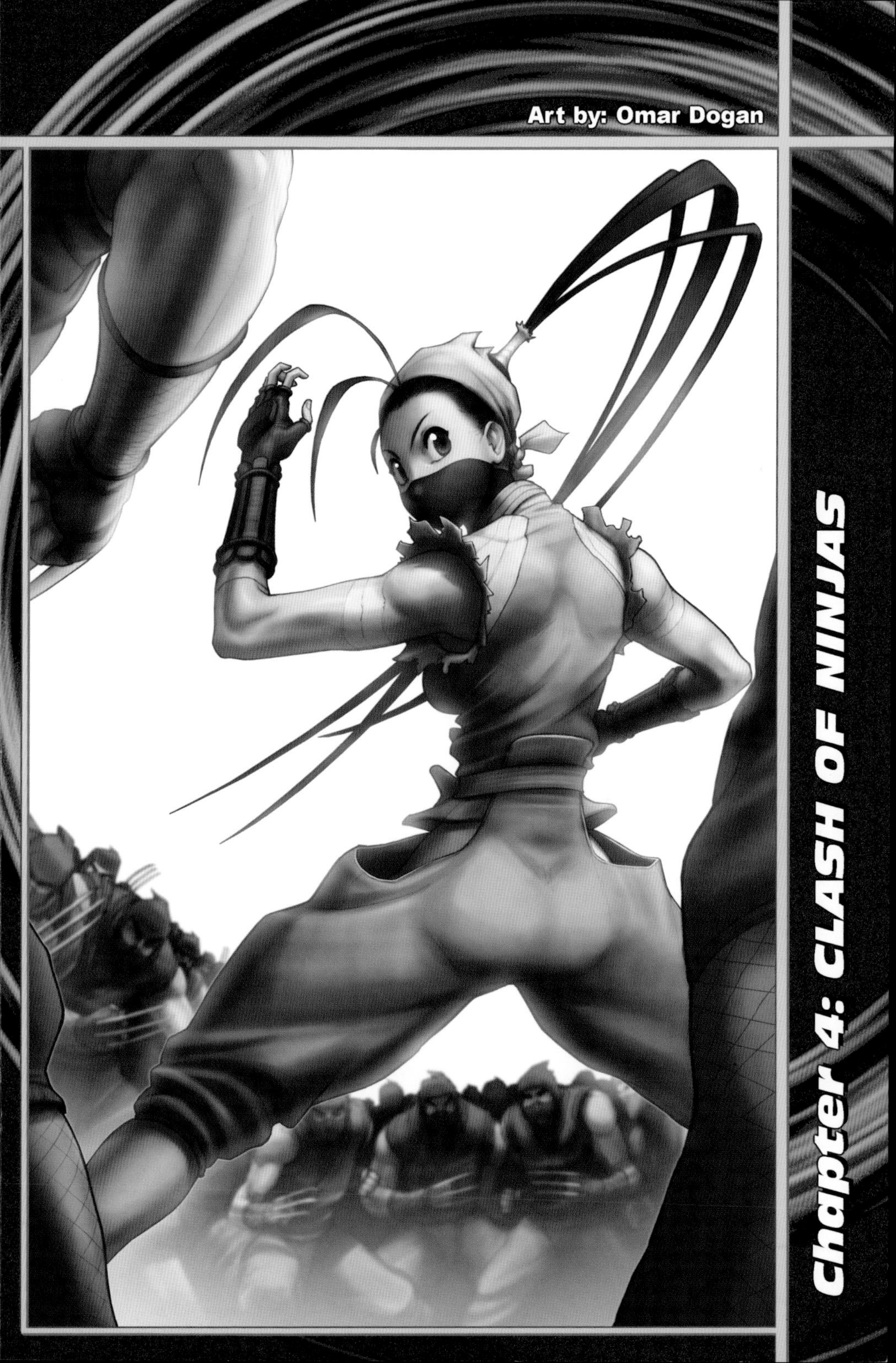
Art by: Omar Dogan

Art by: Omar Dogan

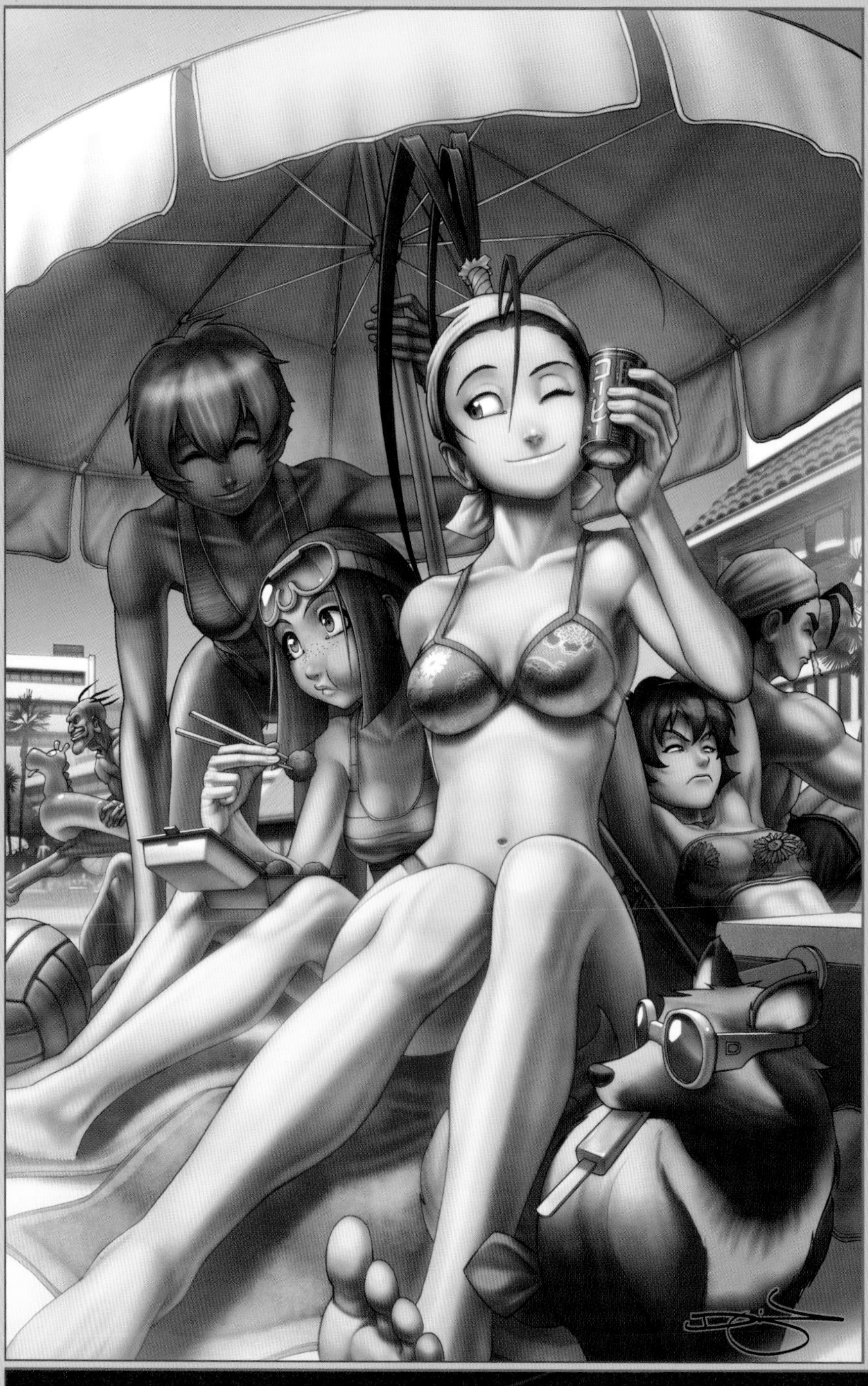

Variant Cover

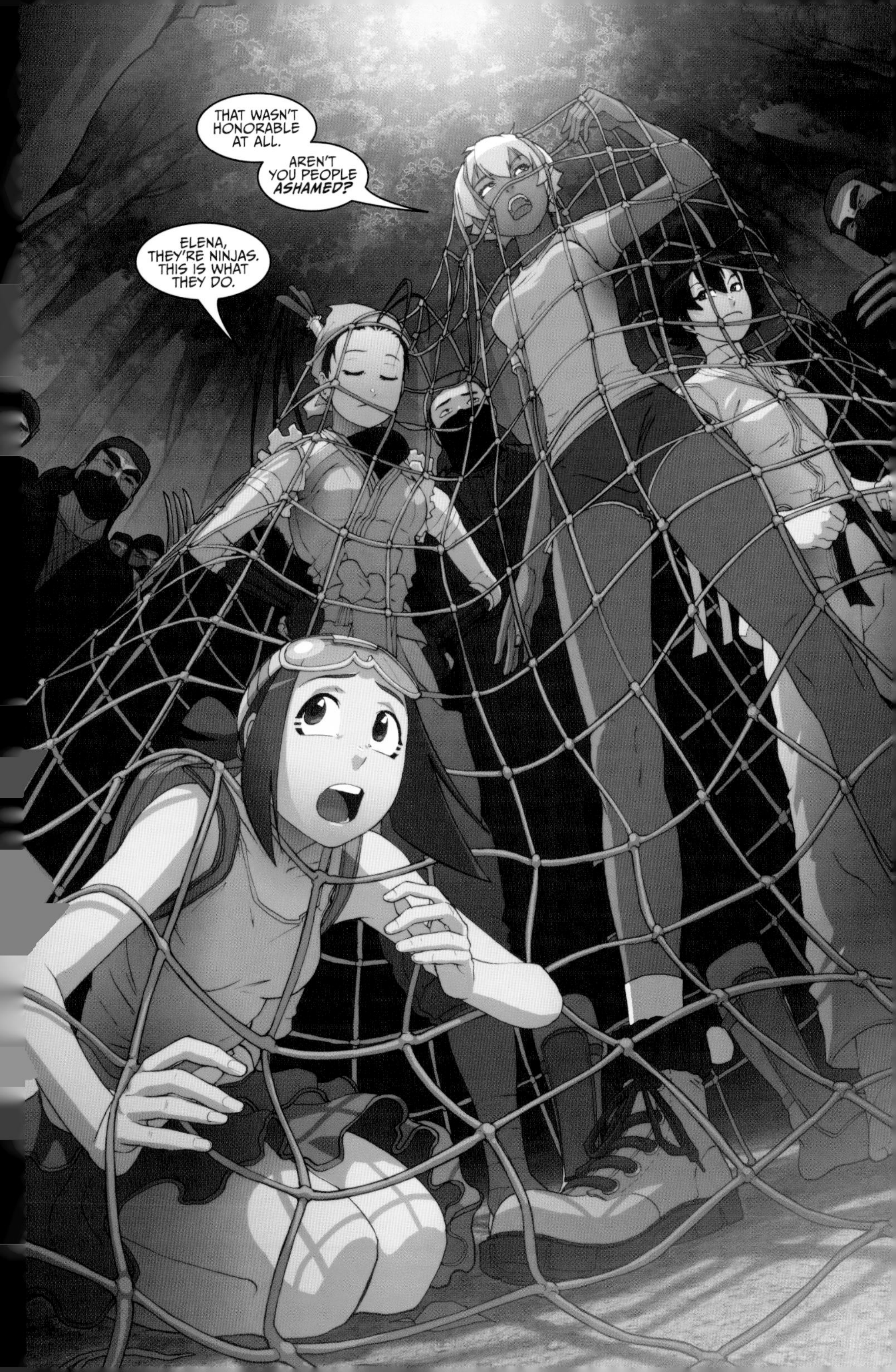
THAT WASN'T HONORABLE AT ALL.
AREN'T YOU PEOPLE ASHAMED?
ELENA, THEY'RE NINJAS. THIS IS WHAT THEY DO.

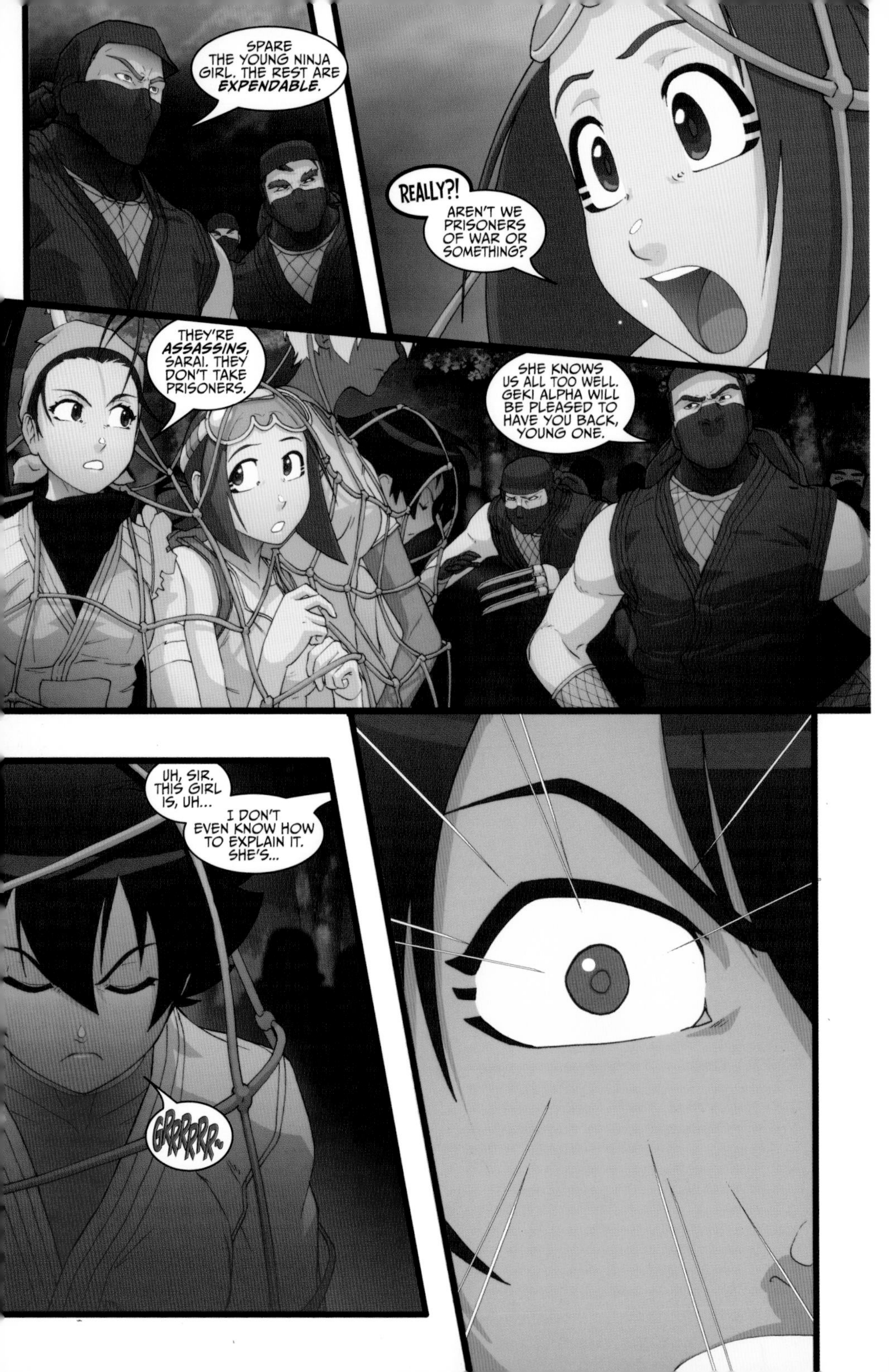
SPARE THE YOUNG NINJA GIRL. THE REST ARE *EXPENDABLE*.
REALLY?!
AREN'T WE PRISONERS OF WAR OR SOMETHING?
THEY'RE *ASSASSINS*, SARAI. THEY DON'T TAKE PRISONERS.
SHE KNOWS US ALL TOO WELL. GEKI ALPHA WILL BE PLEASED TO HAVE YOU BACK, YOUNG ONE.
UH, SIR. THIS GIRL IS, UH...
I DON'T EVEN KNOW HOW TO EXPLAIN IT. SHE'S...
GRRRRRR~

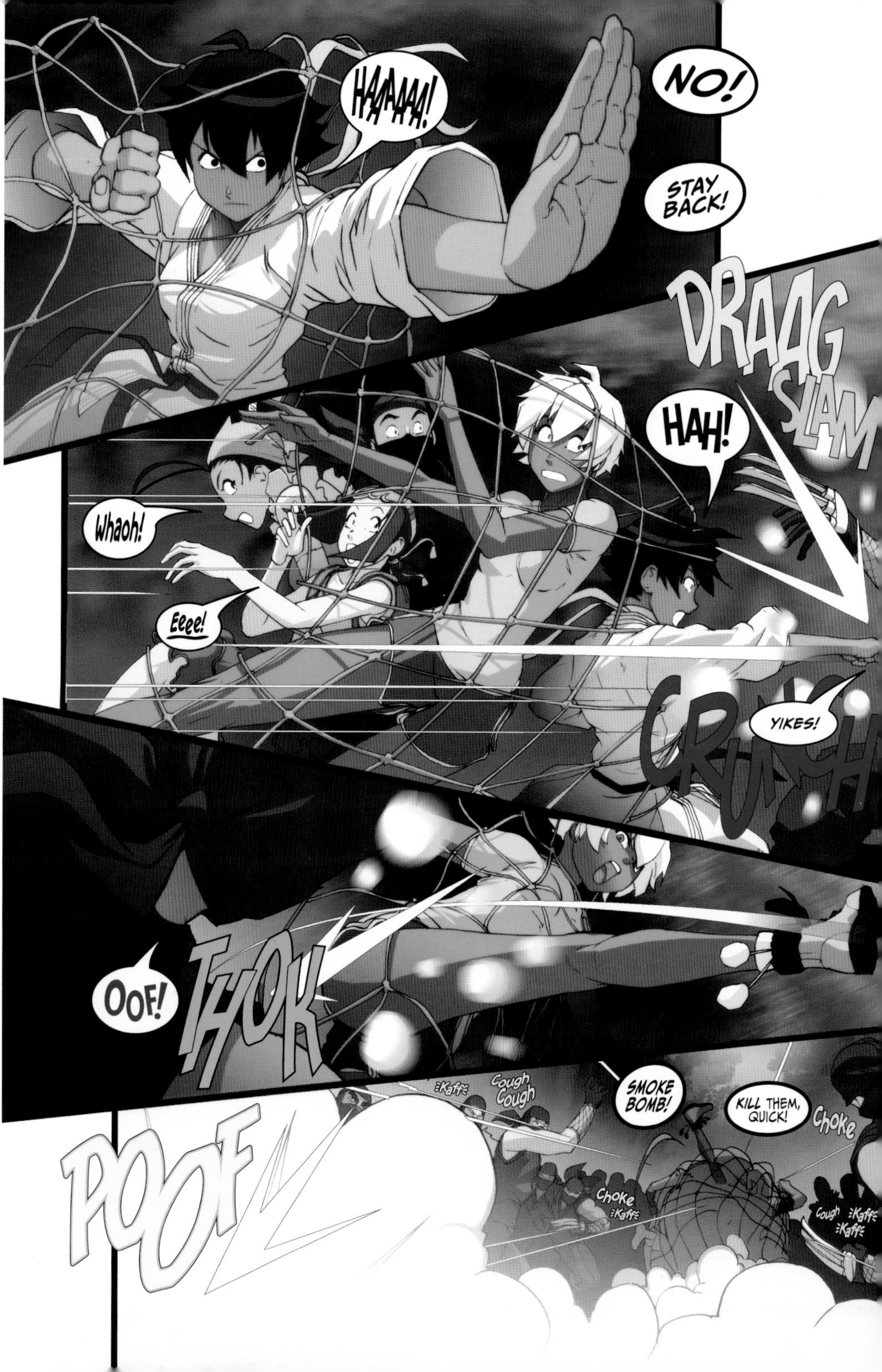
HAAAAAAA!
NO!
STAY BACK!
DRAAG
SLAM
HAH!
Whaoh!
Eeee!
YIKES!
CRUNCH
OOF!
THOK
Kaff
Cough Cough
SMOKE BOMB!
KILL THEM, QUICK!
Choke
POOF
Choke
Kaff
Cough
Kaff
Kaff

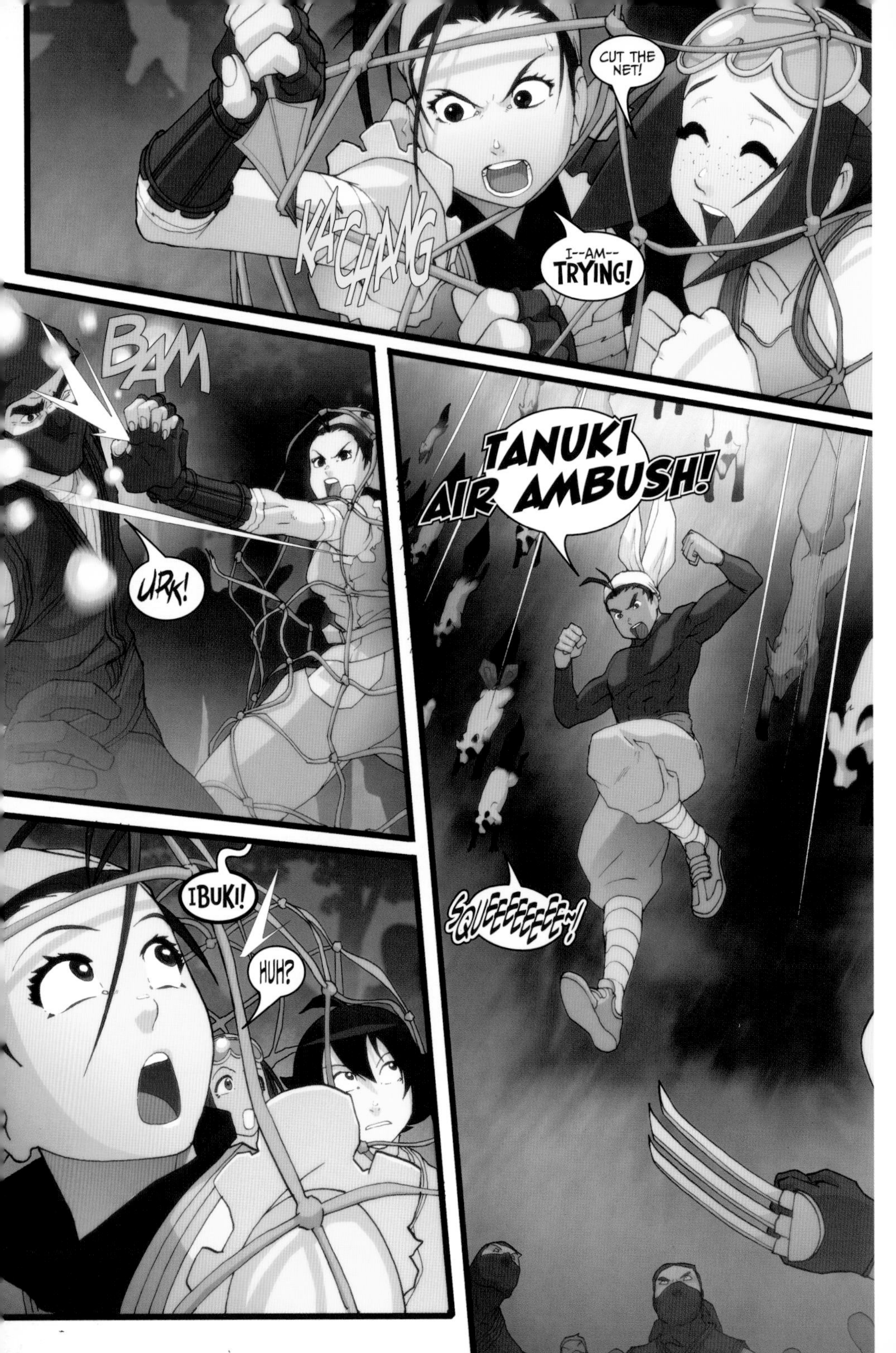
CUT THE NET!
KA-CHANG
I--AM-- TRYING!
BAM
URK!
IBUKI!
HUH?
TANUKI AIR AMBUSH!
SQUEEEEEEEEE~!

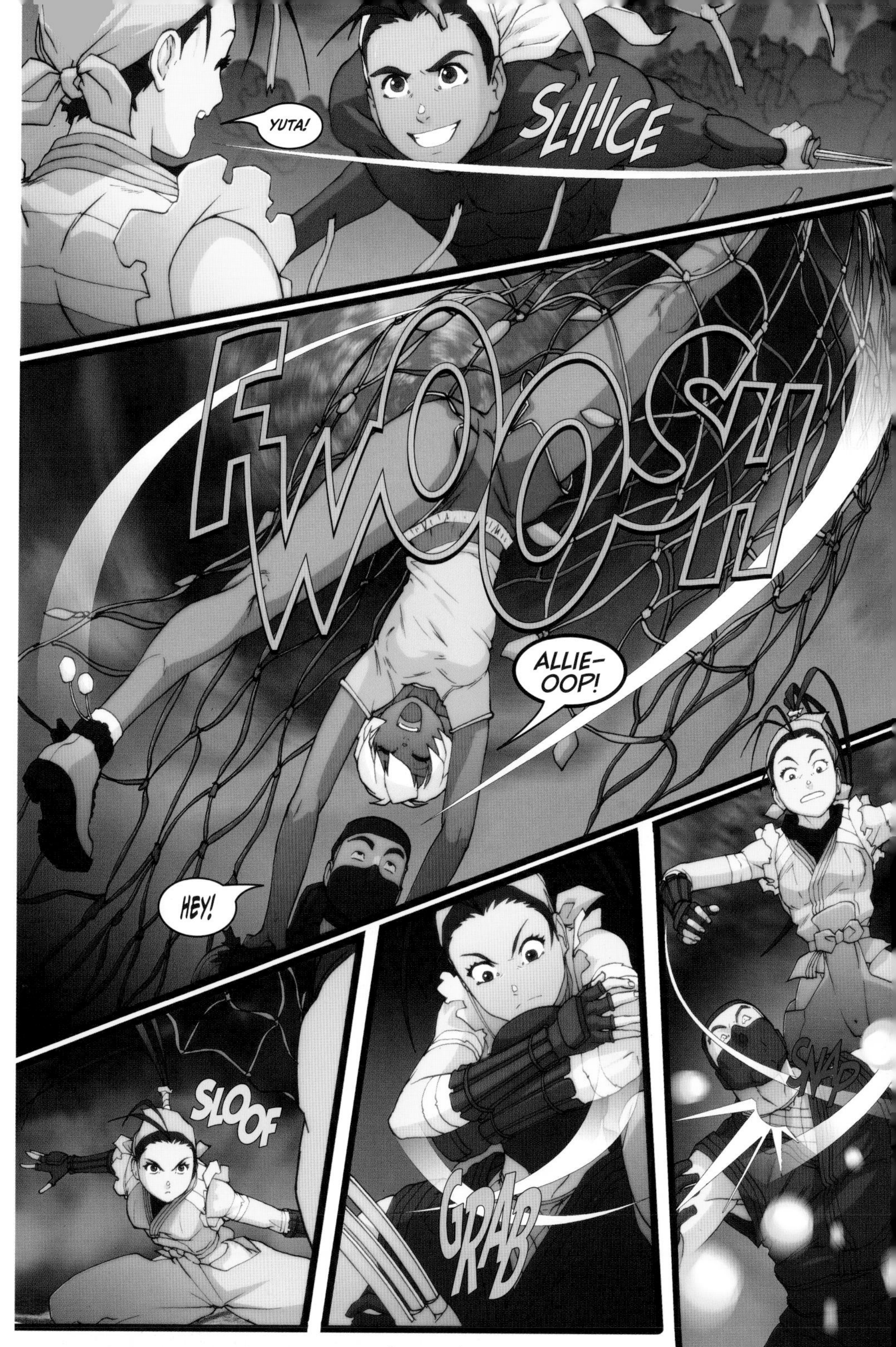
YUTA!
SLIIICE
FWOOSH
ALLIE-OOP!
HEY!
SLOOF
GRAB
SNAP

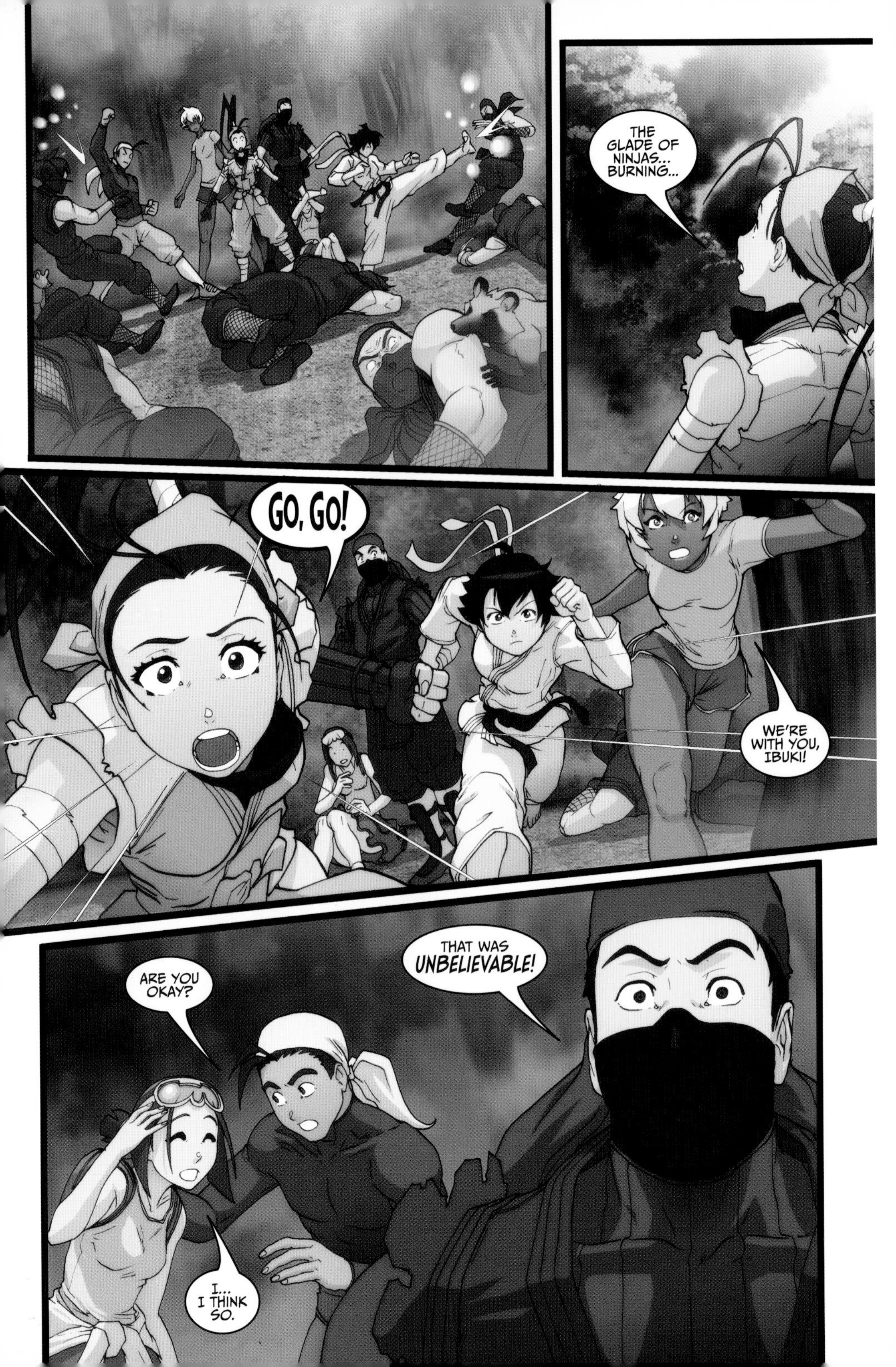
THE GLADE OF NINJAS... BURNING...
GO, GO!
WE'RE WITH YOU, IBUKI!
ARE YOU OKAY?
THAT WAS UNBELIEVABLE!
I... I THINK SO.

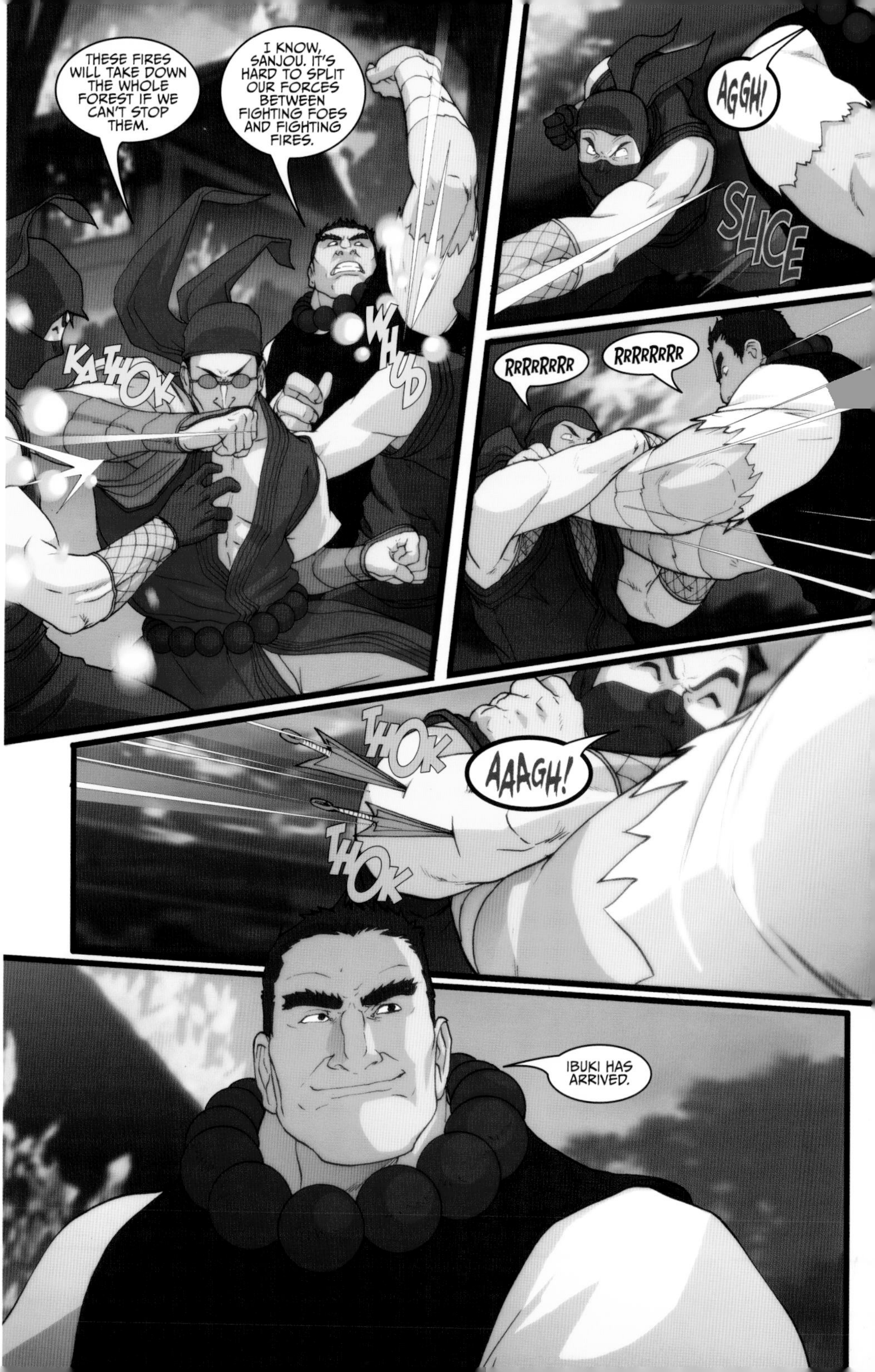
THESE FIRES WILL TAKE DOWN THE WHOLE FOREST IF WE CAN'T STOP THEM.
I KNOW, SANJOU. IT'S HARD TO SPLIT OUR FORCES BETWEEN FIGHTING FOES AND FIGHTING FIRES.
KA-THOK
WHUD
AGGH!
SLICE
RRRRRRRR
RRRRRRRR
THOK
AAAGH!
THOK
IBUKI HAS ARRIVED.

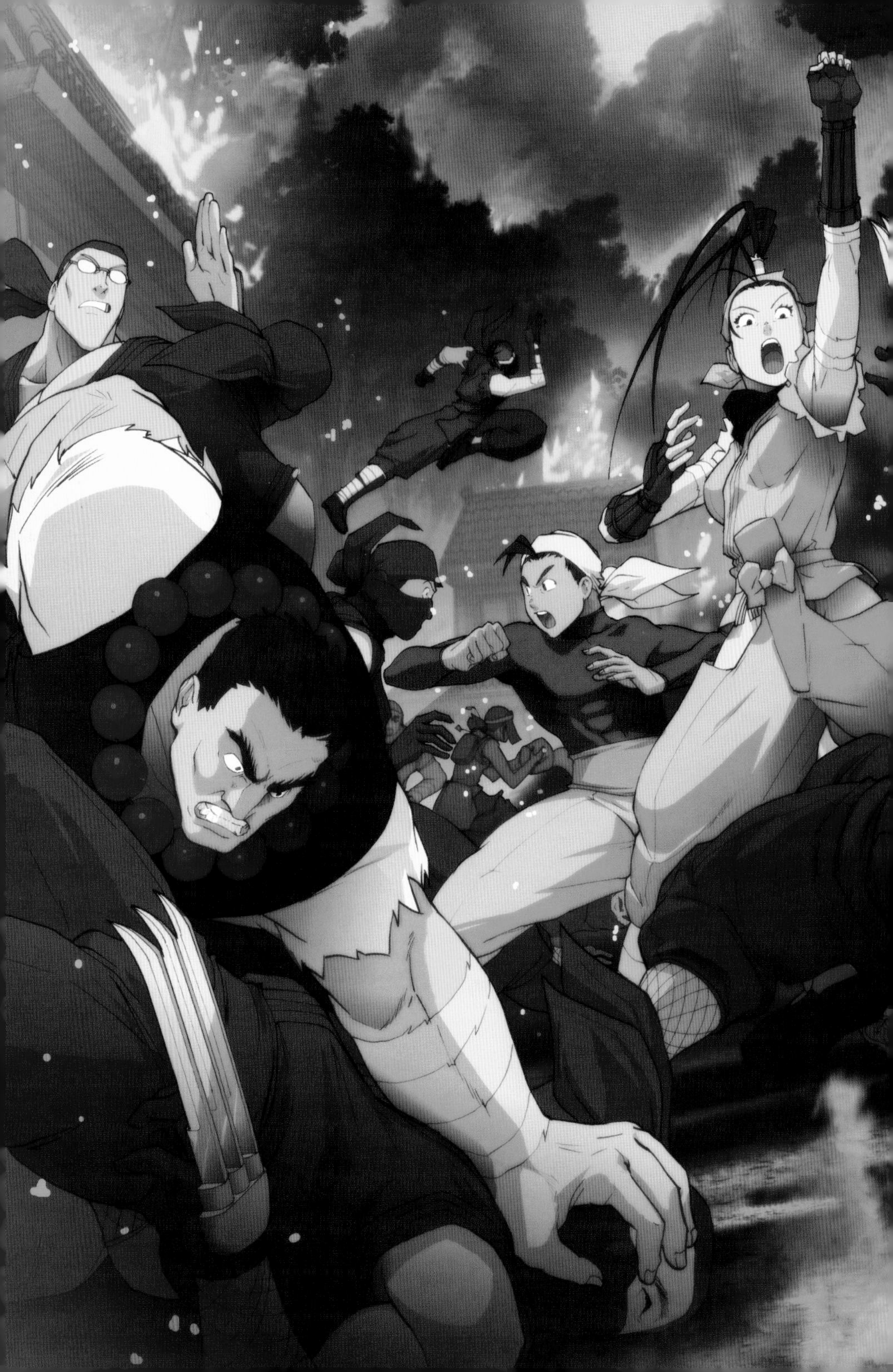

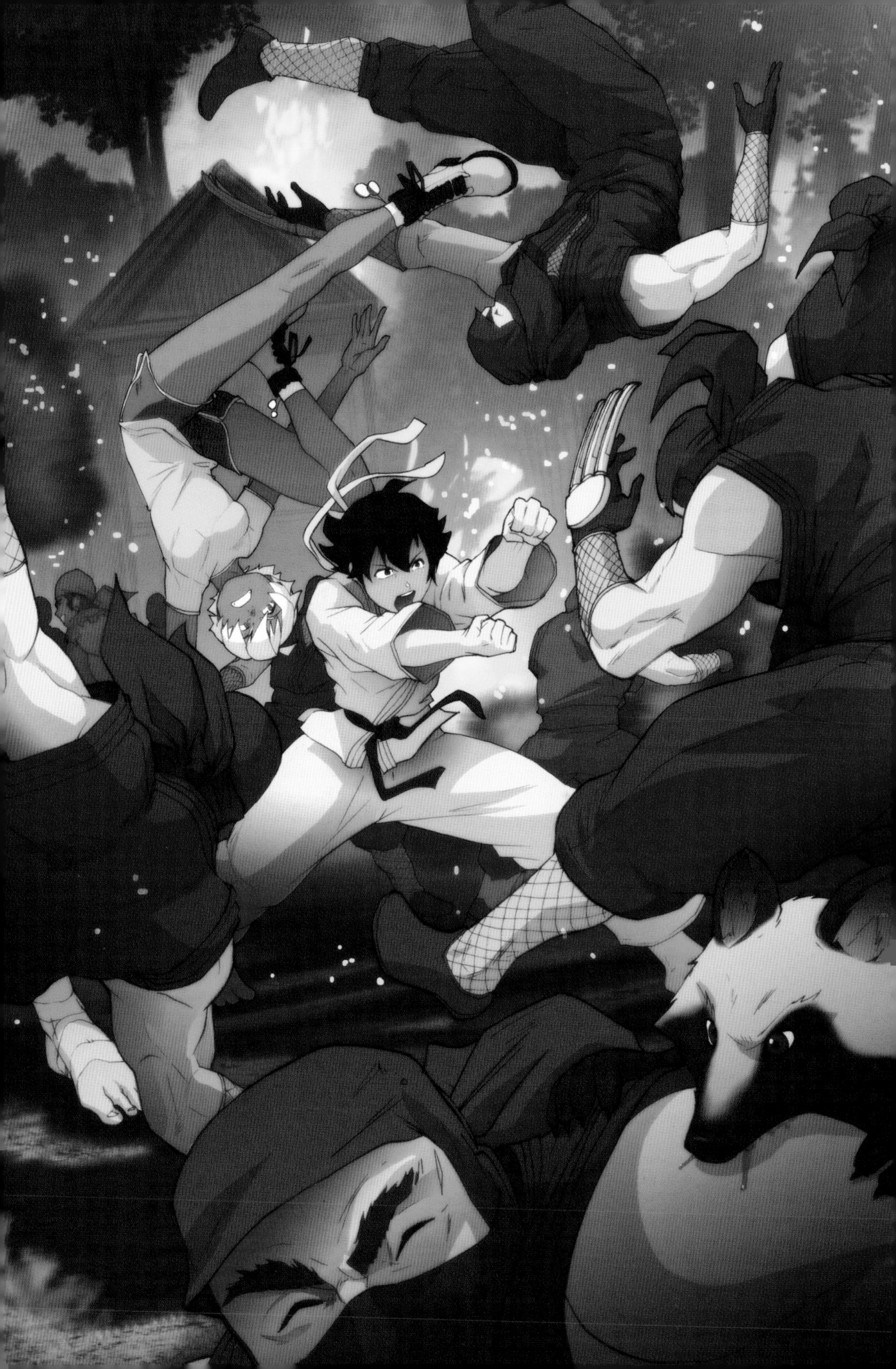

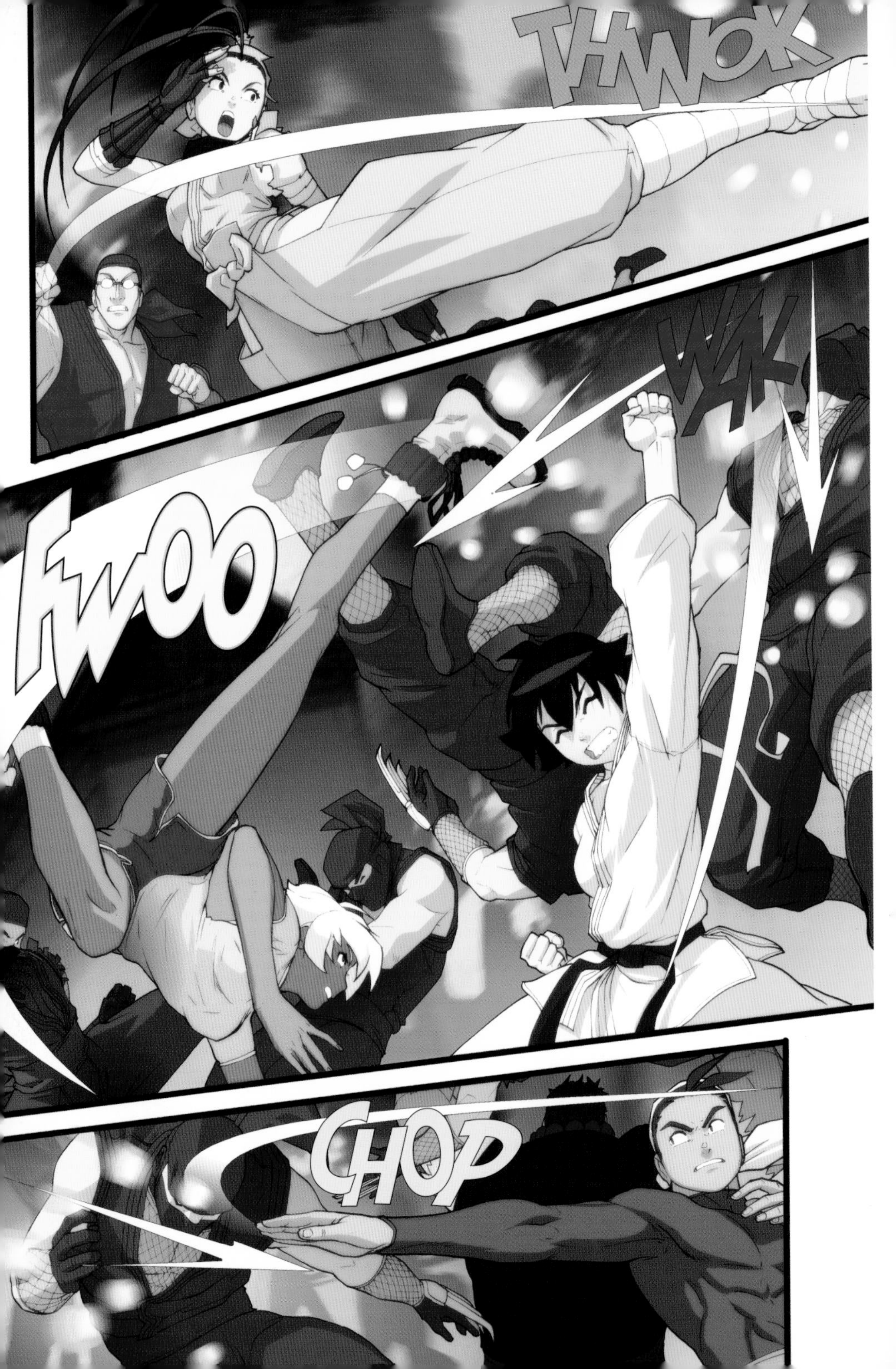
THWOK
WAK
FWOO
CHOP

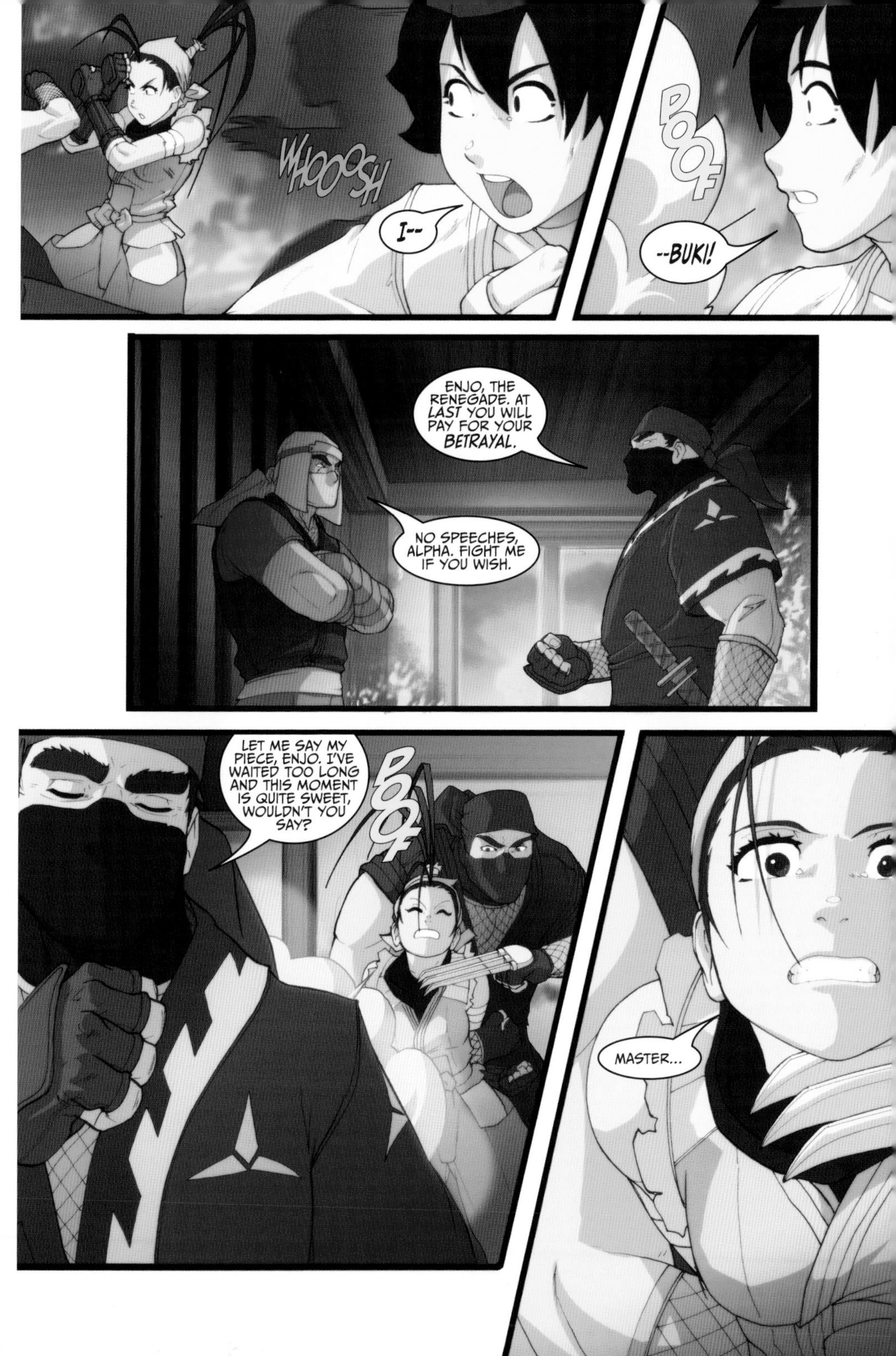
WHOOOSH
I--
POOF
--BUKI!
ENJO, THE RENEGADE. AT LAST YOU WILL PAY FOR YOUR BETRAYAL.
NO SPEECHES, ALPHA. FIGHT ME IF YOU WISH.
LET ME SAY MY PIECE, ENJO. I'VE WAITED TOO LONG AND THIS MOMENT IS QUITE SWEET, WOULDN'T YOU SAY?
POOF
MASTER...

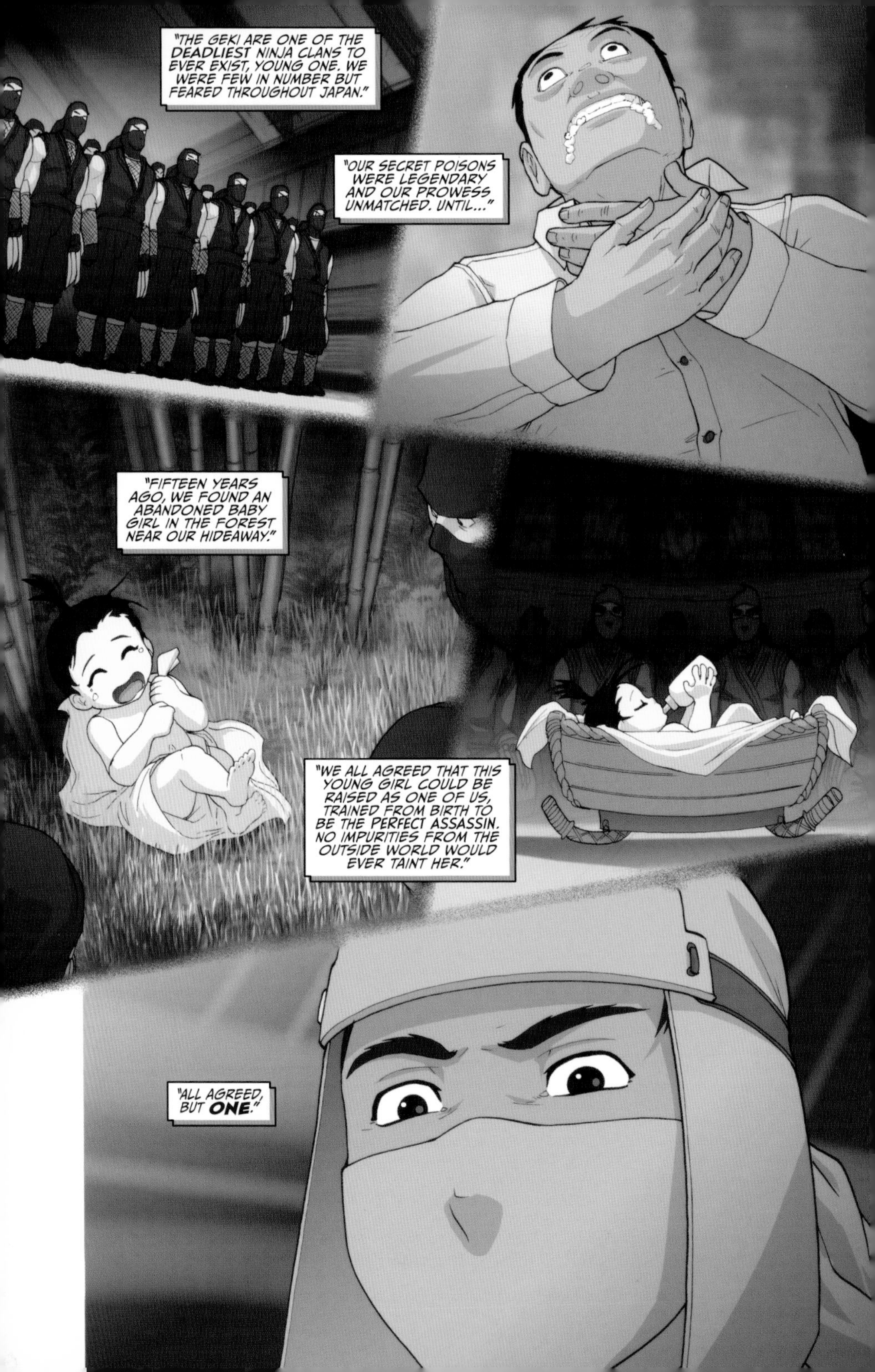
"THE GEKI ARE ONE OF THE DEADLIEST NINJA CLANS TO EVER EXIST, YOUNG ONE. WE WERE FEW IN NUMBER BUT FEARED THROUGHOUT JAPAN."
"OUR SECRET POISONS WERE LEGENDARY AND OUR PROWESS UNMATCHED. UNTIL..."
"FIFTEEN YEARS AGO, WE FOUND AN ABANDONED BABY GIRL IN THE FOREST NEAR OUR HIDEAWAY."
"WE ALL AGREED THAT THIS YOUNG GIRL COULD BE RAISED AS ONE OF US, TRAINED FROM BIRTH TO BE THE PERFECT ASSASSIN. NO IMPURITIES FROM THE OUTSIDE WORLD WOULD EVER TAINT HER."
"ALL AGREED, BUT ONE."

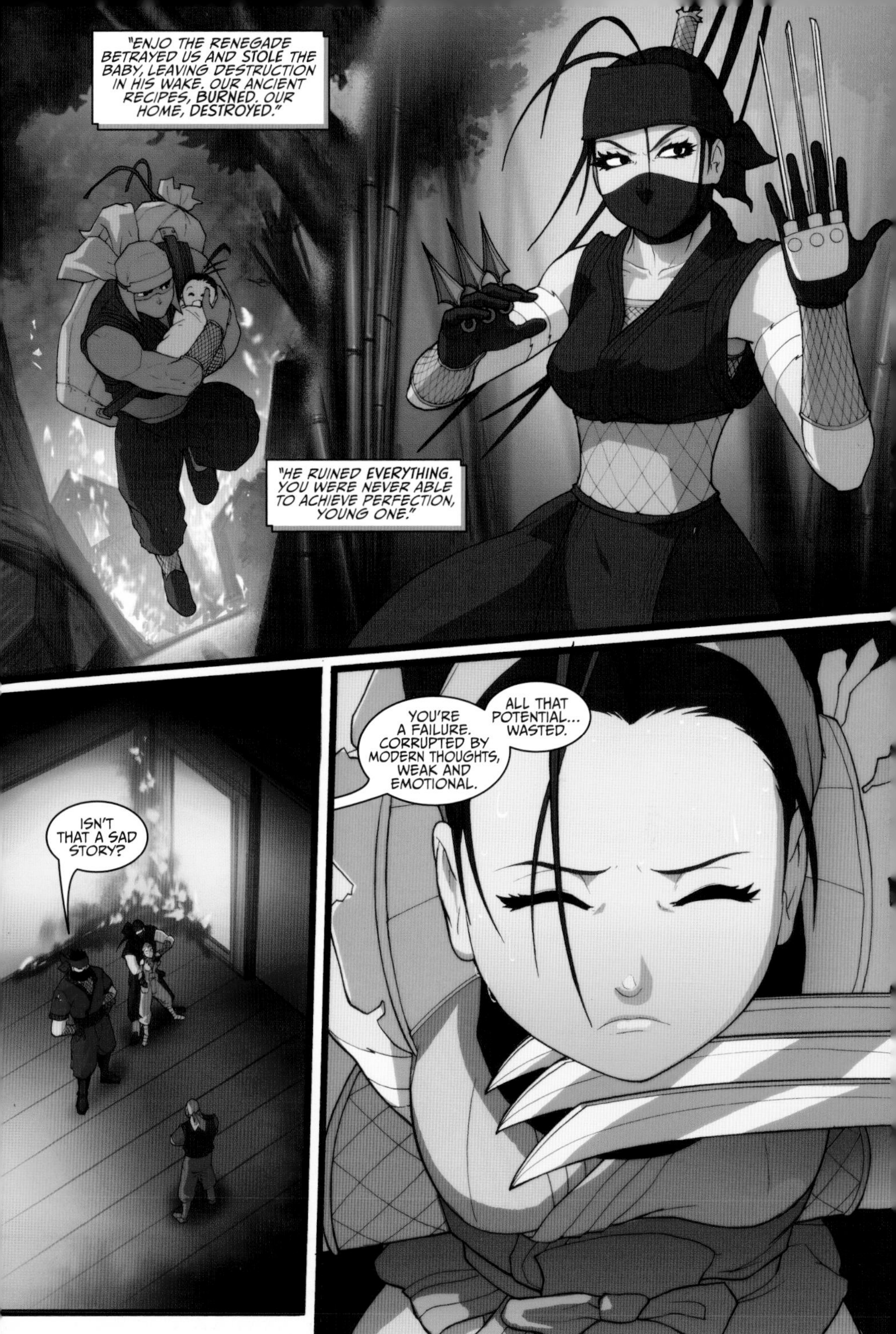
"ENJO THE RENEGADE BETRAYED US AND STOLE THE BABY, LEAVING DESTRUCTION IN HIS WAKE. OUR ANCIENT RECIPES, BURNED. OUR HOME, DESTROYED."
"HE RUINED EVERYTHING. YOU WERE NEVER ABLE TO ACHIEVE PERFECTION, YOUNG ONE."
ISN'T THAT A SAD STORY?
YOU'RE A FAILURE. CORRUPTED BY MODERN THOUGHTS, WEAK AND EMOTIONAL.
ALL THAT POTENTIAL... WASTED.

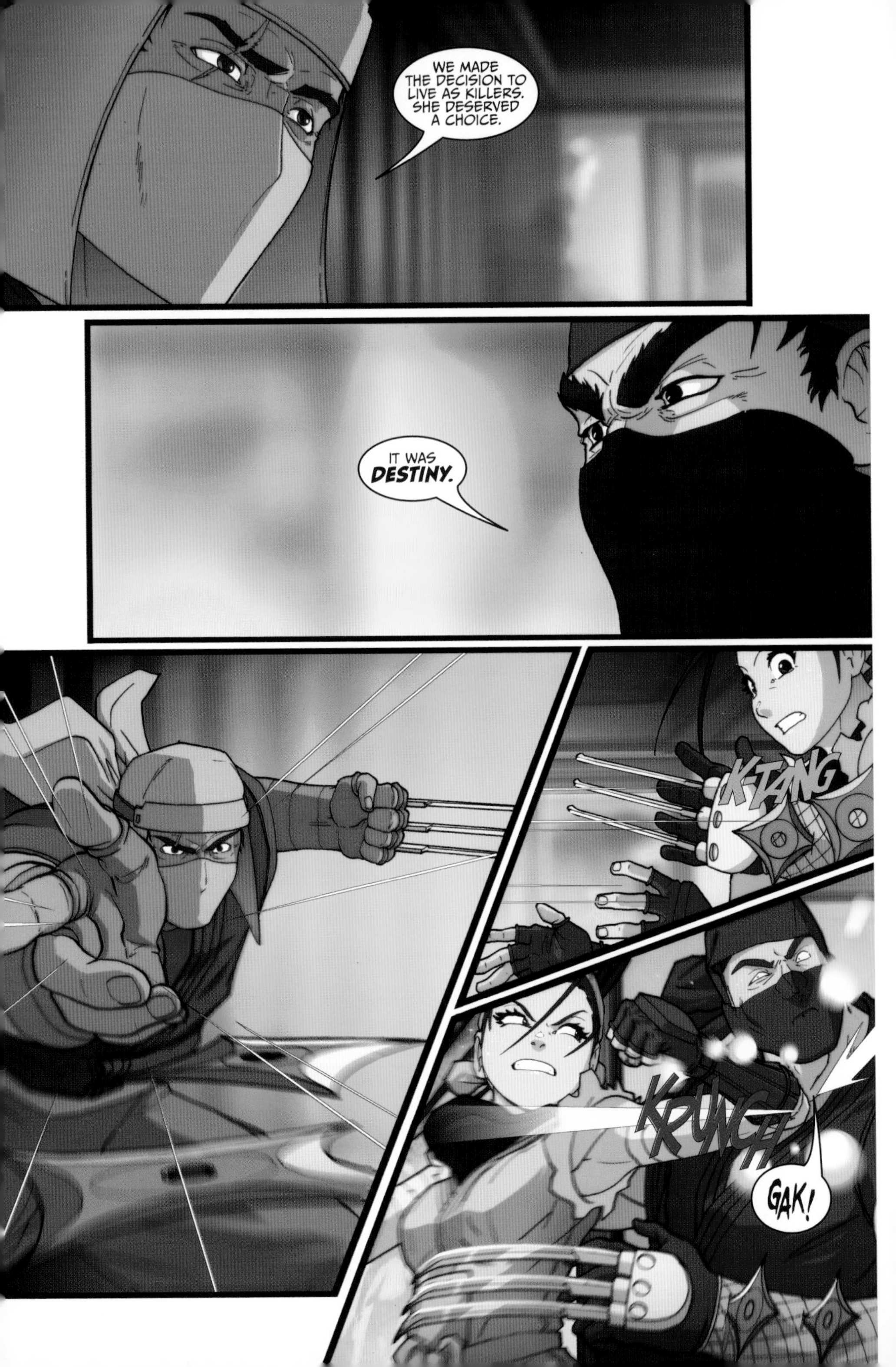
WE MADE THE DECISION TO LIVE AS KILLERS. SHE DESERVED A CHOICE.
IT WAS DESTINY.
KLANG
KRUNCH
GAK!

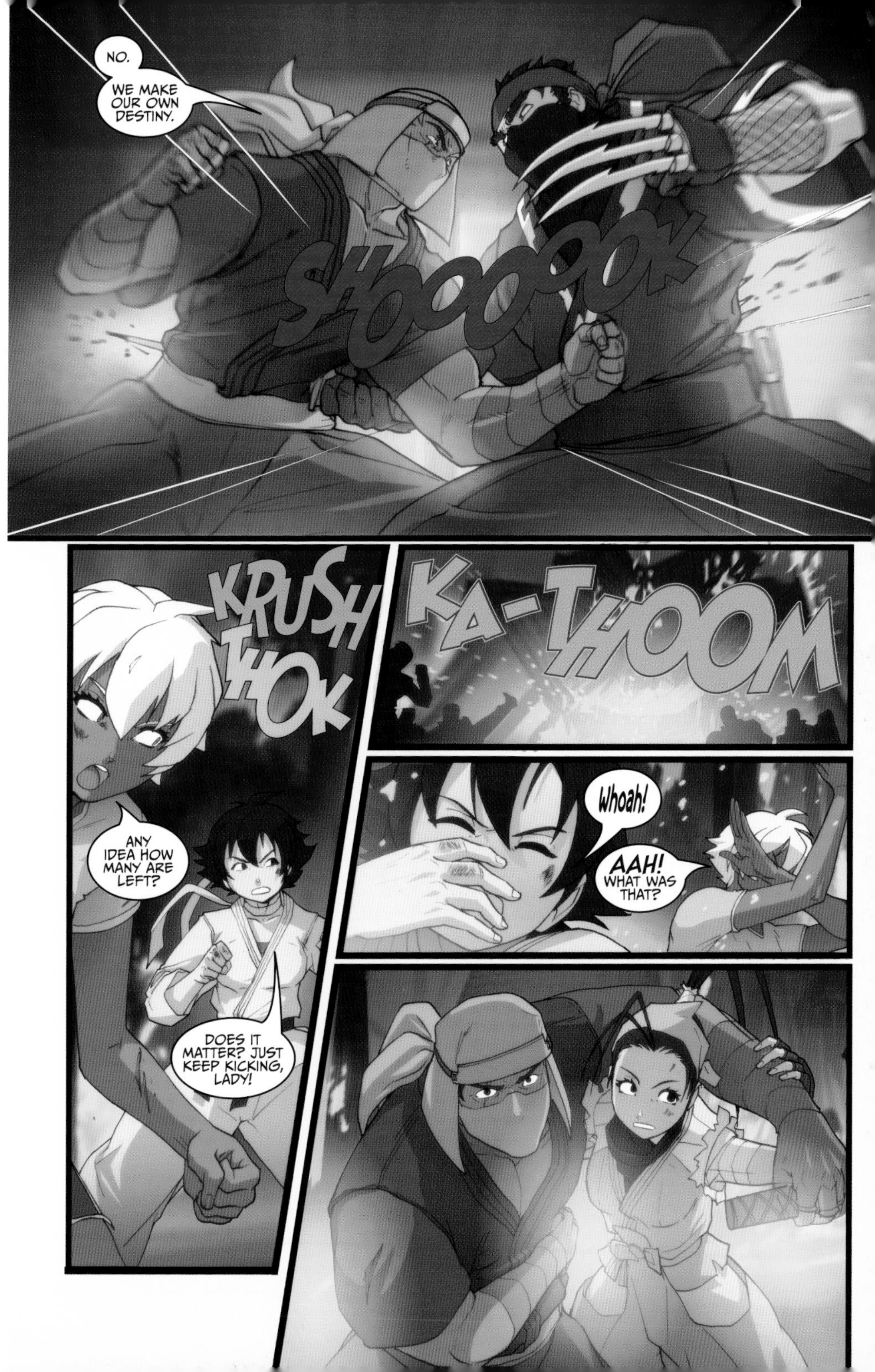
NO.
WE MAKE OUR OWN DESTINY.
SHOOOOOK
KRUSH
THOK
KA-THOOM
ANY IDEA HOW MANY ARE LEFT?
DOES IT MATTER? JUST KEEP KICKING, LADY!
Whoah!
AAH! WHAT WAS THAT?

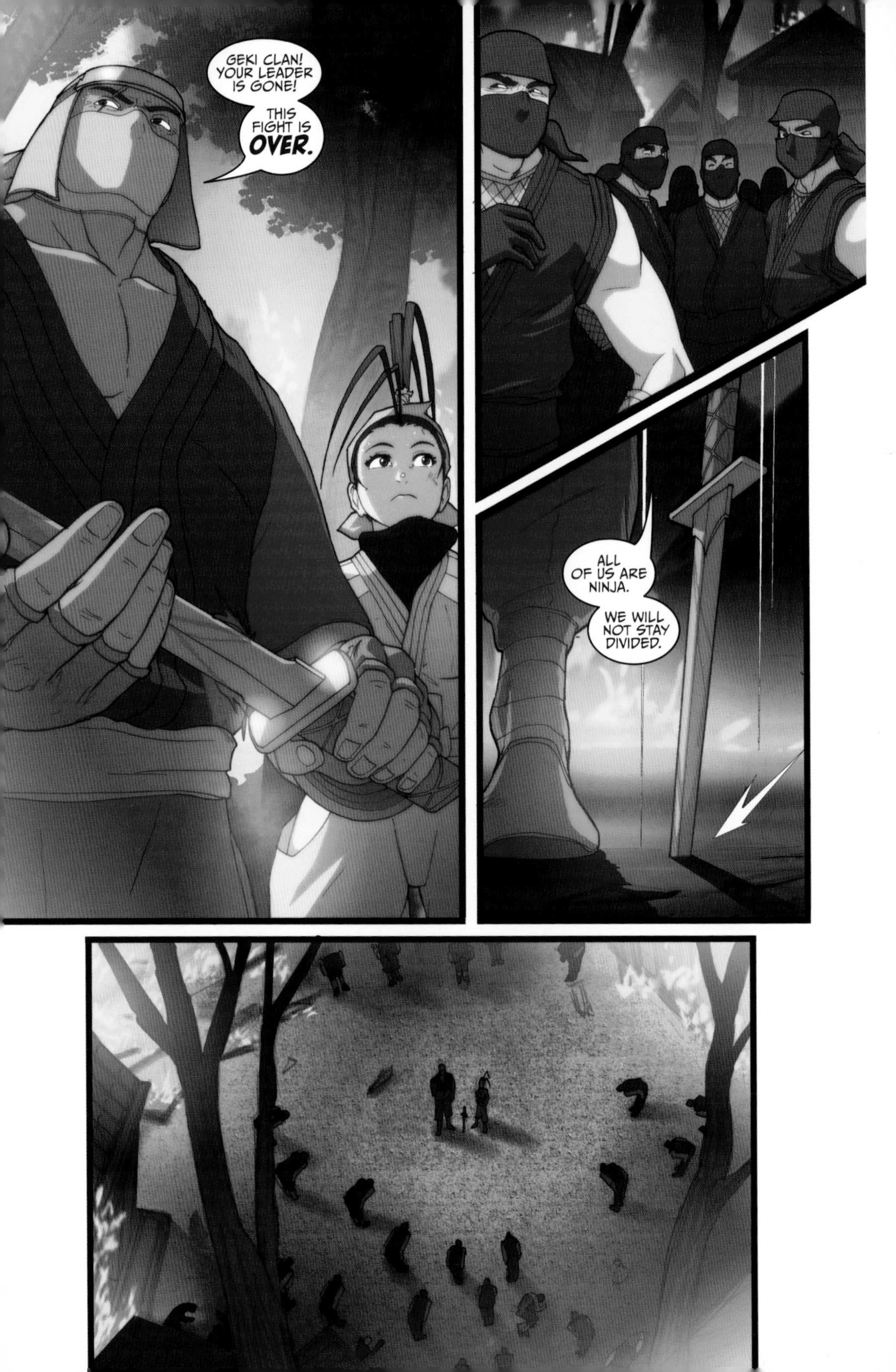
GEKI CLAN! YOUR LEADER IS GONE!
THIS FIGHT IS **OVER.**
ALL OF US ARE NINJA.
WE WILL NOT STAY DIVIDED.

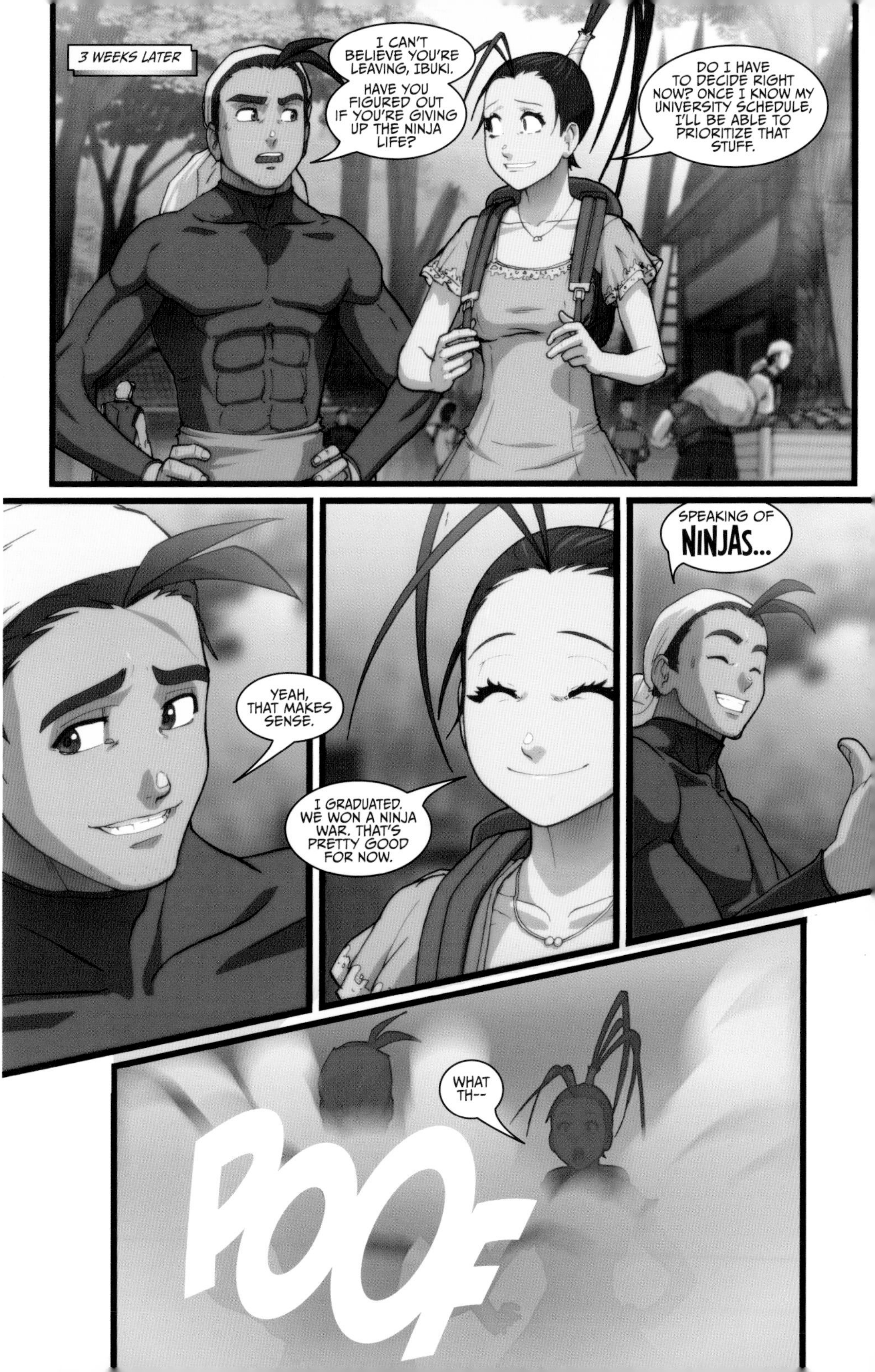
3 WEEKS LATER
I CAN'T BELIEVE YOU'RE LEAVING, IBUKI.
HAVE YOU FIGURED OUT IF YOU'RE GIVING UP THE NINJA LIFE?
DO I HAVE TO DECIDE RIGHT NOW? ONCE I KNOW MY UNIVERSITY SCHEDULE, I'LL BE ABLE TO PRIORITIZE THAT STUFF.
YEAH, THAT MAKES SENSE.
I GRADUATED. WE WON A NINJA WAR. THAT'S PRETTY GOOD FOR NOW.
SPEAKING OF NINJAS...
WHAT TH--
POOF

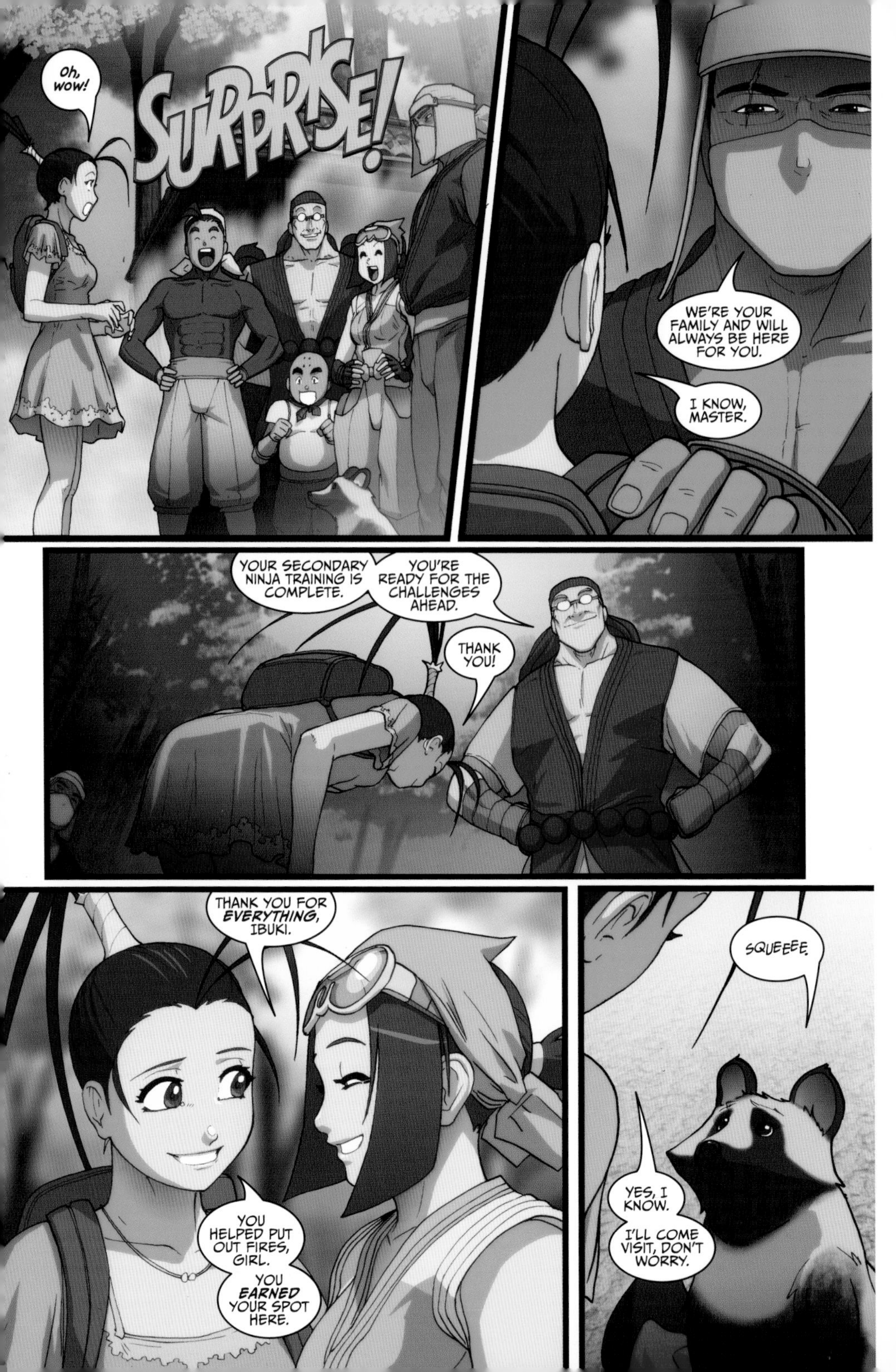
Oh, wow!
SURPRISE!
WE'RE YOUR FAMILY AND WILL ALWAYS BE HERE FOR YOU.
I KNOW, MASTER.
YOUR SECONDARY NINJA TRAINING IS COMPLETE.
YOU'RE READY FOR THE CHALLENGES AHEAD.
THANK YOU!
THANK YOU FOR EVERYTHING, IBUKI.
YOU HELPED PUT OUT FIRES, GIRL.
YOU EARNED YOUR SPOT HERE.
SQUEEEE.
YES, I KNOW.
I'LL COME VISIT, DON'T WORRY.

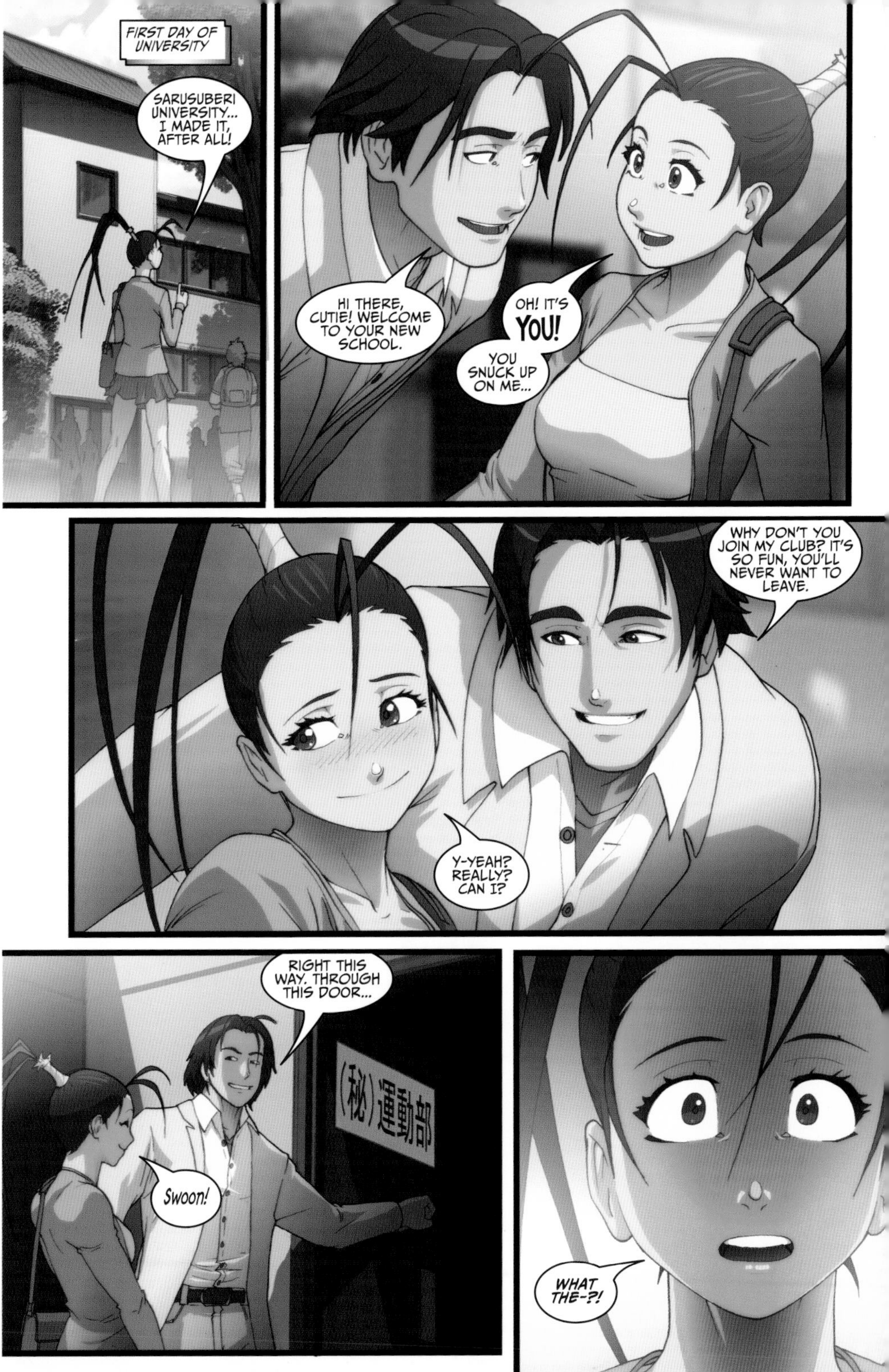
FIRST DAY OF UNIVERSITY
SARUSUBERI UNIVERSITY... I MADE IT, AFTER ALL!
HI THERE, CUTIE! WELCOME TO YOUR NEW SCHOOL.
OH! IT'S YOU!
YOU SNUCK UP ON ME...
WHY DON'T YOU JOIN MY CLUB? IT'S SO FUN, YOU'LL NEVER WANT TO LEAVE.
Y-YEAH? REALLY? CAN I?
RIGHT THIS WAY. THROUGH THIS DOOR...
Swoon!
(秘)運動部
WHAT THE-?!

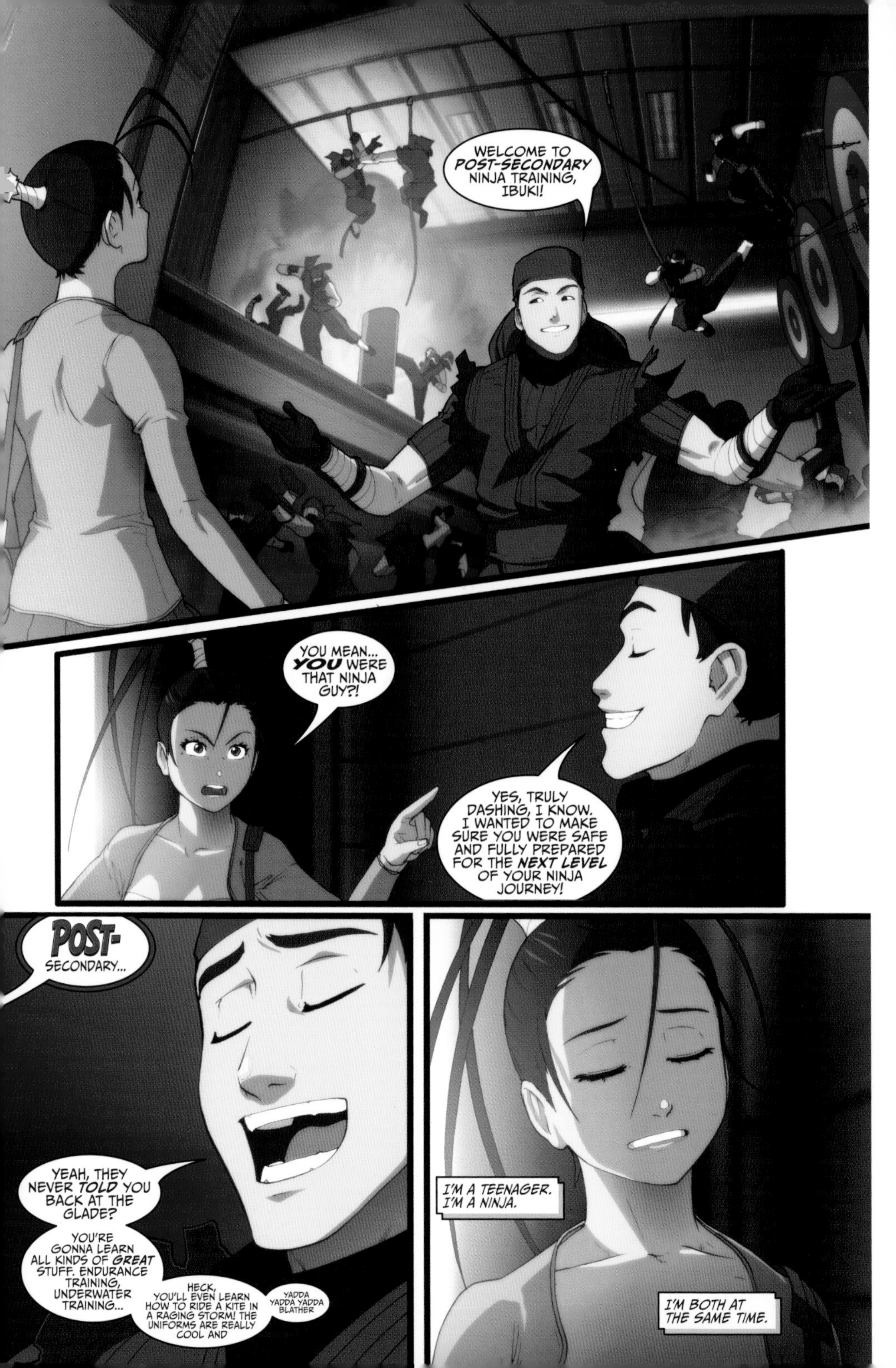
WELCOME TO POST-SECONDARY NINJA TRAINING, IBUKI!
YOU MEAN... YOU WERE THAT NINJA GUY?!
YES, TRULY DASHING, I KNOW. I WANTED TO MAKE SURE YOU WERE SAFE AND FULLY PREPARED FOR THE NEXT LEVEL OF YOUR NINJA JOURNEY!
POST-SECONDARY...
YEAH, THEY NEVER TOLD YOU BACK AT THE GLADE?
YOU'RE GONNA LEARN ALL KINDS OF GREAT STUFF. ENDURANCE TRAINING, UNDERWATER TRAINING...
HECK, YOU'LL EVEN LEARN HOW TO RIDE A KITE IN A RAGING STORM! THE UNIFORMS ARE REALLY COOL AND
YADDA YADDA YADDA BLATHER
I'M A TEENAGER. I'M A NINJA.
I'M BOTH AT THE SAME TIME.

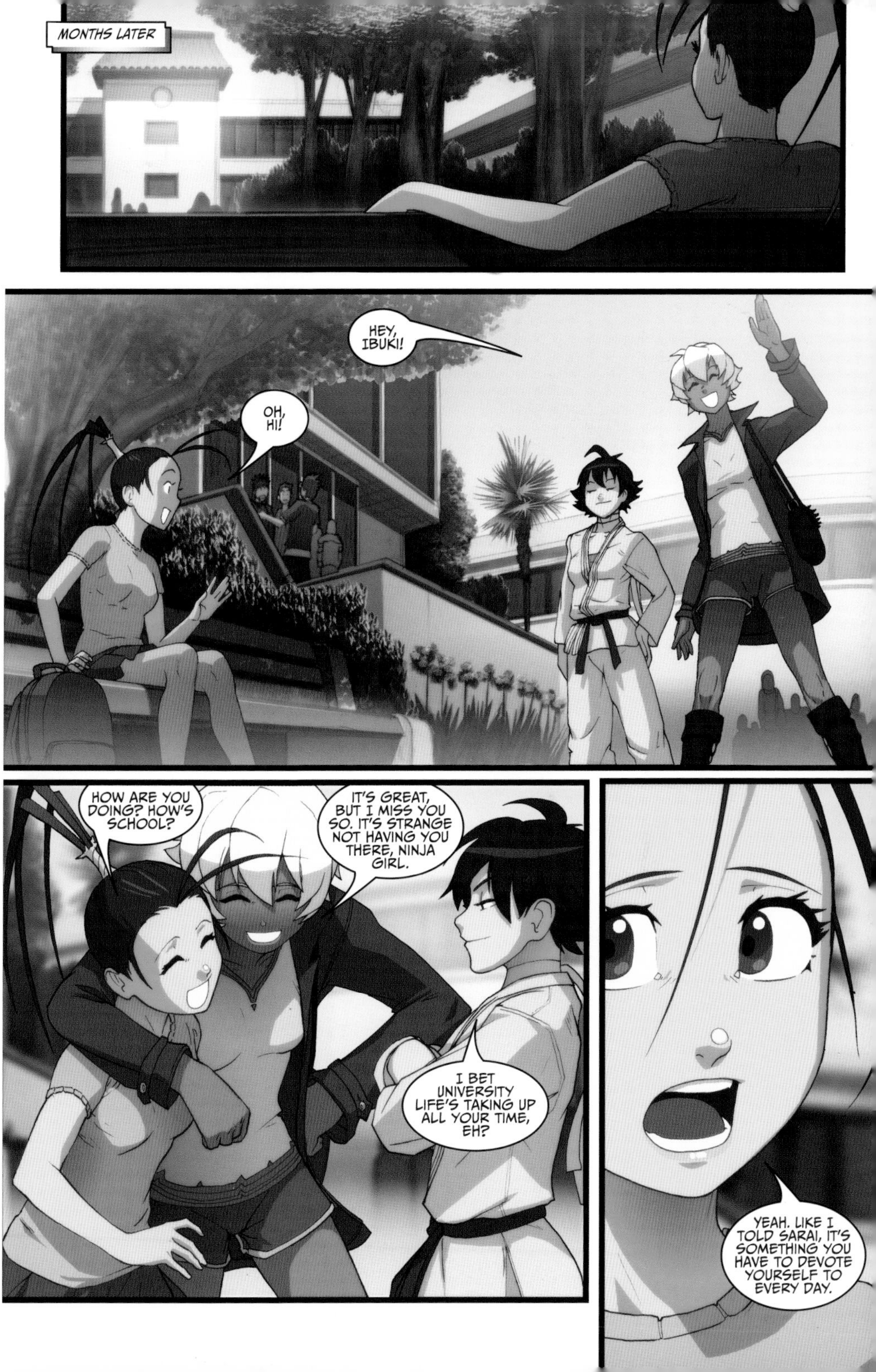
MONTHS LATER
HEY, IBUKI!
OH, HI!
HOW ARE YOU DOING? HOW'S SCHOOL?
IT'S GREAT, BUT I MISS YOU SO. IT'S STRANGE NOT HAVING YOU THERE, NINJA GIRL.
I BET UNIVERSITY LIFE'S TAKING UP ALL YOUR TIME, EH?
YEAH. LIKE I TOLD SARAI, IT'S SOMETHING YOU HAVE TO DEVOTE YOURSELF TO EVERY DAY.

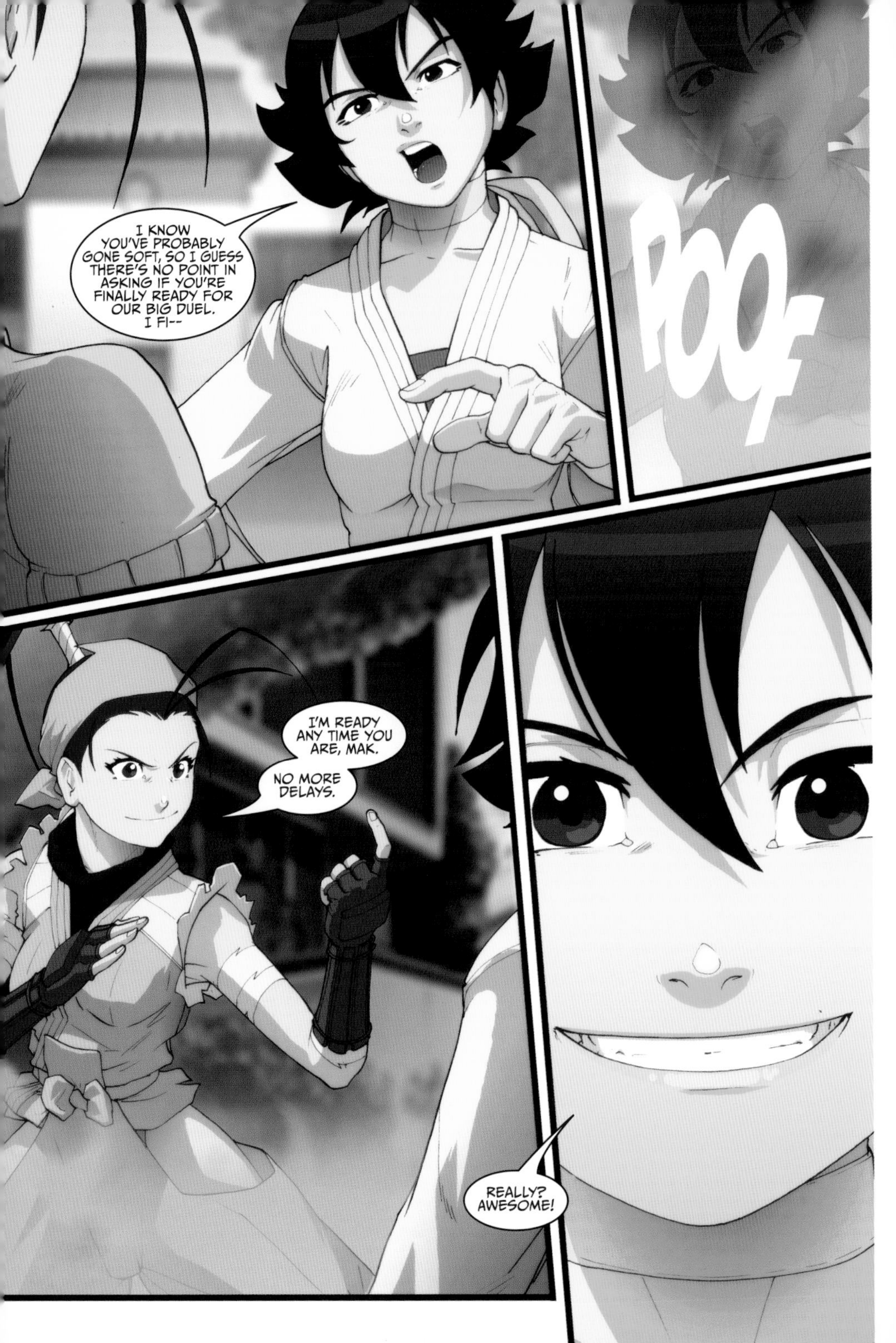
I KNOW YOU'VE PROBABLY GONE SOFT, SO I GUESS THERE'S NO POINT IN ASKING IF YOU'RE FINALLY READY FOR OUR BIG DUEL. I FI--
POOF
I'M READY ANY TIME YOU ARE, MAK.
NO MORE DELAYS.
REALLY? AWESOME!

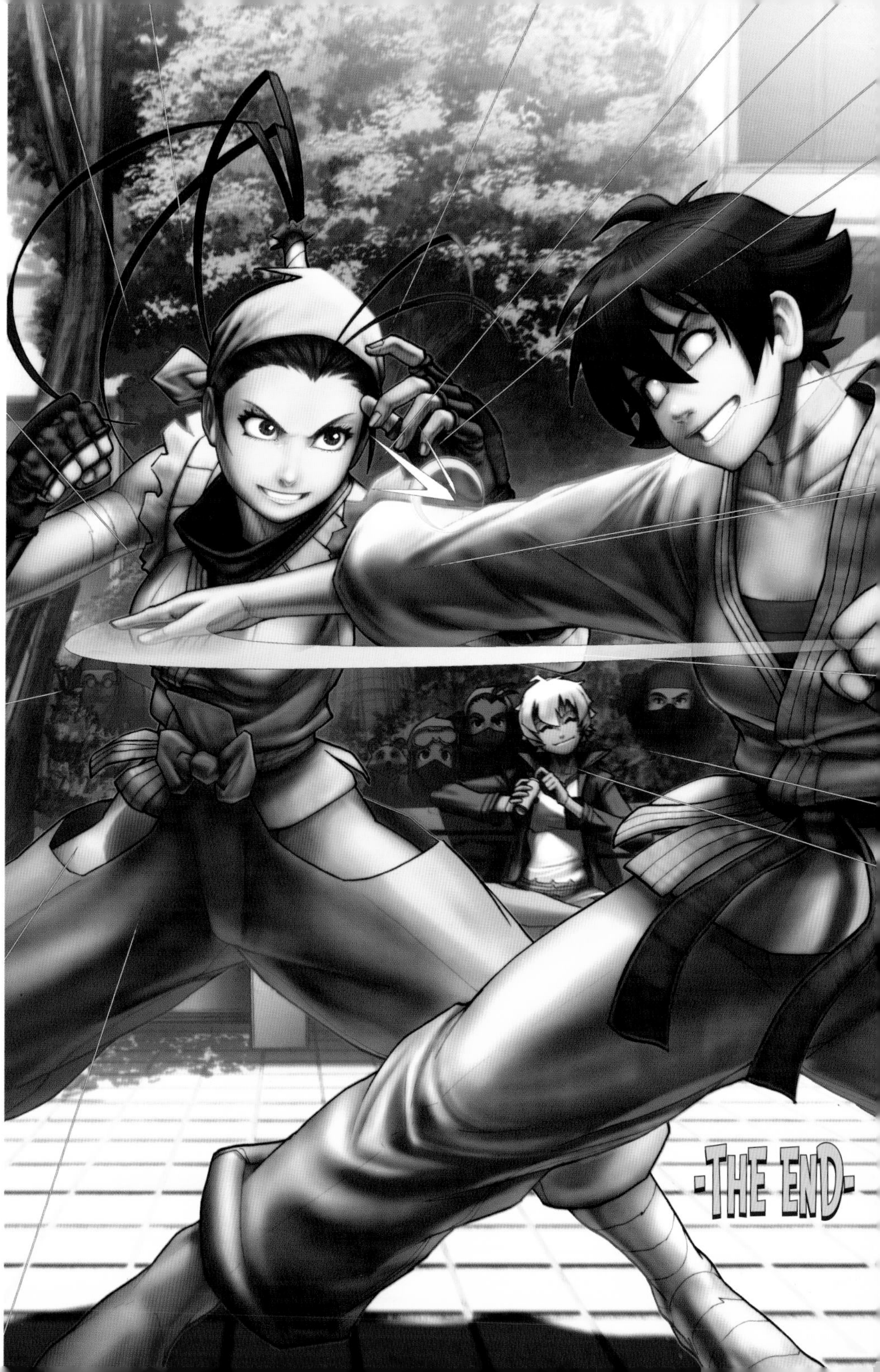
-THE END-

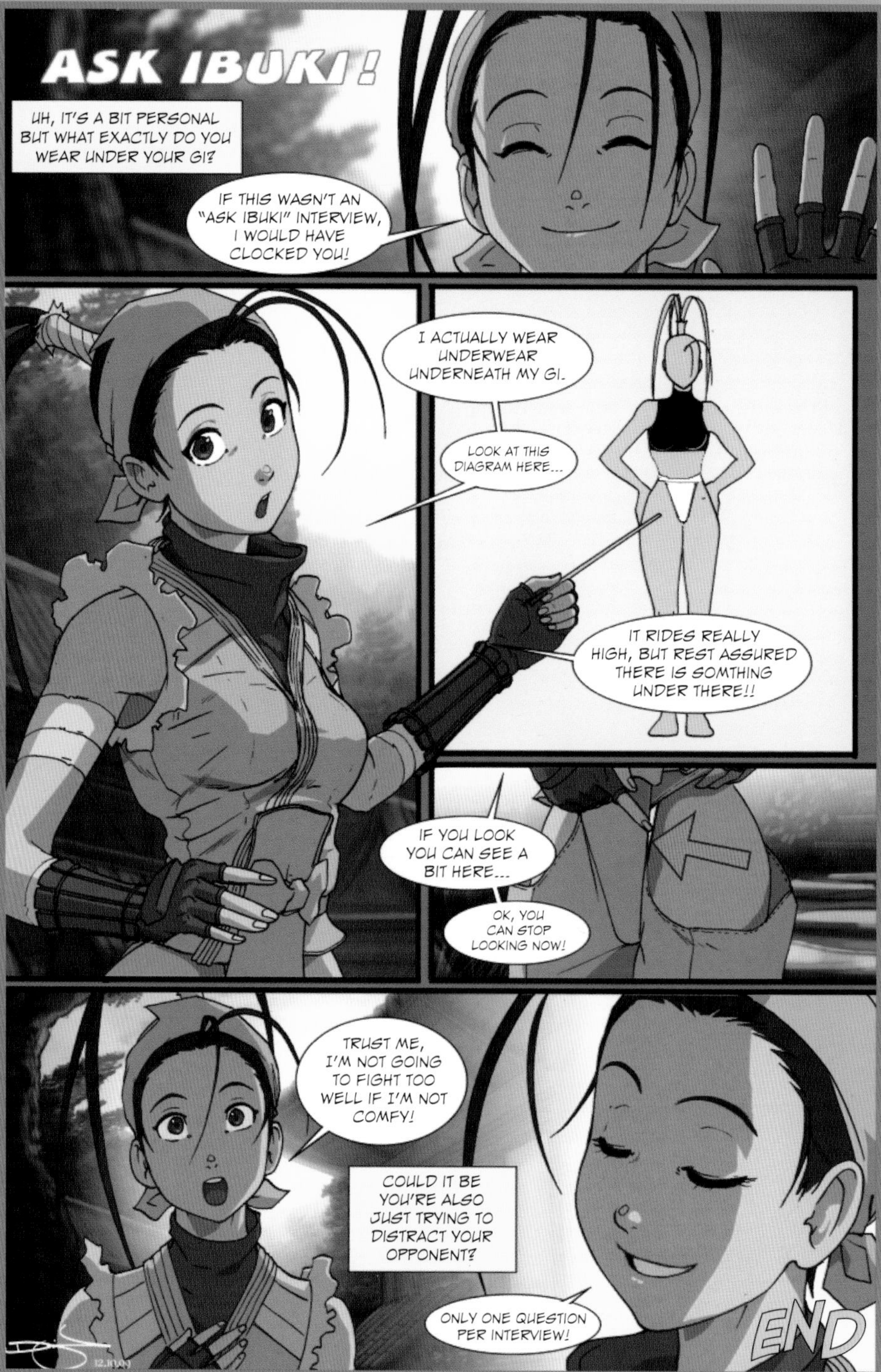
ASK IBUKI!
UH, IT'S A BIT PERSONAL BUT WHAT EXACTLY DO YOU WEAR UNDER YOUR GI?
IF THIS WASN'T AN "ASK IBUKI" INTERVIEW, I WOULD HAVE CLOCKED YOU!
I ACTUALLY WEAR UNDERWEAR UNDERNEATH MY GI.
LOOK AT THIS DIAGRAM HERE...
IT RIDES REALLY HIGH, BUT REST ASSURED THERE IS SOMTHING UNDER THERE!!
IF YOU LOOK YOU CAN SEE A BIT HERE...
OK, YOU CAN STOP LOOKING NOW!
TRUST ME, I'M NOT GOING TO FIGHT TOO WELL IF I'M NOT COMFY!
COULD IT BE YOU'RE ALSO JUST TRYING TO DISTRACT YOUR OPPONENT?
ONLY ONE QUESTION PER INTERVIEW!
END

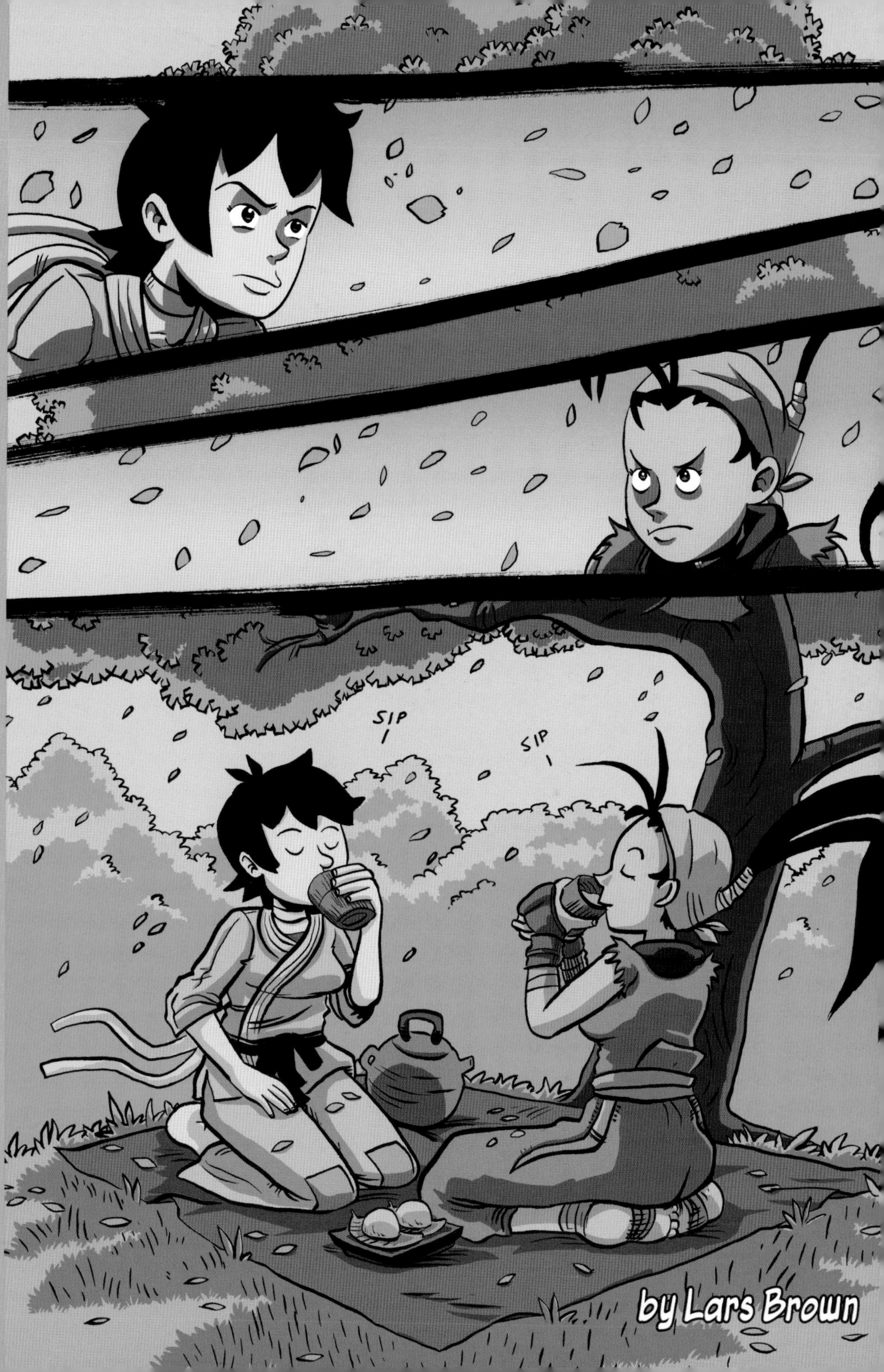
SIP
SIP
by Lars Brown

Art by: Jay Axer

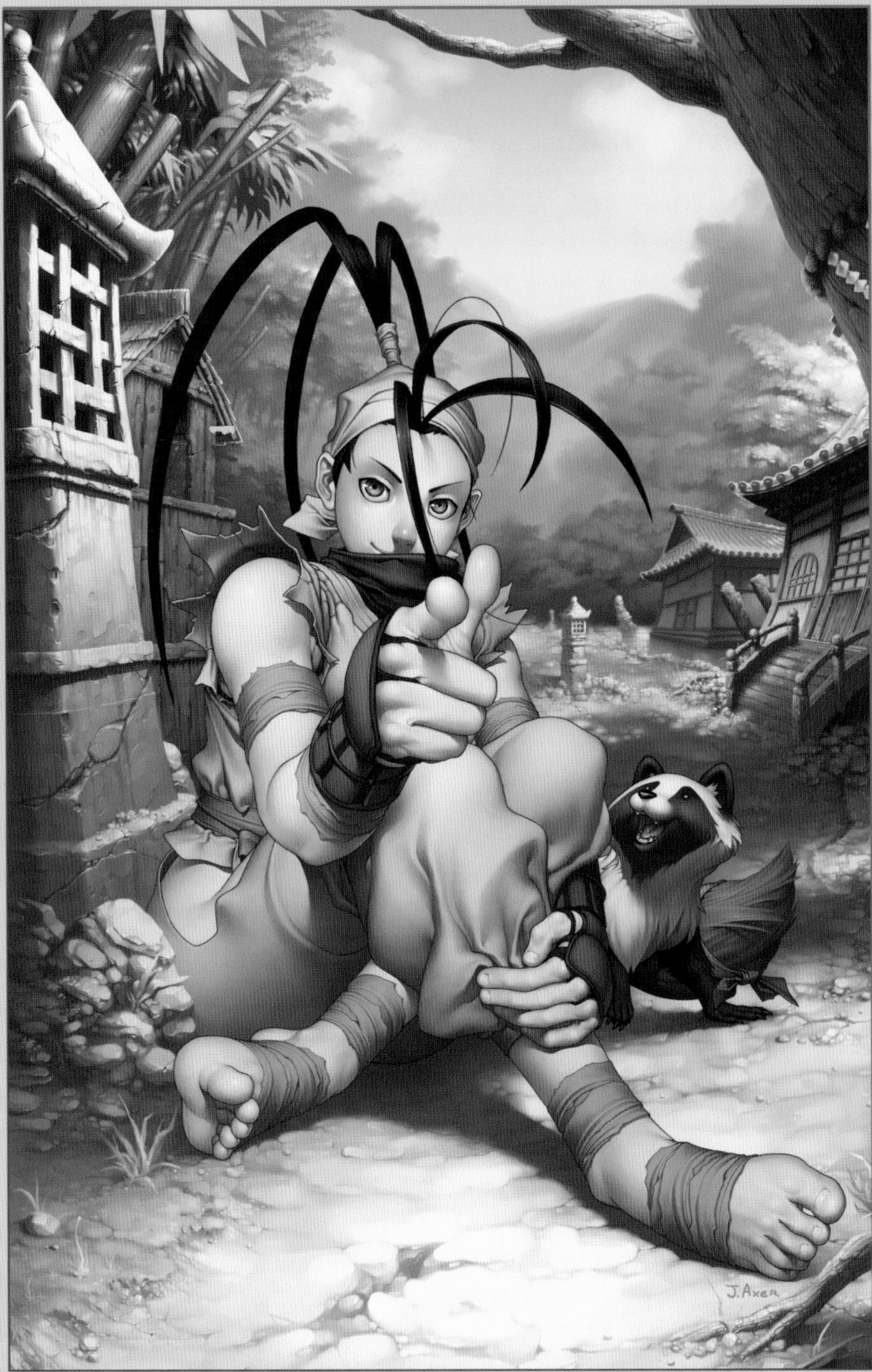
J. Axer

Art by: Judy Jong

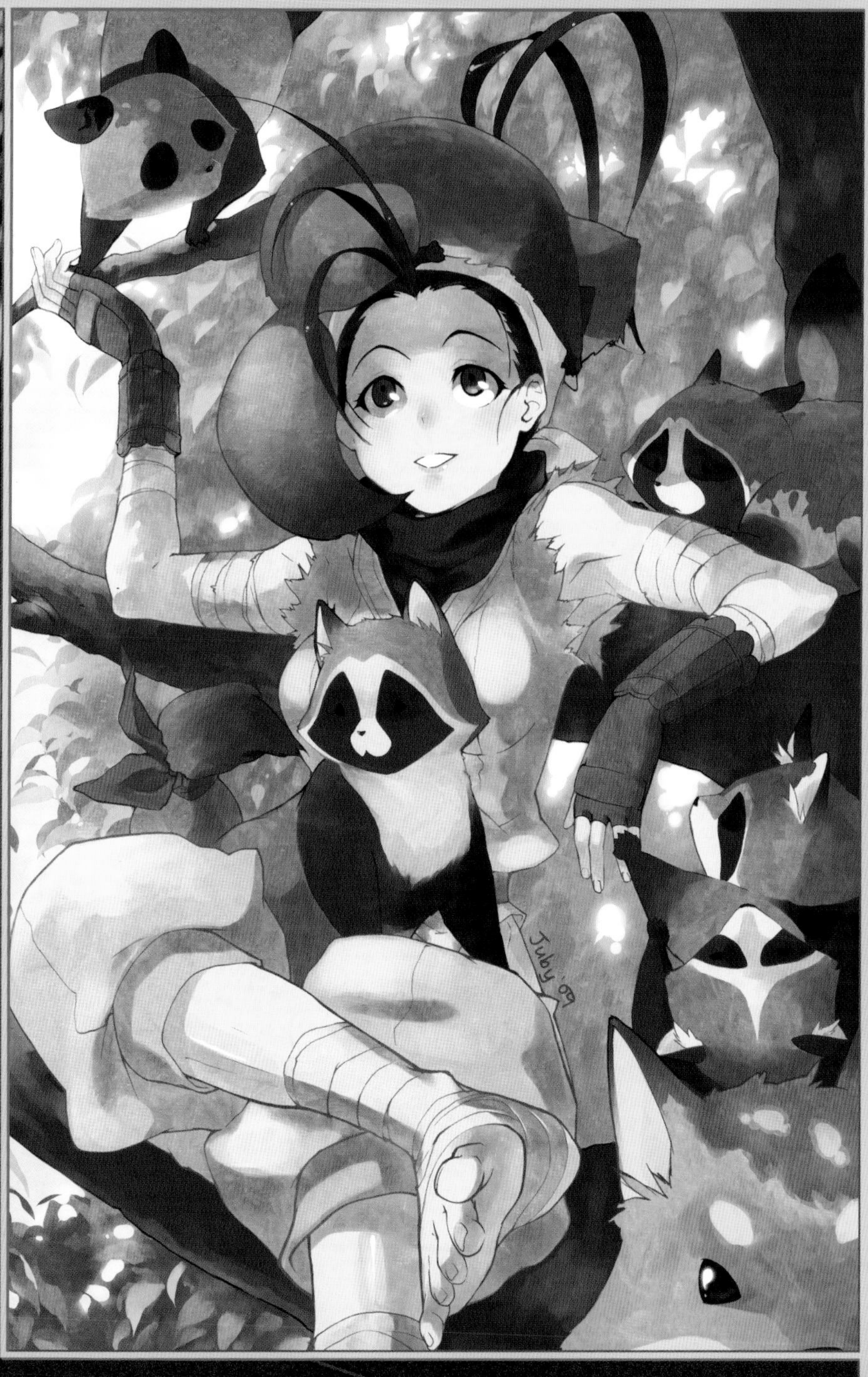

Bonus Gallery

Art by: Adam Warren with Emily Warren

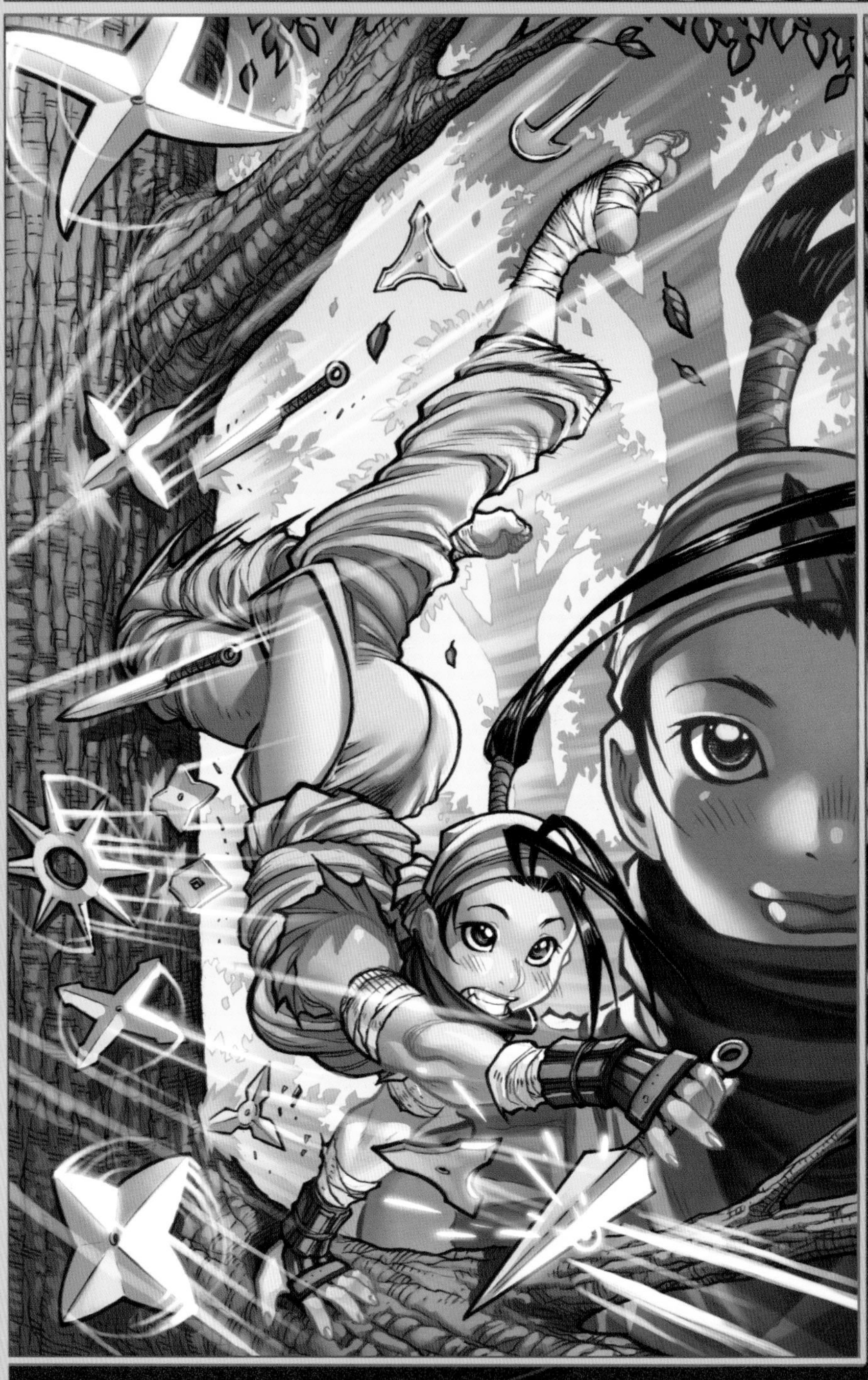

Art by: Jo Chen

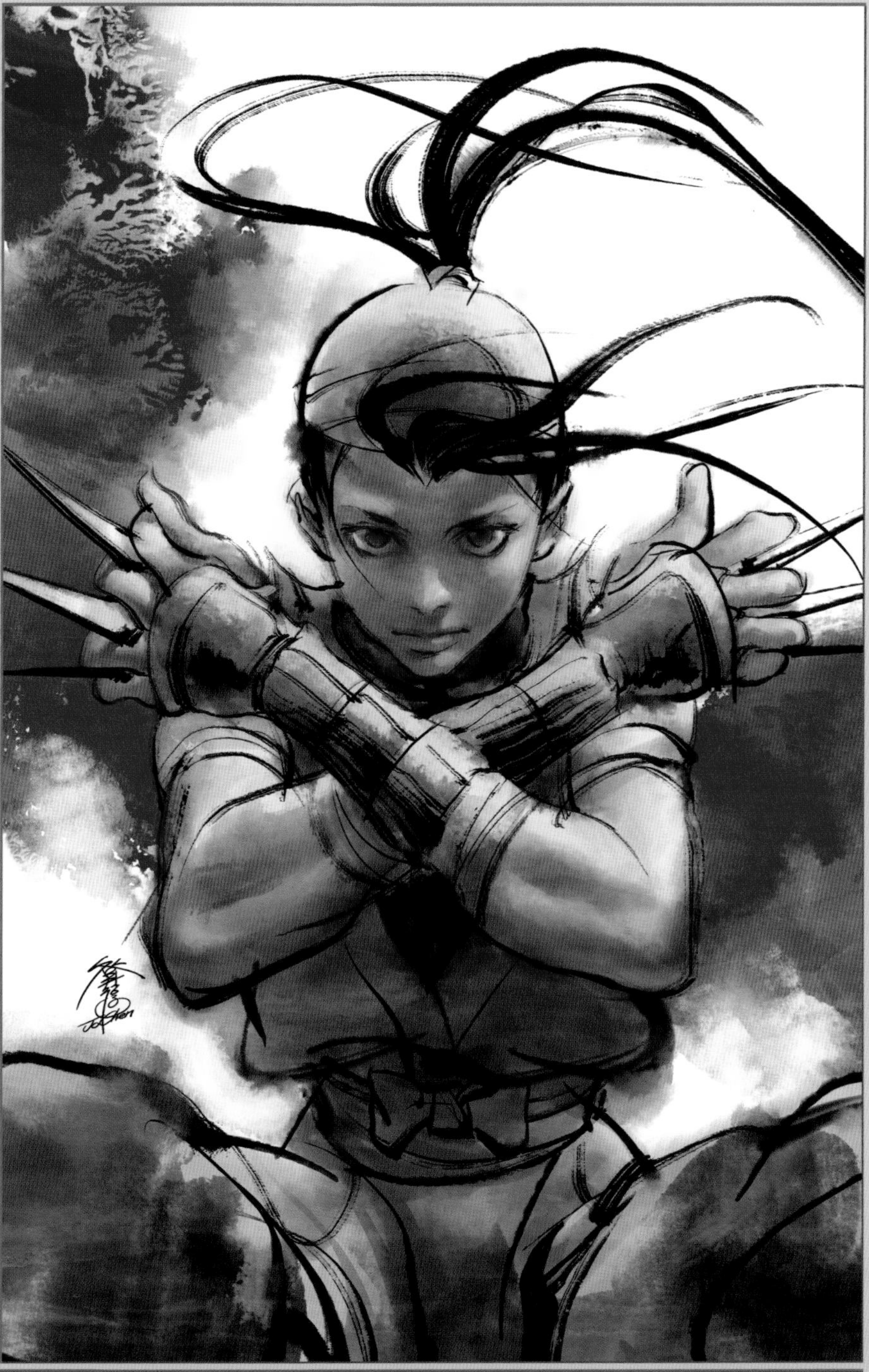

Bonus Gallery

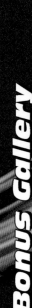

Art by: Omar Dogan

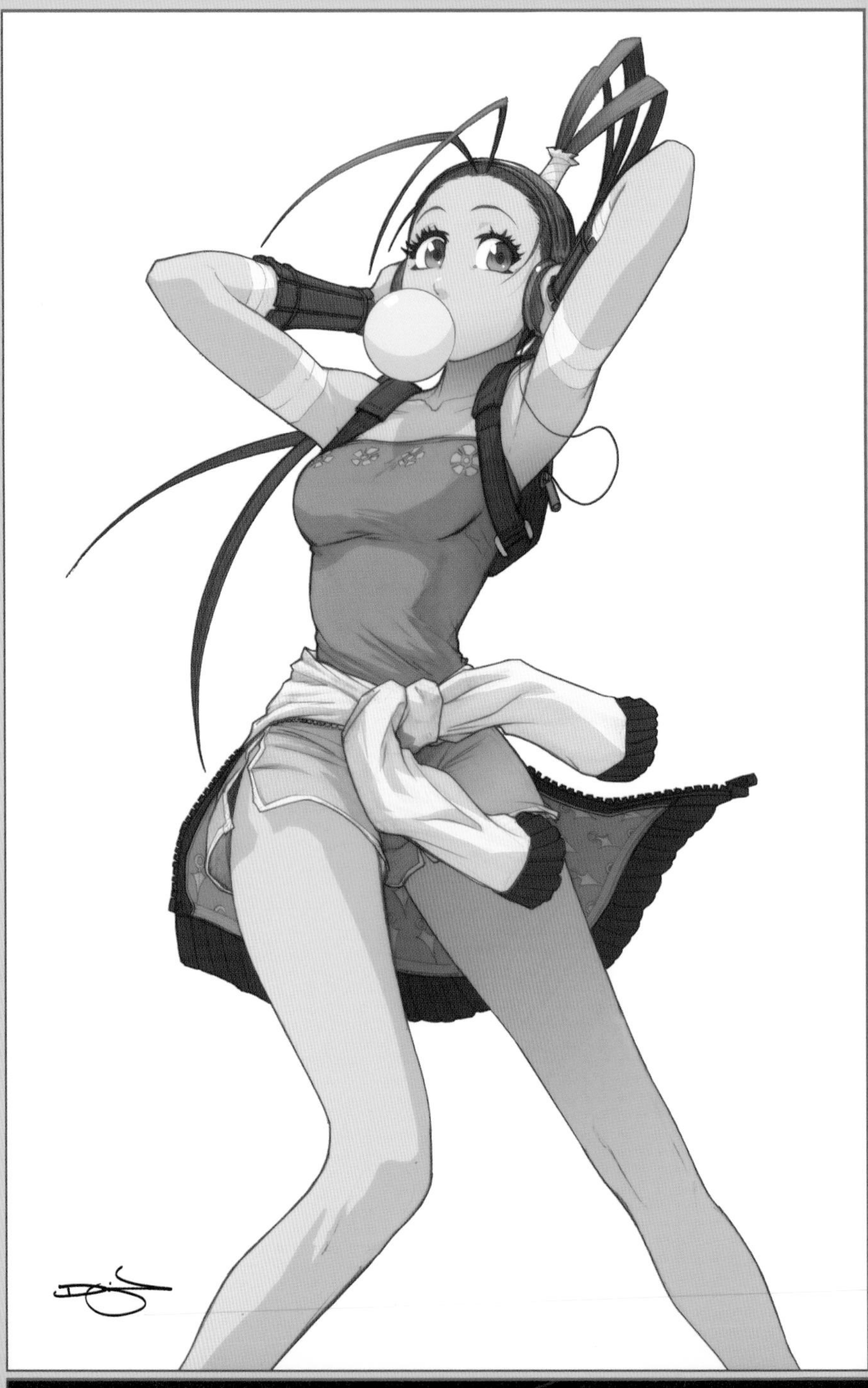

Art by: Omar Dogan

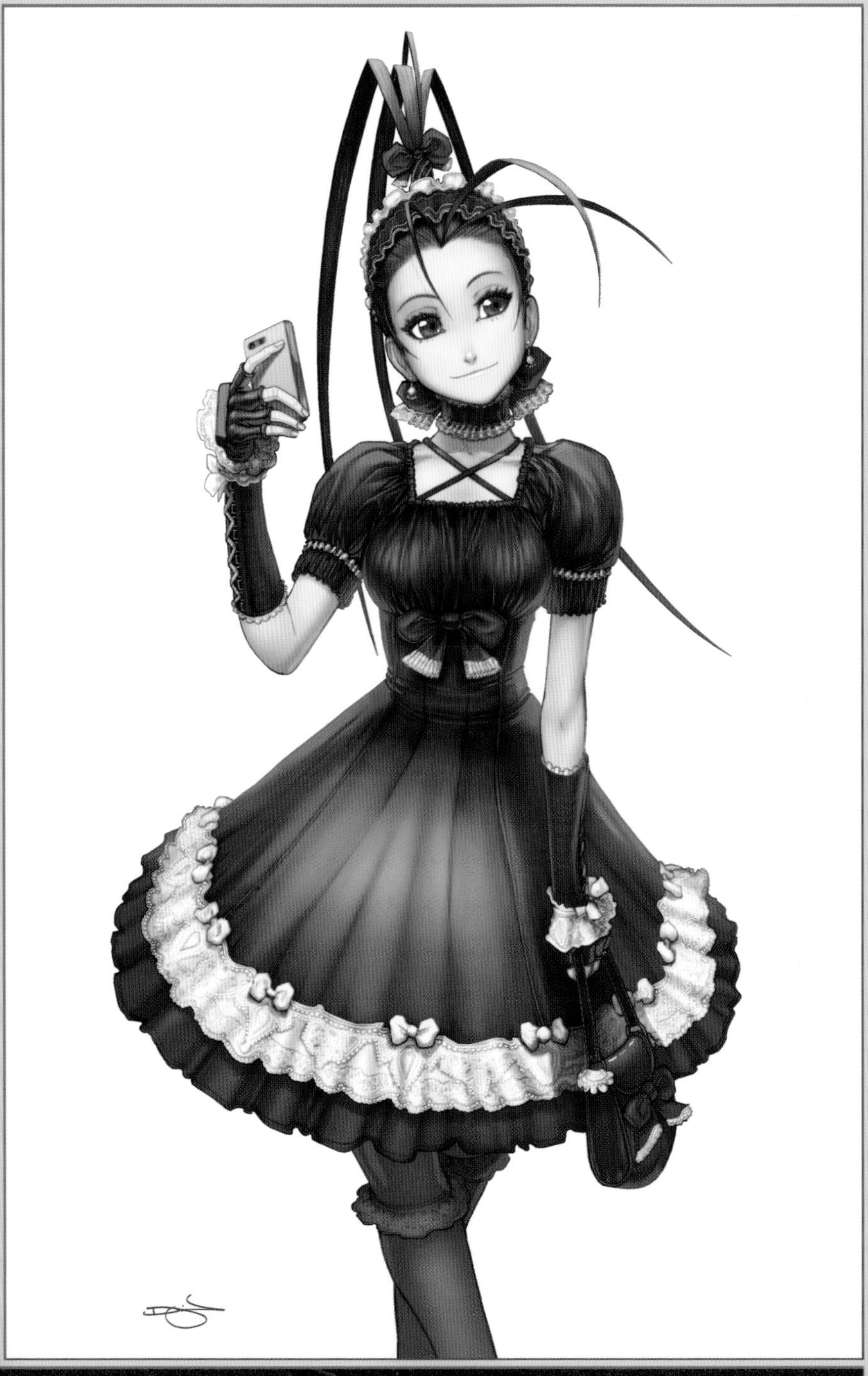

Bonus Gallery

Art by: Omar Dogan

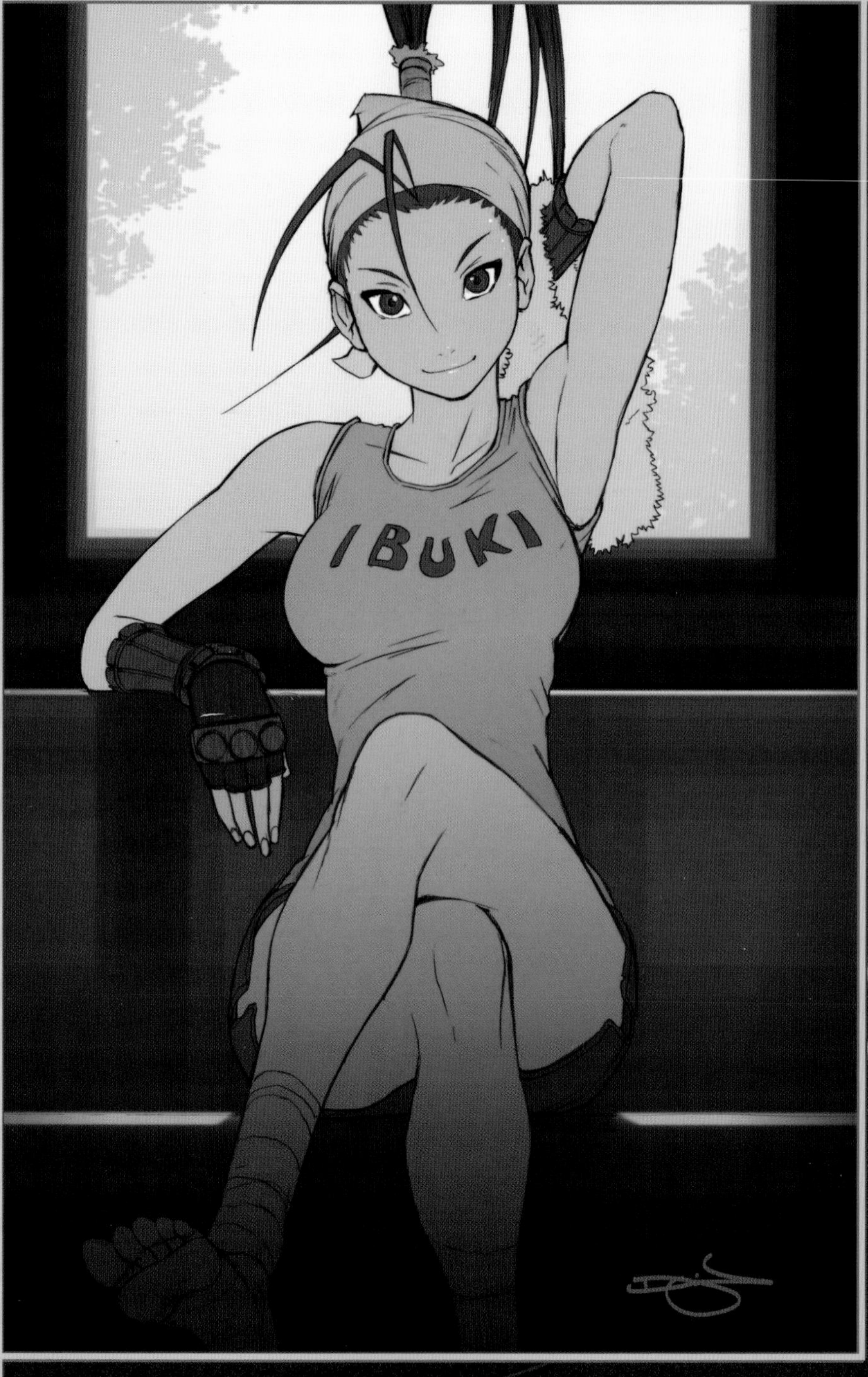
IBUKI

Bonus Gallery

Art by: Edwin Huang with Espen Grundetjern

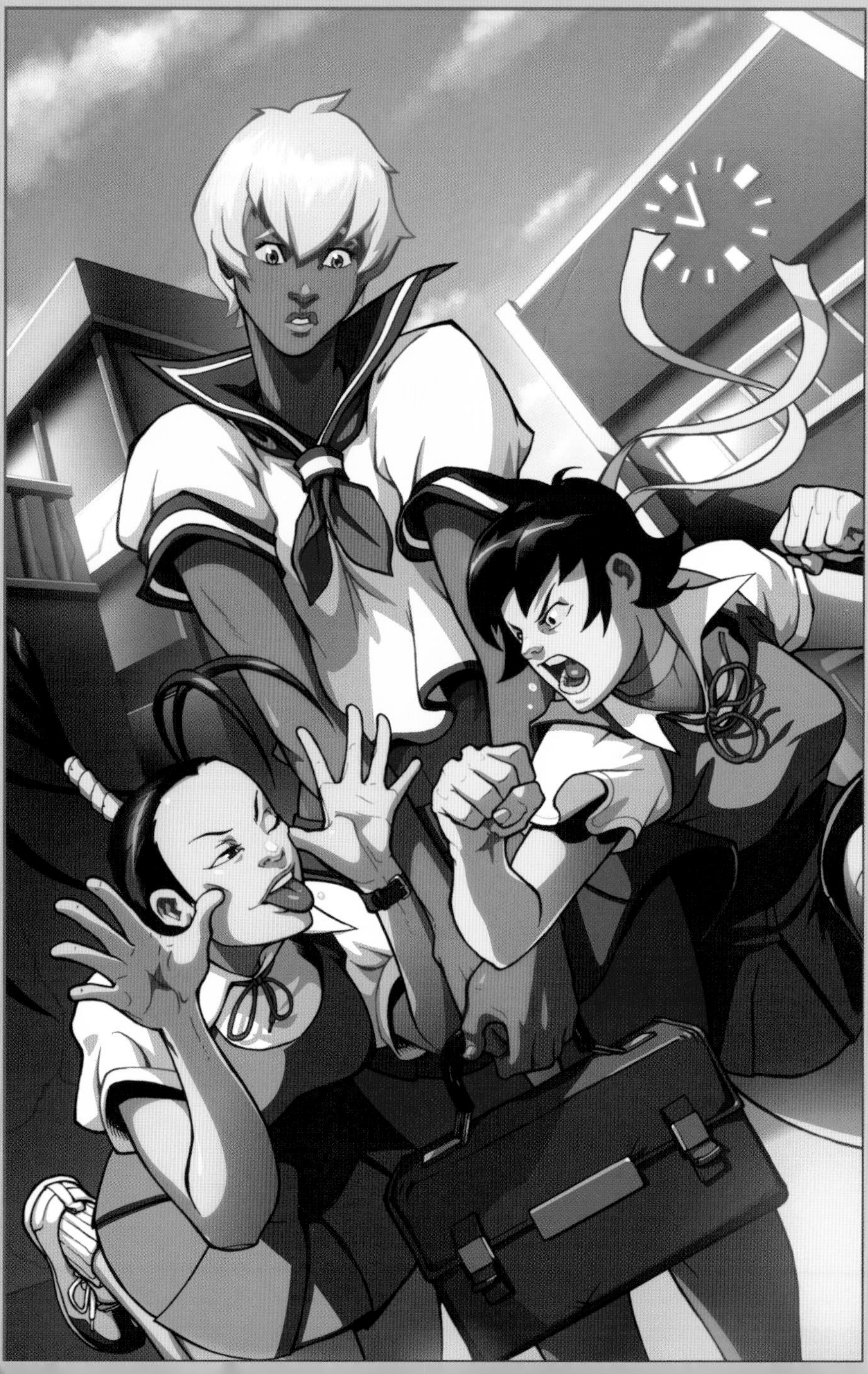

GRAPHIC NOVELS

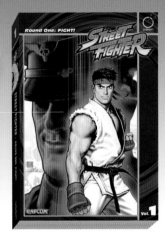

Round One: FIGHT!
STREET FIGHTER
udon
CAPCOM
Vol. 1

STREET FIGHTER VOL.1 TP
ISBN: 978-1-897376-18-8

The New Challengers!
STREET FIGHTER
udon
CAPCOM
Vol. 2

STREET FIGHTER VOL.2 TP
ISBN: 978-0-973865-27-1

Fighter's Destiny
STREET FIGHTER
udon
CAPCOM
Vol. 3

STREET FIGHTER VOL.3 TP
ISBN: 978-0-973865-28-8

Bonus Stage
STREET FIGHTER
udon
CAPCOM
Vol. 4

STREET FIGHTER VOL.4 TP
ISBN: 978-1-897376-00-3

Kick It Into Turbo!
STREET FIGHTER
udon
CAPCOM
Vol. 5

STREET FIGHTER VOL.5 TP
ISBN: 978-1-897376-48-5

Final Round
STREET FIGHTER
udon
CAPCOM
Vol. 6

STREET FIGHTER VOL.6 TP
ISBN: 978-1-897376-49-2

COMPLETE YOUR UDON LIBRARY!

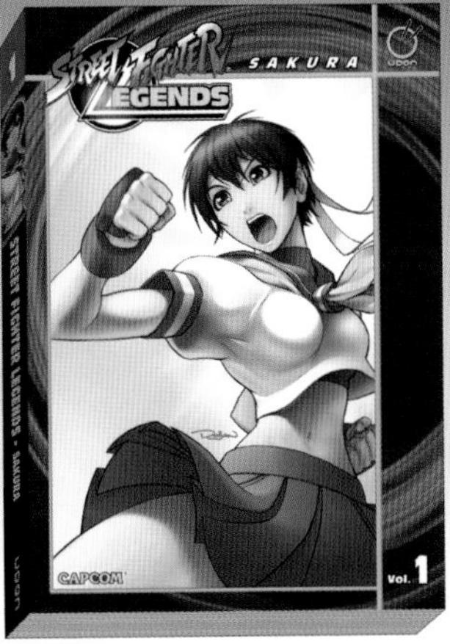
STREET FIGHTER LEGENDS
SAKURA
CAPCOM
Vol. 1

STREET FIGHTER LEGENDS:
SAKURA VOL.1 TP
ISBN: 978-0-978138-64-6

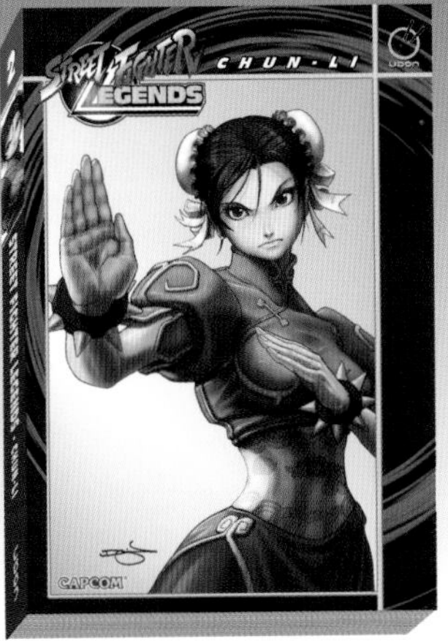
STREET FIGHTER LEGENDS
CHUN-LI
CAPCOM

STREET FIGHTER LEGENDS:
SAKURA VOL.2 TP
ISBN: 978-0-978138-65-3

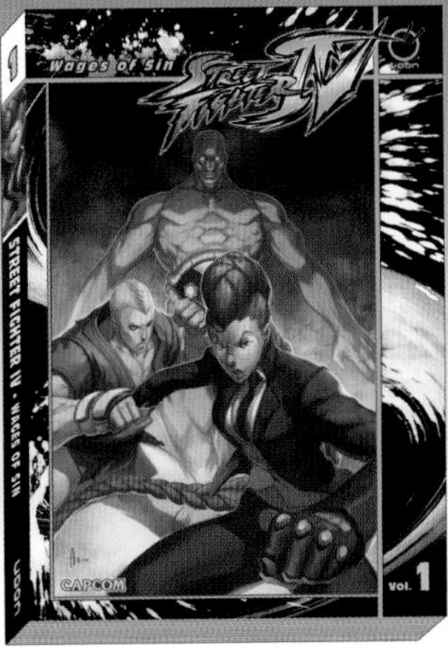
Wages of Sin
STREET FIGHTER IV
STREET FIGHTER IV - WAGES OF SIN
CAPCOM
Vol. 1

STREET FIGHTER IV VOL.1
ISBN: 978-1-897376-59-1

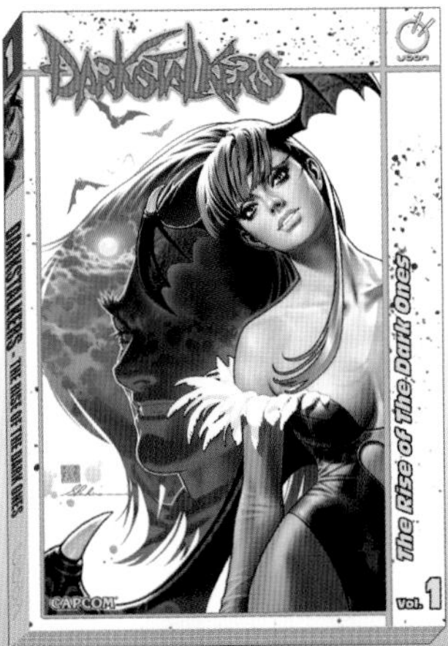
DARKSTALKERS
The Rise of The Dark Ones
CAPCOM
Vol. 1

DARKSTALKERS VOL.1
ISBN: 978-0-973865-21-9

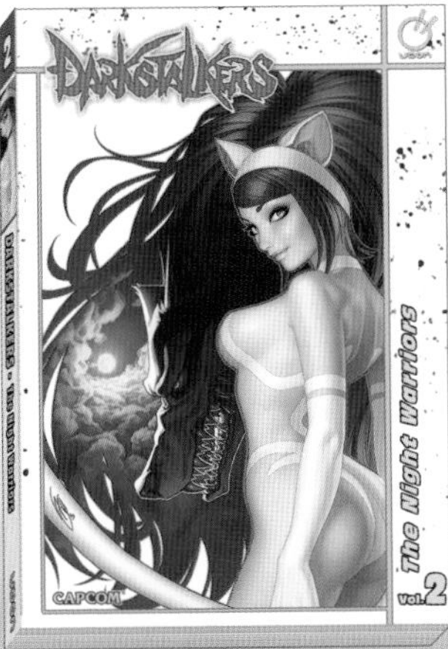
DARKSTALKERS
The Night Warriors
CAPCOM
Vol. 2

DARKSTALKERS VOL.2
ISBN: 978-1-926778-02-0

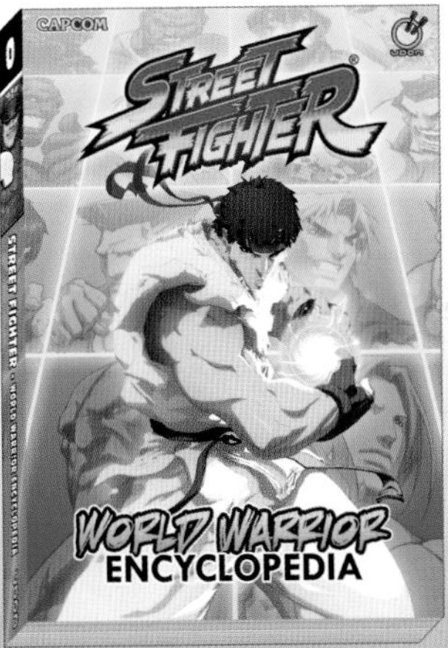
CAPCOM
STREET FIGHTER
WORLD WARRIOR
ENCYCLOPEDIA

STREET FIGHTER:
WORLD WARRIOR ENCYCLOPEDIA
ISBN: 978-1-926778-01-3

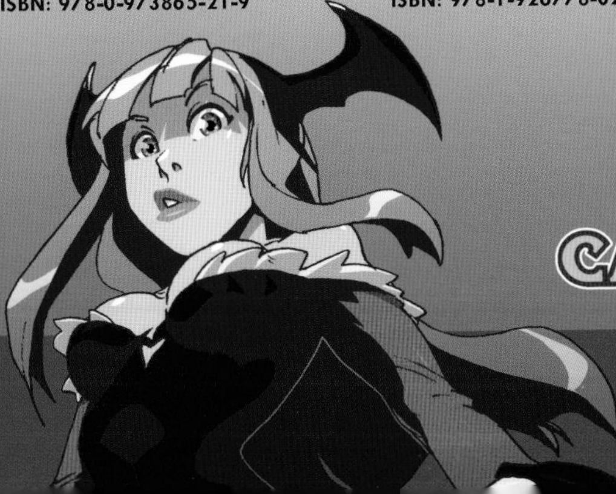

CAPCOM UDON

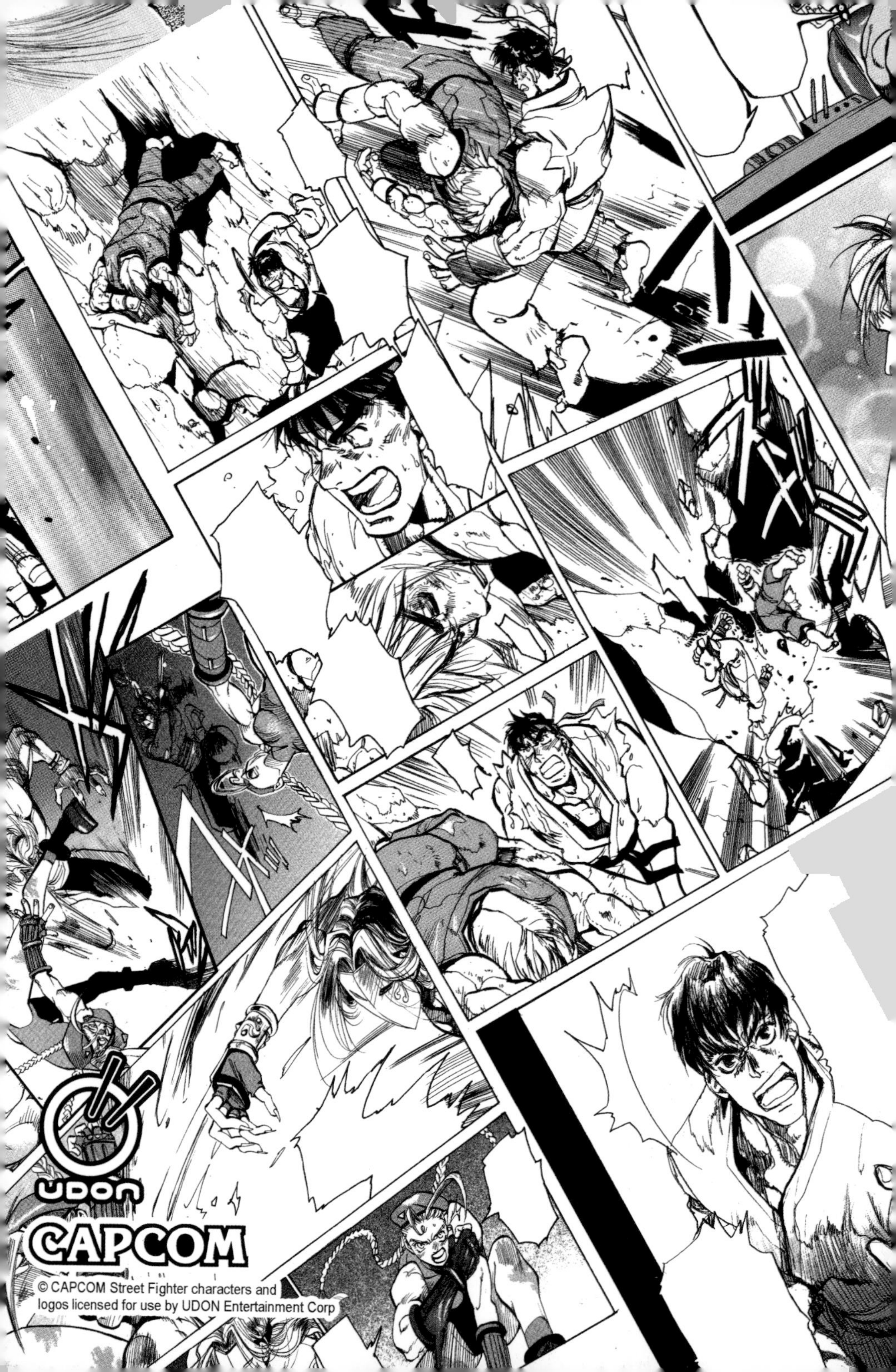

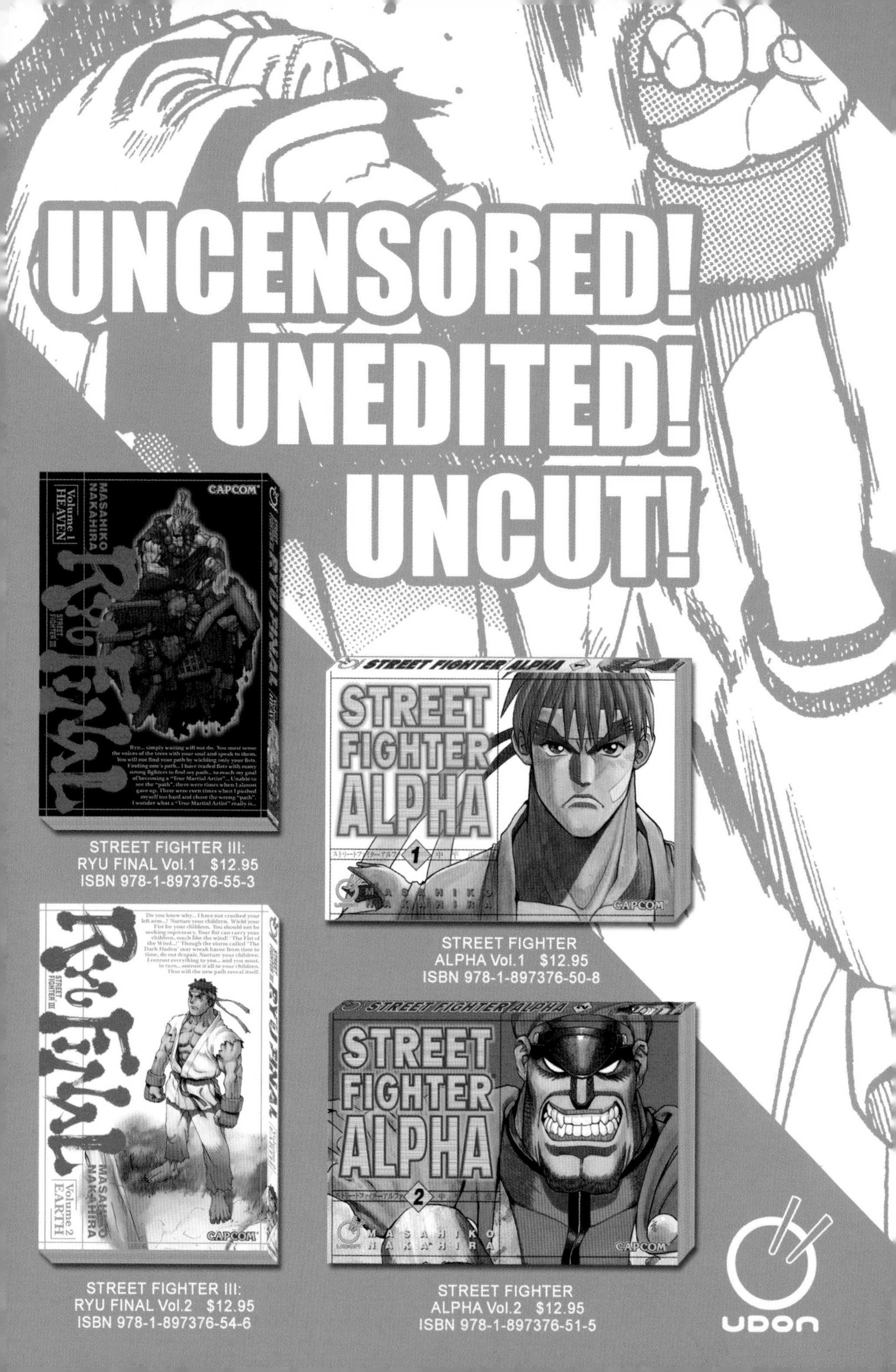

UNCENSORED!
UNEDITED!
UNCUT!
STREET FIGHTER III:
RYU FINAL Vol.1 $12.95
ISBN 978-1-897376-55-3
STREET FIGHTER
ALPHA Vol.1 $12.95
ISBN 978-1-897376-50-8
STREET FIGHTER III:
RYU FINAL Vol.2 $12.95
ISBN 978-1-897376-54-6
STREET FIGHTER
ALPHA Vol.2 $12.95
ISBN 978-1-897376-51-5
UDON

Volume 3: Ibuki
CREDITS
Cover Art: Omar Dogan

Story by:
Jim Zubkavich

Art by:
Omar Dogan

Letters by:
Marshall Dillon

MAKOTO BONUS STORY:
Written by: Ken Siu-Chong
Art by: Omar Dogan

ORO BONUS STORY:
Written by: Ken Siu-Chong
Art by: Alan Wang with Gary Yeung

Managing Editor: Matt Moylan
Project Manager: Jim Zubkavich
Marketing Manager: Stacy King
UDON Chief of Operations: Erik Ko

For CAPCOM Licensing:
Toshi Takumaru, Taki Enomoto, Emi Nakai, Yoshinori Ono of CAPCOM Co., Ltd.
Seon King, Steve Lee, Joshua Izzo, David Crislip,
Brian Oliveira, Francis Mao, Grant Luke, Will Hirsch, Seth Killian,
and Christian Svensson of CAPCOM U.S.A. Inc.

Special Thanks To:
Shoei, Kinu Nishimura, Edayan, Ikeno, Shinkiro, Bengus, Akiman
Adam Warren, Jo Chen, Judy Jong, Jay Axer, Tom Liu, Marc Mostman

STREET FIGHTER® Legends : Volume #3. November 2010. First Printing. © CAPCOM Street Fighter characters and logos licensed for use by UDON Entertainment Corp. Published by UDON Entertainment Corp. Office of publication P.O. BOX 5002, RPO Major Mackenzie, Richmond Hill, ONT, L4X 07B, CANADA. The entire content of this book are © 2010 UDON Entertainment Corp. Any similarities to persons living or dead is purely coincidental. No portion of this comic book may be used or reproduced by any means (digital or print) without written permission from UDON Entertainment except for review purposes.

Printed in Hong Kong.

ISBN13#: 978-1-926778-13-6   ISBN10#: 1-926778-13-8

Licensed by
CAPCOM

Printed by Suncolor Printing Co., Ltd.
e-mail: suncolor@netvigator.com

An
UDON ENTERTAINMENT
Production
www.udoncomics.com